ANUNNAKI

Gods No More

PACIFIC BASIN #21
11,000 B.C. DELUGE #187
ANUNNAKI DEMI-GOD NIN- PUABI OF UR IRAQ
(GENES)   PAGE # 217

ANUNNAKI
Gods No More

Sasha (Alex) Lessin, Ph. D. (Anthropology, U.C.L.A.)

DEDICATION

I dedicate this book to my teacher, Zecharia Sitchin, who made the truth of human existence available to us, and to my wife, Janet Kira Lessin, who encouraged me to share some of Sitchin's findings in this book.

Published by CreateSpace

ISBN-13:
978-1479372218

ISBN-10:
1479372218

CONTENTS

Part II

Part III: PERUSE THE APPENDIXES

PREFACE: PARADIGM PLANETARY PEACE

The giant gods of the ancient world and the successors they choose created mind-sets that shackle us to short desperate lives. These so-called gods rocketed to Earth from a planet they called Nibiru. Nibirans stand way taller and live way longer than we. The ETs said they bred us as short term slaves and soldiers. We killed in their names: Allah (= Sumerian, Nannar), Yahweh (sometimes = Enlil, at times Adad or even Enki), Ishtar (Inanna) and Adanoi (Enki)– mining expedition personnel all, all Nibirans. We Earthlings are one species, designed to slave in mines, armies, businesses, schools, governments, farms, factories, and building projects for ETs and the "royal" lines of ever-murderous hybrid rulers they begat.

The alternative history Zecharia Sitchin, Neal Freer, Michael Tellinger, Andy Lloyd, Michael Cremo and Richard Thompson articulate about our origins and development shatter the fetters of the lies with which the elite the false gods chose keep us in war, greed, poverty, shortened lives. Lies of church and state now hide hoard information, necessities and survival plans as Earth faces immediate danger from space debris.

We feel our oneness with all people and together survive when we see we're all kin, descended from the same ancestors, ancestors from two different planets. When we accept our hybrid origins, we can nullify what the elites the Nibirans imposed on us demand. We can instead cooperate with all and drop hate for others the gods scripted on us. We survive together when we jointly plan for the periodic return of Nibiru, its astronauts, and the debris that lurks at its Lagrange point, 180 degrees from Nibiru on its orbit around its subdwarf primary star, Nemesis.

When I studied for my doctorate in anthropology at U.C.L.A. in the 60s, my professors taught that gradual physical then socio-cultural evolution caused all human development.

In physical evolution, they said a Miocene or Pliocene anthropoid primate evolved into a hominid, *Homo Erectus,* which in turn had evolved from simpler primates over millions of years. My anthropology teachers said *Homo Sapiens*–that's us--gradually evolved from Erectus [Clark, D., W., 1959, *History of the Primates*:178].

Socioculturally, anthropologists said we evolved with technology we ourselves developed. They thought we proliferated as we planted and bred cereals from local grains, tamed indigenous wild sheep, goats, cattle, donkeys and horses, invented tools and machines, developed medicine, constructed irrigation and transportation systems, built cities and developed ever-more effective mathematics, astronomy, chemistry, metallurgy, architecture and engineering.

Modern information proves the anthropologists wrong about our physical evolution: we didn't evolve incrementally from simpler primates on Earth. We've found no gradually intermediate skeletons of primates that link modern humans from tarsier-like ancestors from which Twentieth Century anthropologists thought we evolved. Several advanced hominids co-existed with Erectus. Erectus and its contemporaries may have been survivors of astronomically-caused extinction events during human settlement on Earth long before 400,000 years ago when the scientist Enki and crews of seven - twelve foot tall Homo Sapiens colonized Earth from Nibiru Reject the view that we're an entirely indigenous species that evolved only from simpler forms native to this planet.

Reject also anthropologists' old view that the technologies we invented caused our social evolution. We actually developed socially when the ETs gave us advanced technologies. 60s anthropologists had noted mysterious uplevelings of civilizations every 3,600 years or so, improvements ancient inhabitants of Iraq–then called Sumer–wrote that the Nibiran gods gave them. Anthropologists of the 60s believed these gods imaginary.

My Chairman at U.C.L.A. said technological innovations Sumerians themselves developed explained social evolution. Their innovations, he said, allowed more population growth, sedentariness, material goods, specialization and leisure, all of which caused social evolution. Neither he nor I ever considered as real–let alone the source of cultural evolution "gods" Sumerians said gave them the genes, inventions, crops and livestock that let them increase their numbers and master the environment. In the thrall of evolutionary anti-creationism, we dismissed what Mesopotamians, Egyptians, Indians, Norse, Chinese, Tibetan, Central and South Americans said about gods who rode Celestial Chariots, threw thunderbolts and periodically boosted our civilizations with crops, herds, devices, laws and knowledge. [Goldschmidt, W., 1959, *Man's Way*: 110 -117]

Sociologist C. W. Mills showed how power elites control Earth and collaborate to perpetuate competition and war. These elites descended from the bloodline of Enki whom Sumerians said was a god, albeit a flesh-and blood god. 300,000 years ago, Enki combined his genes with those of Erectus to breed goldmining slaves. 13,000 years ago, he fathered Ziasudra (Noah in *The Bible*), ancestor of the elite that to this day rule Earth. The elite still employ a master-slave, god-worshiper code (with them in master status and we in slave–albeit economic slave--status) to run humanity. Ziasudra's descendants--today's elite--passed their mandate to dictate "from Sumer through Egypt to Israel through David and the messiahs, fostered by the Essene communities in Canaan.

"Jesus was an Essene as was his wife, Mary Magdalene, information the Catholic Church suppressed. Catholics instead perpetuated slave-code fear and subservience. They hid the truth of our hybridization and persecuted and brutalized the human-centered strain of the bloodline [that's most of us]." [Gardiner, L., 2000, *Bloodline of the Holy Grail*; quote from Freer, 2004, *Sapiens Rising*]

In 2000, Cody and Robin Johnson brought me to a seminar led by Sumerian scholar, Zecharia Sitchin. Sitchin displayed evidence in clay and stone of astronomical, geological and biological knowledge Sumerians said gods gave them, knowledge our scientists only verified many millenia later. Sitchin disproved both the theistic and evolutionary dogma perpetrated by the elite. His findings solved the mysteries of missing hominid links and the periodic leaps in our social and industrial evolution. No missing physical links existed because we emerged suddenly, when Enki and his cohorts blended their genome and Erectus'. We got stronger tools and weapons when a Sumerian "god" showed the Hittites how to mine and refine iron.

Sitchin's work breaks the elite's stranglehold on us. I attended Sitchin seminars and read everything he, Tellinger, Lloyd, Cremo and other revisionists wrote. Thanks to these revisionists, we can revise our dismissal of "myths" as superstition. Sumerians labeled Nibirans' aircraft, submarines, helicopters, spaceships, weapons and computers with their own metaphors or words the Nibirans taught them as skyships, celestial chariots, arks, whirlbirds, brilliances, and MEs and recorded the history and science the Nibirans taught them. We can now evaluate what these ETs said and not dismiss tales of gods as superstitious myth.

"Sitchin advanced a coherent paradigm of our genesis to rewrite our beginnings and astronomically, evolutionarily, paleontologically, archaeologically and redefine ourselves. His thesis corrects creationism, redefines Darwinism. Sitchin read Sumerian as well as Hebrew, was steeped in the history and had material from the Middle East rediscovered only last one hundred and fifty years." [Freer, N., 2004, *Sapiens Arising*]

In *Anunnaki: Gods No More*, I review our ancient history and sense of who we are, how we got here, and how the new paradigm of Earthlings' unique two-race genetics frees us from the model the ETs imposed on us. The new view frees us the physical and economic slavery, hierarchic obsession, derogation of women, gold lust, antagonistic religions and nations the Nibirans and the hybrid elite they created dictated.

Free of short, desperate lives, we'll create our future. We shall activate our latent Anunnaki genes, scientifically improve our own genome and take our place in the civilization of the galaxy.

(Images in this book were downloaded from www.google.com)

Cover art courtesy of Richard Fields

I. "GODS" CAME FROM THE PLANET NIBIRU

READ WHAT SITCHIN SAID[1b]

Zecharia Sitchin

Zecharia Sitchin translated clay tablets, statue bases and monuments scribes inscribed in ancient Sumer (now Iraq). The inscriptions said how extraterrestrial gods created and conditioned us. This information can free us to end war, persecution, short lives, famine, disease and pollution.

Sumerian scribes pressed or stamped writing called *cuneiform* into clay tablets.

The tablets show the Sumerians' version of our solar system's history for the last 4.5 billion years. 300,000 years ago, the tablets say, the ETs added their genes onto *Homo Erectus'* to create Earthling-slaves. 13,000 years ago, as the ETs' planet, Nibiru, neared Earth, the Antarctic icesheet slid into the South Sea and caused the Deluge, the ETs let most of the hybrid Earthlings drown. ETs also nuked Sodom and Gomorrah in 2024 B.C. and decimated the Earthlings of Sumer with radiation. Nibirans with advanced weaponry and biological pathogens murdered hundreds of thousands of Earthlings.

(ANUNNAKI'S)

Sitchin with enlargement of a clay tablet Sumerians made for ETs from Nibiru who entered our sun-system and saw Uranus and Neptune (shown between the two standing figures).

Sumerians lacked telescopes; the clay depiction validates the assertion that the ETs came to Earth from space beyond Neptune.

The ETs, whom the scribes called "gods" (the Bible's *Elohim*), dictated the tablets and statue tags. Statues show the ETs looked like 7- 12 foot (and taller) Swedes with space-age weapons. These so-called "gods" lived millions of Earth years. They said an atmospheric crisis 445,000 years ago on Nibiru drove them to Earth for gold. Most Nibirans left Earth in 2024 B.C..

Nibirans shaped our societies, bodies, thoughts and consciousness. They scripted us to obey males ranked in hierarchy, to disdain underlings and perpetrate violence.

445,000 ago, Ea (Ptah, Buzur, Hephaestus, Vulcan and Adoni), a Nibiran Sumerians called *Enki,* rocketed to Earth with fifty men. 50 Medics, 600 miners and 300 astronauts and administrators followed them. The Expedition sought gold to refine to floating monoatomic white powder of gold and create a superconductive shield for Nibiru's decaying atmosphere. Sumerians named the Nibirans *Anunnaki*–those who came from the sky. Israelites called Nibirans *Anakin* and *Nefilim;* Egyptians called Nibirans *Neter* (Watchers).

Enki

The Anunnaki found gold aplenty in Africa and South America. Enki incited the African miners to strike, then pressed Enlil (aka Yahweh), the Expedition Chief, to pardon the strikers. Enki would, he said, breed short-term mining slaves to replace the striking Nibirans.

Enlil, Commander Earth

To make the slaves, Enki added his genes, his sister Ninmah's mitochondrial DNA and genes of Homo Erectus. Enki thought the Creator-of-All designed Erectus to evolve into *Homo Sapiens*. Ningiszidda–Enki's son, Ninmah and Enki expedited the Creator's design; they made hybrid Earthlings who could breed. We were like Nibirans, though they had longer heads and bigger brains. Enki made our men with foreskins Nibiran men lack.

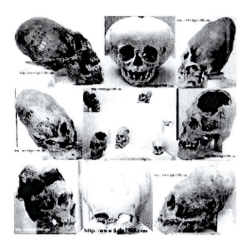

Nibiran skulls? These were found in ancient strata on Earth.
ANUNNAKI SKULLS

Enki created us hybrids short, too. We were short-- under six foot tall--versions of the 7- 12 foot tall. He shortened our lifespans vs the Nibiran livespan; his earliest hybrids might last several hundred years, whereas Nibirans lived millions of years. Earth's orbit, smaller than Nibiru's, may also shorten Earthlings' lives. [ZS, *Giants*: 294 -347]

Nibiru revolves around Nemisis, a dark subdwarf star more massive than Jupiter. Nemesis nears our Sun, at the Kuiper Belt, 48 Astronomical Units from Earth, every 10,800 Earth years. Nibiru circles Nemesis but did not our sun. Instead, every 3,600 years Nibiru passes though our inner solar system between Jupiter and Mars. One of Nibiru's years (the time Nibiru takes to circle Nemesis) is thus 3,600 Earth years--long enough for 180 generations of Homo Sapiens Earthlings to live and die. [Lloyd, *Dark Star*: 176 -181, 225 - 228]

Enki created our ancestors. He and the Nibirans on Earth begat babies with each generation of us Earthlings. Nibirans trained us to mine gold and copper. We tended their crops, livestock and mansions. From 300,000 years ago until the Great Flood, millions of us toiled for the ETs in South Africa.

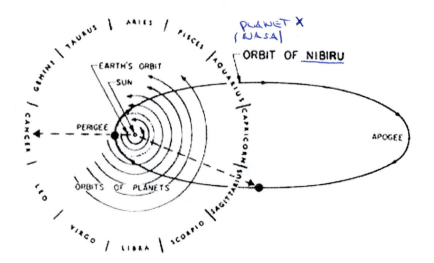

After the Flood, 13,000 years ago, Expedition bosses had us call them "gods." They made us build temples, palaces, hangars and cities in Sumer, Egypt, Mesoamerica and South America. They taught us astronomy, metallurgy, mathematics, agriculture, herding, writing, architecture and geology to support cities and palaces. They owned and ruled us.

Commander Enlil's descendants, whom Sitchin called *Enlilites*, ruled the Earthlings of Sumer and India. Chief Scientist Enki's descendants, whom Sitchin called *Enkiites,* ruled the Earthlings of Africa, Basara (then called Edin) on the Persian Gulf and Bagdad (then called Babylon). Enlilites and Enkiites pitted Earthling armies against each other. The pushiest Enkiites, Babylon's god Marduk (aka Ra and Nimrod) and his demigod son Nabu, raised fifth-columns in Canaan and sent Earthling armies to wrest the Sinai Spaceport from the Enlilites. In 2023 B.C., Enlilites nuked the Spaceport and the cities south of the Dead Sea to keep the Spaceport from the Enkiites.

Fallout from the bombs spread to Enlil's Sumer but not Marduk's Babylon; Babylon nestled north of the nuclear cloud. Sumer's Enlilite gods fled, but their Earthlings in Sumer, except for those at Edin, whom Enki saved, died. Marduk ruled Sumer for awhile.

The ETs and the bloodlines of hybrids closest to them genetically (they begat babies on each generation of hybids) still rule Earth. They chain us in matrices of religion, war and business. Power hierarchies dedicated to Yahweh and Allah compete to the death.

Sumer's history warns us to cast off the hierarchical godspell and mind-set of the Nibirans--Enlil, the patriarchal and genocidal Nibiran Commander who left Earth in 2024 B.C. as well as woman-degraders Marduk and Nannar and mass-killer Inanna who stayed on Earth.

Nibirans taught us to war, fight, enslave, slave, defoliate and pollute. Each Nibiran god made us obey blindly. Some Earthlings fled mines and cities of the gods, hid in hinterlands far from ET abuse and wars, no longer fodder for spears, arrows, chariots, explosives, lasers, gas and biological agents.

Science confirms what the ETs saw and charted when they rocketed to Earth from beyond the parts of the solar system Earthlings could see. The Nibirans saw Earth as they neared it from space outside Neptune's orbit. They saw Earth recede as they rocketed to rejoin Nibiru as it moved past Neptune to orbit around Nemesis.

Nibirans gave us physics, astronomy and biology better than we have now. Just nowadays, researchers verify genetic, metallurgical, geological, mathematic and astronomical data. We validate with hard data predictions and principles inscribed on the ancient Sumerian tablets dictated, say the Sumerians, by ETs.

The truth of our origins frees us from the "godspell." Philosopher Neal Freer defines *godspell* as our yearning for Nibirans' return and rule. But Earthling religions under the spell of gods obsessed on genealogical status, hierarchy, male rule and war. They trained the Nibiran in each of us, the part that fights, kills and grasps.

The Erectus in us--the short-lived hominid the Nibirans altered--resonates with Gaia, this planet and with a natural cooperativeness and capacity for interspecies empathy the Nibirans lacked. When we know and balance our Nibiran and Gaian energies, we break the godspell, become peers rather than servants of the gods. We embrace both our Nibiran and our Erectus natures, our capacities to strive and compete as well as capacities to support, encourage, love and celebrate every consciousness.

NIBIRU HIT EARTH 4 BILLION YEARS AGO

Our Solar System grew from a gas cloud that circled its own center counterclockwise, cooled, and formed both our sun and a dimmer pair-star, a subbrown dwarf–Nemesis. Both the sun and Nemesis developed planets that circled them. Tiamat, the very watery planet that would become Earth orbited the sun between the orbits of Jupiter and Mars.

The ancient *Enuma Elish* describes how, four and a half billion years ago, our sun created Tiamat, then Mercury. The sun then, says the Enuma, sent Mercury with water and gold to Tiamat. Planet-pairs formed: Venus with Mars, Jupiter with Saturn, Uranus with Neptune. These planets orbited the Sun counterclockwise, as did Tiamat. "There was no planet between Venus and Jupiter, where the Earth now resides and Pluto was a moon of Saturn."

Tiamat lacked a partner-planet, but one of her moons, Kingu, enlarged. Kingu started to partner with Tiamat. Then Kingu could orbit the Sun, not Tiamat.

But, four billion years ago, before Kingu could orbit the Sun, either Nibiru or Nemisis invaded the Sun' inner planetary system. (I call the invader Nibiru, but it could be Nemesis.) Nibiru changed the planets' orbits. When it approached Tiamat," both Tiamat and Nibiru sprouted moons. [Lloyd, Dark Star: 41, 122 -124]

Nibiru's gravity tore off a piece of Neptune and pulled the piece clockwise, Nibiru's direction, into space near Neptune. That's how Neptune's moon, Triton, formed and why, unlike other moons in the System, Triton orbits its planet clockwise.

Nibiru's Apparent Orbit
PLANET X (NASA)

In the first Proto-Earth/Nibiru meeting, the planets didn't hit but Nibiru's smaller moons ("winds") struck Tiamat, "fracturing her midst, extinguishing her life." Nibiru's small moons shattered into apparently retrograde [clockwise] orbiting comets." Kingu, our moon, "turned into a lifeless circler, doomed forever to circle Earth." Kingu didn't orbit the sun, as it would've had Nibiru not invaded the Solar System. [Lloyd, *Dark Star*: 122 -124; ZS, *Giants*:111 - 114].

When Nibiru pierced our Solar System, it lost three of its moons and tore four moons from Uranus. When Nibiru passed Uranus, it tilted Uranus's orbit. Nibiru pulled Gaga, Saturn's largest moon, into clockwise orbit (between Neptune and Uranus).

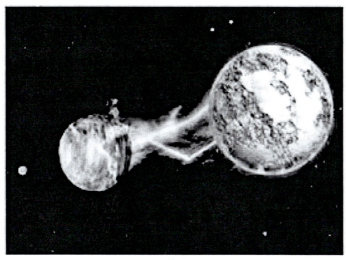

PACIFIC BASIN

We call Gaga Pluto.

One orbit of Nibiru into the inner solar system forced all Tiamat's new sprouting moons from counterclockwise orbit into apparent clockwise orbit. Tiamat's new moons circled Nibiru (instead of Tiamat). They formed apparently "retrograde orbiting comets." Nibiru's perigee sucked off Kingu's air and blocked Kingu's orbit around the Sun. Kingu remained Earth's moon.

Evil Wind, one of Nibiru's moons, struck Tiamat. Then Nibiru itself hit Tiamat and gouged a huge gap, the Pacific Basin, in it. Chunks of Tiamat, now asteroids, careened into space as did gobs of water, which became comets of the Kuiper and Oort Belts of comets. Nibiru knocked what was left of Tiamat into its current position, between Mars and Venus. Earth's what the collisions left of Tiamat.

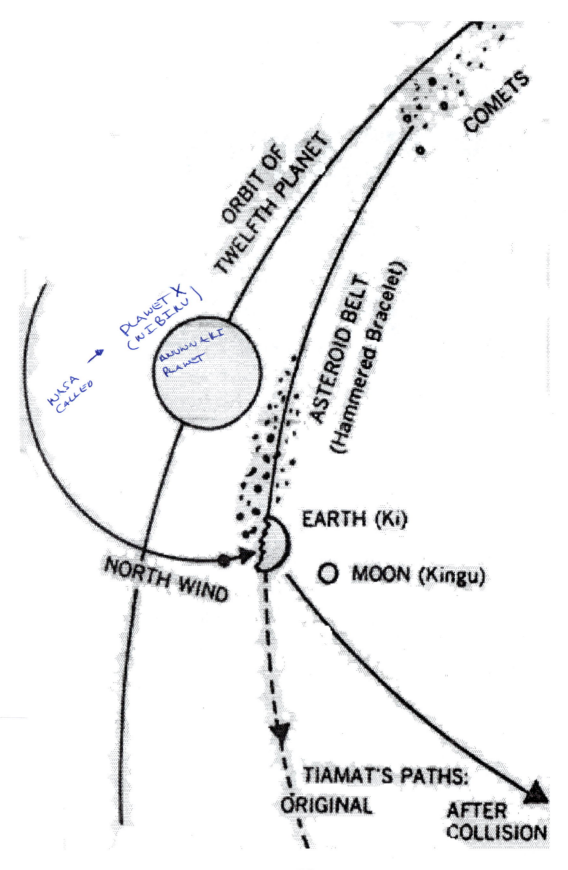

ORBIT OF TWELFTH PLANET

COMETS

ASTEROID BELT (Hammered Bracelet)

PLANET X (NIBIRU)

ANUNNAKI PLANET

NASA CALLED

EARTH (Ki)

O MOON (Kingu)

NORTH WIND

TIAMAT'S PATHS:
ORIGINAL

AFTER COLLISION

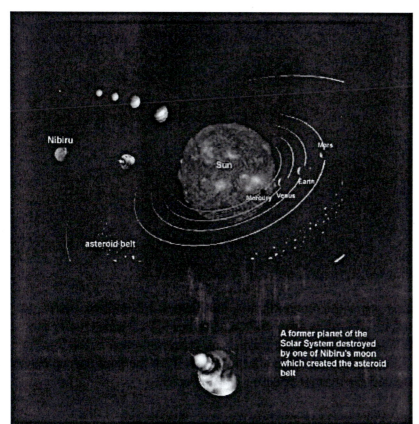

(NIBIRU) PLANET ✳ (NASA)

Nibiru and other planets' size ccompared

A Nibiran moon struck Proto-Earth, created the Pacific Basin

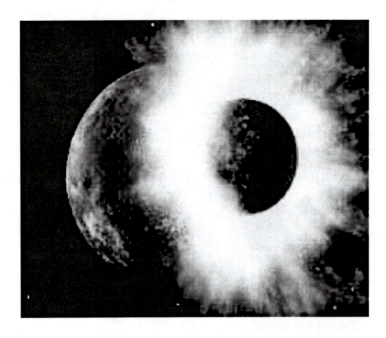

Earth's crust formed 4 billion years ago on continents, but formed 200 million years ago under the Pacific. The crust,12 - 45 miles deep on land, lies but 3.5 - 5 miles under the Pacific Ocean. When Evil Wind and Nibiru hit Tiamat, no crust remained in the Pacific Gap, only a gaping hole. After collisions, silt ran into the gap from the land and volcanoes spewed lava into it; they created the thinner crust under the Pacific.

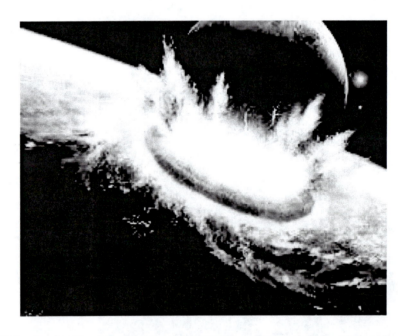

Evil Wind and Nibiru broke Earth's crust into slabs. Then Earth "attained the shape of a globe dictated by forces of gravity. Waters gathered into the cavity on the torn-off side. Dry land appeared on the other side of the planet. Breakup of the Earth's crust, plate tectonics, differences between continental and oceanic crusts, emergence of a Pangaea [a single continent] from under the waters, the primordial encircling ocean" led our scientists to confirm the Nibiran model of Earth formed after Evil Wind then Nibiru hit Tiamat. [ZS, *Genesis*:96 -105].

The tilt of Earth 21 - 24 degrees on its rotational axis–the basis of our seasons and shifting days the equinoxes (apparent stand-stills of the Sun's and other stars' positions) due to Earth's wobbles--were caused either by the collision of Nibiru and its moon with Tiamat or the massive meteor that struck Earth 65 million years ago. [ZS, *Time*:62]

When Evil Wind and Nibiru hit Tiamat, they gave it rare molybdenum, needed for enzymatic reactions. Nibiru and Evil Wind set a "single genetic code for all terrestrial life." In the Pacific, waters and life-seeds of Nibiru and Tiamat evolved together. [ZS, *12th Planet*: 255 -256; 2010, *Giants*: 109-114].]

Nibiru stabilized into a clockwise 3,600-year orbit. But in 10,900 B.C., Uranus drifted away from the Sun and sped Nibiru toward Earth sooner than 3,600 years. As Nibiru flew by, Uranus caught Miranda, a moon of Nibiru. Miranda, now a moon of Uranus, circled it instead of Nibiru. From 10,000 B.C. on Uranus slowed Nibiru's orbit to 3450 Earth years rather than 3600. Nibiru returned to perigee in 7450, 4000, and 556 B.C. and next returns to the inner solar system in 2900A.D. rather than 2012 as it would on its earlier 3600-year orbit (though the debris 180 degrees from Nibiru on Nibiru's orbital path, its far LaGrange point moving in harmonic procession always opposite Nibiru, is upon us now). Nibirans can communicate with and even travel to Earth both before and after Nibiru's perigee. The Infrared Imaging Satellite and the Naval Observatory confirmed Nibiru's existence 1983 -1984. "NASA attempted to hush-up" Nibiru's discovery in an published then denied the IRAS sighting. [Freer: *Sapiens Rising*. Part 1; Lloyd: *Dark Star*: 75; ZS, *End*: 315 - 317]

Sumerians drew Nibiru as a winged disk and a cross. They say it crosses our orbital plane and the space between Mars and Jupiter. Drawings of Nibiru also show radiation heat. "Thick atmosphere protects Nibiru against the long periods of cold while deep in space when the planet is farthest from the Sun as well as hot periods when it is closest to the Sun. Their wounded atmosphere brought the Anunnaki [Nibiran Mining Expedition personnel] from Nibiru to Earth." When Nibiru nears the sun, people on Earth see Nibiru without telescopes. [Tellinger, M., *Slave Species*: 88]

Nibiru's perigee's the "cross" we and Nibiru both suffer and enjoy. We suffer when Nibiru sweeps through the Oort Cloud of comets which shower Earth "causing a clockwork extinction pattern [Lloyd, *Dark Star*: 58]. We suffer Nibiru-caused rain, floods, earthquakes but we also enjoy technology Nibirans give us. Nibirans lose some of their gold shield when Nibiru nears us.

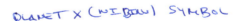

PLANET X (NIBIRU) SYMBOL

Nibiru's also the "winged globe. Rulers of Sumer and Akkad, Babylon and Assyria, Elam and Uratu, Mari and Nuzi, Mitanni and Cannan, Hittite Kings, Egyptian Pharohs, Persian Shar's--as well as the ancient Hebrews–thought Nibiru the home of the supreme god. All the peoples of the ancient world considered the nearing of Nibiru a sign of upheavals, great changes and new eras, expected to cause rains and flooding, [due to] its strong gravitational effects, which include an arrest in Earth's spin on its own axis for one day. Earthlings thought when they saw Nibiru, peace and justice would settle upon Earth and the Lord shall judge among the nations and repute many people in rains, inundations and earthquakes."

Nibiru appears "from the south and moves clockwise." It first aligns with Mercury "30 degrees" to the ecliptic. As it nears Earth, Nibiru rises another 30 degrees," crosses Jupiter's orbit and reaches perigee at "the Place of Crossing" where Nibiru struck Tiamat. It can be seen with telescopes "slightly south of the ecliptic" [the plane to the sun's inner planets]. Then Nibiru starts "back into distant space." to its aphelion, 20,000 astronomical units from our sun, around Nemesis. Nibiru crosses the ecliptic north of Sagittarius. [Lloyd, *Dark Star*:78 -83; ZS, *12th Planet*: 237 -246]

II. NIBIRU'S POLITICS SCRIPTED EARTH

Enki wrote[2]: "After eons of time [on Nibiru] our own species sprouted, by our own essence an eternal seed to procreate. As our numbers grew, to many regions of Nibiru our ancestors spread. Some tilled the land, some four-legged creatures shepherded.

"Rivalries occurred, encroachments happened; clashes occurred, sticks became weapons. Clans gathered into tribes, then two great nations each other faced. The nation of the north against the nation of the south took up arms. What was held by hand to thrusting missiles was turned. Weapons of thunder and brilliance increased the terror. A war, long an fierce, engulfed the planet; brother amassed against brother. There was death and destruction both north and south. For many circuits [3,600 Earth-year orbits of Nibiru around Solaris] desolation reigned the land; all life was diminished."

Nibiru's North vs South War

NUCLEAR WARS

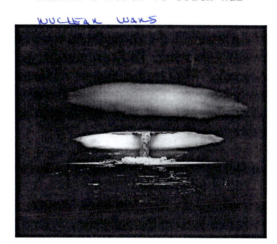

654,000 years ago, "truce was declared; then peacemaking conducted. *'Let the nations be united, the emissaries said to one another; let there be one throne on Nibiru, one king to reign over all. Let a leader from the north or from south by lot to be chosen, one king supreme to be. If he be from north, let south choose a female to be his spouse. Let their firstborn be the successor; let a dynasty thus be formed, unity on Nibiru forever to establish.'*

King An, who united Nibiru, created a military dictatorship--hierarchical male-centered, patrilineal. "By lots was he chosen; his decrees in unity were accepted. For his abode he built a splendid city Agade [Unity] was its name. Governors for each land he appointed; restoration and reclamation was their task."

Since the nuclear wars killed many more men than women, An had men take principle and secondary wives, official concubines too. An's dynasty set The Law of Succession: THE KING'S HEIR, A SON HE HAS WITH HIS HALF SISTER--THE PRINCIPAL WIFE--RULES WHEN THE KING DIES. This law will long plague Earth, for it legitimized the contribution of line of female-transmitted DNA in the Merovingian French royals descended from Jesus and Mary Magdalene. [ZS, *Enki*: 25-26; Tellinger, *Slave Species:* 98].

500,000 years ago, Nibiru's protective shield weakened. The thick atmosphere thinned. This forced Nibirans to mine Earth for gold to powder Nibiru's air, save their atmosphere, and keep the heat they needed. [Tellinger, *Slave Species*: 88]

NIBIRU'S PERIL DROVE MINERS TO EARTH 450,000 YEARS AGO

Nibiru used to near Earth and the sun (perigee), every 3,600 years. "For a time in cold is Nibiru engulfed; for part of its circuit by the Sun strongly is it heated. A thick atmosphere Nibiru envelops, by volcanic eruptions constantly fed. All manner of life this atmosphere sustains. In the cold period the inner heat of Nibiru it keeps about the planet, like a warm coat that is constantly renewed. In the hot period it shields Nibiru from the Sun's scorching rays." [ZS, *Enki*: 24]

By the reign of Enshar, the sixth king descended from An, "Nibiru's air has thinner been made, the protective shield diminished," scientists said. Enshar's son, Duuru, failed to create an hereditary heir, but the Council of Counselors made his adopted son, Lahma, King. To Lahma, "In the councils of the learned, to heal the breach in the atmosphere, were two suggestions. *Use gold, within the Hammered Belt [Asteroids] abundant. To finest powder, gold could be ground, lofted high to heaven, suspended it could remain.[3] With replenishment, the breach it would heal. Let celestial boats [rockets] the gold to Nibiru bring over. Let weapons of Terror [nukes] be created, the missiles the volcanoes to attack, their dormancy to bestir, their belching to increase, the atmosphere to replenish, the breach to make disappear.*"

"For a decision Lahma was too feeble; what choice to make he knew not."

Every 3,600 years, Nibiru, as it orbited the Sun, lost more oxygen. Lahma vacillated for four orbits (204,000 Earth years) whether to nuke the volcanoes or send miners to the Asteroids. While he pondered, Nibiru's air bled into space. [ZS, *Enki*: 32 - 33]

PRINCE ALALU KILLED NIBIRU'S KING LAHMA

Prince Alalu, descended from Nibiru's forth king, Anshurgal (and a concubine) attacked Lahma atop the palace tower. *"We need a king who acts now. Not you; you dither. I'm taking over now, before we lose all our air."* Alalu hurled the King from the tower. *"Now I'm King."*

ALALU GAVE DAUGHTER TO EA FOR FEALTY FROM ANU

ANU, a prince descended from King An's youngest son (Enuru) spoke against Alalu's claim. Anu said he, not Alalu, should rule.

Anu

Alalu told Anu, *"Wed our children--my daughter Damkina; your son Ea; I rule and civil war we forestall."*

Anu agreed; he canceled the betrothal his daughter Ninmah had with Enki, Nibiru's greatest scientist. Instead of Nimah, Ea wed Damkina [ZS, *Giants*: 249].

Ninmah pined for Enki, but sought solace in sex with Anu's heir, her (and Ea's) half-brother Enlil, a dashing military man. When Ninmah bore Enlil's son Ninurta (later known as Ishum, then Mars), Anu forbade her marriage to anyone ever.

Enlil, who before the Anu-Alalu marriage deal, would've succeeded Anu as Nibiru's King, lost his claim to the throne. The first male born of Enki and Damkina, Anu and Alalu agreed, would rule Nibiru and merge the descent lines of both Alalu and Anu.

Enki and Damkina had a boy, Marduk. The pact between Anu and Alalu pledged Marduk, not Enlil, would one day rule Nibiru. Deal in place, Anu pledged fealty to Alalu. Alalu, now King, made Anu his Cupbearer. [ZS, *Wars*: 84]

When Enki and Damkina married, Anu bowed to Alalu. The first male Enki and Damkina begat, Anu and Alalu agreed, would rule Nibiru and join the lines of both grandfathers, Alalu and Anu.

Ea and Damkina begat a boy, Marduk. THE PACT BETWEEN ALALU AND ANU, PROCLAIMED MARDUK, WOULD ONE DAY RULE NIBIRU. PLANET X

ANU WRESTLED & DEPOSED ALALU

King Alalu didn't-- though he tried--save Nibiru's air. To create overcast that would hold the air, he nuked the volcanoes, but this didn't yield enough overcast so he explored the gold-shield option. Earth and its asteroids contain most of the gold in the solar system, so Alalu sent a rocket for Earth for gold to powder and spread over Nibiru's atmosphere, but the ship crashed into an asteroid; all aboard died. Nine more Nibiran years (nine sars, orbits of Nibiru around the Sun, 32,400 Earth years) passed and Alalu still hadn't stopped Nibiru's air loss.

Cupbearer Anu seethed when Alalu failed to protect and replenish Nibiru's atmosphere. He cited Nibiru law and proclaimed himself rightful king. He challenged Alalu.

"Anu gave battle to Alalu. To hand-to-hand combat, with bodies naked, Alalu he challenged."

"Alalu in combat was defeated; by acclaim Anu was hailed as king."[ZS, *Enki*: 24 - 39]

III. ALALU PROVED EARTH'S GOLD

ALALU NUKED TO EARTH, SAID *GOLD'S HERE*, THREATENED NIBIRU

Alalu launched a missile-loaded rocket for Earth and with the nuclear missiles blasted through stones of the Asteroids. He landed in the Persian Gulf and waded ashore.

In the Gulf, he confirmed gold and targeted Nibiru with missiles. "The Speaker-of-Words he stirred up; toward Nibiru the words to carry, "*On another world I am, the gold of salvation I have found. The fate of Nibiru is in my hands. To my conditions you must give heed! Return my throne*" [ZS, *Enki*: 60]

On Nibiru, the Council[5] heard Alalu's demands. "Two royal princes--the Commanders of the Weapons" protected the palace with "two divine weapons--the Royal Hunter and the Royal Smiter. The gateway to the palace was flanked by 'Eaglemen' [uniformed astronauts] with the Winged Disc emblem of Nibiru centrally displayed. The Council heard Alalu's transmission in the Throne Room where Anu sat on his throne, flanked by his Foremost Son Enlil seated on the right and his Firstborn Son, Ea seated on his left. Anyone present could speak but Anu's word was final." Enlil impugned Alalu's data; he and the Council begged Anu, *"Resist Alalu."* Anu had Enlil beam Alalu back, *"Prove ample gold on Earth."* [ZS, *Giants*: 129]

Enki said he'd rocket to Earth and see if it had enough gold to send miners. *"If from gold dust of Earth a shield for Nibiru its atmosphere to save,"* said Enki, *"let Alalu Earth rule as King. For kingship on Nibiru, let him wrestle Anu. Let me in a chariot* [rocket] *to Earth journey, a path through the Bracelet* [Asteroids] *with water, not fire I shall fashion. On Earth, from the waters let me the precious gold to obtain; to Nibiru back it will be sent."* [ZS, *Enki:* 66]

Anu sent Enki with Alalu's grandson, pilot Anzu (an astro-navigation expert), and fifty men to Earth. Enki had pre-empted the job half-brother Enlil coveted. Enlil seethed while Enki and Anzu rocketed for Earth. [Sitchin, J., *Website*]

EA, WITH WATER, WON EARTH

Enki blasted rocks in the asteroid belt with a water canon, fed with water he took from his ship's engine.

Asteroid Belt

"*Critical Water depleted,*" Anzu warned; "*engine failure immanent.*" Mars' waters could save them.

Enki and Anzu landed on Mars which had water and an air too. "The water was good for drinking but the air was insufficient for breathing; they needed their Eagle's helmets to breathe." On Mars, they drew water from a lake." [Sumerian clay tablets show water on Mars long before Twenty-First Century scientists found water traces there]. [Tellinger, *Slave Species:* 432]

Rocket's water renewed, Enki launched for Earth, "its gold Nibiru's fate for salvation or doom containing." [ZS, *Enki:* 71]

"'*The chariot must its speed reduce or in Earth' thick atmosphere it will perish*' said Anzu. They circled the planet a few times slowing before they entered the atmosphere hurtling toward the solid ground. The gravity played havoc with their ship and they moved too fast for a dry landing. "443,000 years ago, they splashed into the Persian Gulf. Alalu guided them ashore. [Tellinger, *Slave Species:* 443]

Enki built houses at Eridu, the head of the Persian Gulf, near modern Basara[6].
From Gulf waters, he sifted some gold. He made a plane, and with his personal pilot Abgal, tested all over Earth for more gold. Anu beamed Enki, "*Send us Alalu's ship with all gold you gathered.*" The Nibiran scientists messaged, "*Get more gold quick.*"

ENKI HID ALALU'S NUKES, FIRED PILOT ANZU

Enki and Abgal entered Alalu's rocket. In it, they found seven nuclear missiles. They hid them in a cave in the African Great Lakes area.

Anzu, the interplanetary pilot and Alalu's grandson, saw no missiles when he came to ready Alalu's rocket to return to Nibiru. He told Enki, *"Most missiles Alalu stole to Anu I must return and some I must fire at rocks in the Belt."*

"This rocket you cannot with such attitude pilot, radiation missiles must not in interplanetary space discharge." Enki said, *"I replace you Anzu; stay on Earth with Alalu. Abgal, who pilots my plane, will return Alalu's rocket to Nibiru."* [ZS, *Enki*: 82]

ENKI SENT ABGAL TO NIBIRU WITH GOLD SAMPLES

Enki routed a return through the Asteroids and Abgal flew the rocket to Nibiru with sample gold. Scientists processed it into "the finest dust, to skyward launch it was hauled away. A shar [one orbit of Nibiru around the Sun, 3,600 Earth years] did the fashioning last, a shar did the testing continue. With rockets was the dust heavenward carried, by crystals' beams was it dispersed.

(1 SHAR IS 3,600 EARTH YEARS)

"[But] when Nibiru near the Sun came, the golden dust by its rays disturbed; the healing in the atmosphere dwindled, the breach to bigness returned."[ZS, *Enki*: 86]

Anu sent Abgal to Earth for more gold and Enki sent him back to Nibiru with the meager gold from the Gulf.

"Enki traced the [Persian Gulf's] gold to its nearest prime source–the gold lodes, huge veins deep in the rocks of Abzu [Africa]. Jubilant, he announced his find to Nibiru." [ZS, *Giants*:99, 138]

On Nibiru, Enlil, angry that Enki led Mission Earth,
demanded Enki prove vast, extractable gold on land.
*"False hope Enki gave already that gold quantity from
Earth's waters could Nibiru's atmosphere save,"* he said.

Anu gave in: *"You Enlil, my legal successor are. Of
Earth take charge; gold there assess for yourself."*

Enlil landed on Earth
and saw Enki's find.
Enlil beamed back to
Nibiru that, despite
initial doubts, Earth had gold enough to save Nibiru's
atmosphere.

But the basic rivalry between Enki and Enlil (that plagues Earth
to this day) surfaced again.

Anu

~ 34 ~

IV. NIBIRANS MINED & SETTLED EARTH

ANU, ENLIL & ENKI DREW FOR NIBIRU, EARTH, SEAS & MINING

"Father Anu", Enlil beamed from Earth to Nibiru, *"affirm succession. I, son by your half-sister Antu, rank Enki, though, he, your eldest be."*

"Come," Enlil implored,*" to Earth in person and deal with Alalu, too, who claims rule here over Nibiru too."*

So, 416,000 years ago, Anu flew to Earth.

On Earth, he put three straws in his right hand, held them out to Enki and Enlil: *"Whoever draws the long straw rules Nibiru. Draw the short straw and you command Earth. Middle-sized straw: run mining and sea transport."*

"By their lots the tasks they divided; Anu to Nibiru to return, its ruler on the throne to remain.

"The Edin [Sumer] to Enlil was allotted, to be Lord of Command, more settlements to establish, of the skyships and their heros charge to take. Of all the lands until they the bar of the seas encounter, the leader to be." Enlil, "Lord of Command" extended King Anu's military dictatorship to Earth. Enlil, who preceded Enki as Anu's successor on Nibiru, now ruled Enki on Earth too. [4] [ZS, *Enki*: 92 - 93]

"To Enki the seas and the oceans as his domain were granted, lands beyond the bar of the waters by him to be governed, in the Abzu [Africa] to be the master, with ingenuity the gold to procure." [ZS, *Enki*: 92 - 93]

Enlil's first act as Commander conciliated Ea. Enlil forever gave Enki Eridu, the settlement at Basara and gave the title, *En.Ki*, Earth's Lord, on Ea [ZS, *Wars*: 81]

ANU BEAT ALALU, BANISHED HIM TO MARS WITH ANZU

When Anu and his sons divided rule of Nibiru and Earth, "Forward toward Anu Alalu stepped, shouted, *'Mastery of Earth to me was allotted; that was the promise when the gold finds to Nibiru I announced! Nor have I the claim to Nibiru's throne forsaken.'"* [ZS, *Enki* : 93]

Anu wrestled Alalu. They grappled. [Sitchin, *Wars*: 86]

"Anu on the chest of Alalu with his foot pressed down, victory in the wrestling thereby declaring, *'I am King'"*

But when Anu lifted his foot from Alalu, "swiftly he the manhood of Anu bit off, the malehood of Anu Alalu did swallow.!" [ZS, *Wars:* 94]

Enlil tied Alalu while Enki gave Anu first-aid, who groaned, "*Maroon Alalu on Marsh, I shall, to Mars, to slowly die from my seed,* " His flesh killed anyone who ate it. So Anu, enroute to Nibiru, left Alalu with food and tools on Mars. On Mars also, Anu left Anzu to tend the ex-King as he died. [Tellinger,, *Slave Species*: 438]

NINMAH SAVED ANZU ON MARS, BUILT MARSBASE

On Nibiru, Anu ordered freight rockets to shuttle from Earth and its moon, as well as other planets and satellites between Nibiru and the sun. He sent daughter Ninmah with doctors to Earth. *"On Mars stop,"* he said, *"If Anzu lives, to him give men to there a base start."*

On Mars Ninmah found Alalu and Anzu dead but she revived Anzu. To honor Alalu who found the gold that could save Nibiru, "The image of Alalu upon the great rock mountain [Cyndonia] with beams they [Ninmah's crew and Anzu] carved. They showed Alalu wearing an eagle's helmet; his face they made uncovered." [ZS, *Enki*: 104].

ALALU FACE ON PLANET MARS

Cydonia, Mars

Before she left Mars for Earth, Ninmah, as Anu had ordered, gave Anzu twenty astronauts from her company and told them to build a way-station for the gold freighters.

ENKI & ENLIL BOTH WANTED NINMAH

To his scribe, Enki dictated this segue of the background of his relationship to his half-siblings, "Enki and Enlil and Ninmah, offspring of Anu the three leaders were, by different mothers. Enki was the Firstborn Son; a concubine of Anu's was his mother."

Enki

"Enlil by Antu, the spouse of Anu, was born; the Legal Heir he thus became. Ninmah by another concubine was mothered, a half sister of the two half brothers she was. Beautiful she was, full of wisdom, quick to learn. Ea, as Enki was then named, by Anu to espouse Ninmah was chosen, thereby their offspring son the legal successor thereafter to become.

"Ninmah of Enlil, dashing commander, was enamored; by him she was seduced. A son from Enlil's seed Ninmah bore, Ninurta. Anu angered; as punishment he Ninmah ever to be a spouse forbade! Ea his bride-to-be by Anu's decree abandoned; a princess named Damkina [Alalu's daughter] he instead espoused; a son, an heir to them was born, Marduk." [ZS, *Enki*, 112-113]

Ninmah and her doctors, en route to Earth from Nibiru, left Anzu with astronauts on Mars, then rocketed to Eridu on Earth. There, Enlil, obsessed with besting Enki, courted her. He and Enki both wanted babies with her. Their half-sister, and only half-sister on Earth, Nibiran law held that only boys with Ninmah would build their royal lines.

Enlil told her he'd bring Ninurta and build a center in Sumer for her doctors. He flew them to his place in Lebanon, perfect, he said, for her seeds from Nibiru. They'd make "euphoric elixer" from fruit from her seeds.

At his place, he held and "with fervor kissed her, '*Oh my sister, my beloved*!' He whispered. By her loins he grabbed her." But "Into her womb his semen he did not pour"[ZS, *Enki*: 108].

Enlil

COUNCIL EXILED ENLIL FOR SUD RAPE

For many months, hurt and angry, Enlil mooned about his gardens. He saw Sud, Ninmah's gorgeous assistant, bathe in his stream with other women from the medical team and invited Sud to get high on elixir made from seeds Ninmah brought. "Sud drank, Enlil drank too; to her Enlil of intercourse was speaking. Unwilling was the lass. Enlil laughed and embraced her, kissed her. His semen into her womb he poured.

"To Ninmah, Sud's commander, the immoral deed was reported. *Enlil, immoral one, for your deed judgement you shall face.'* So did Ninmah to Enlil in anger say.

"In the presence of fifty Anunnaki, Seven Who Judge assembled. On Enlil a punishment decreed: *Let Enlil from all cities be banished. Let him exiled be.* In a skychamber [plane] they made Enlil leave the Landing Place [Lebanon] to a "Land of No Return" in Africa." The Tribunal told Abgal, the pilot, to choose Enlil's site. [ZS, *Enki*: 112 - 114]

Abgal, recall, had helped Enki hide Alalu's nuclear missiles.

ABGAL BETRAYED ENKI, SHOWED ENLIL "ALALU'S NUKES"

In Africa, at the site he'd chosen for Enlil, Abgal secretly defected from Enki and allied with Commander Enlil. Enki thought the nukes hidden, but, Abgal told Enlil, *"At the right time, seize the missiles and prevail over all rivals. With the weapons your freedom obtain!"* [ZS, *Enki*: 114]

THE SEVEN MADE ENLIL WED SUD

While Enlil viewed the missiles in Africa, in Sumer, Sud's womb swelled. Enki and Tribunal sympathized with her and asked if she'd marry Enlil. If he made her Royal Wife, she would. So he returned to Lebanon, married her, and professed sexual conservatism. He kept secret his knowledge of the nukes' secret cave. Sud, now called *Ninlil* (Lady of Command), bore Nannar, the first Nibiran Royal born on Earth, then Adad. [ZS, *Handbook*: 7; *Giants*: 15; *Lost Realms*: 116].

ENKI & NINMAH BRED GIRLS TILL SHE CURSED HIM

Ninmah spurned Enlil. Now she could explore with former fiancee Enki. Enki told her, *"Come with me in the Abzu* [Africa], *your adoration of Enlil abandon."* In Africa, "Enki to her words of loving spoke, sweet words he spoke, *'You are still my beloved'* to her he said, caressing. He embraced her, he kissed her, she caused his phallus to water. Enki his semen into the womb of Ninmah poured. *'Give me a son,'* he cried." If he could begat a son with Ninmah, the boy "would be considered a rival to Enlil and the sons of Enlil."

But Ninmah bore a daughter with whom Enki begat another daughter, whom he asked to begat a son with him. Ninmah "was enraged, her pride wounded. "She brewed an irresistibly delicious and intoxicating elixir full of deadly herbs. As Enki drank" she cursed him. He fell to the ground, cup in hand. She wanted him to suffer.. He began to shrivel up and age rapidly, his skin turning a putrid yellow. Anu was forced to plead with her to relinquish her curse and invoke healing magic. Enki recovered and begged Nimah's forgiveness, but she never again let herself trust men." "To distance himself from Nimmah's vulva Enki by raised arm swore; from her curse Enki was freed. To the Edin Ninmah returned." [Ferguson, 1995; 32 -33; ZS,:*Enki*: 115-116]

Enki consoled himself; he flew Ereshkigal (Enlil's son Nannar's daugher) to Cape Agulhas on South Africa's tip where Enlil sent her to run the Cape's astronomical, climate and earth-monitoring station.

Enroute Enki seduced her. Then he sent to Nibiru for his wife, Damkina, and their son, Marduk.

Alalu, recall, had seized the Nibiran Throne and wed his daughter Damkina to Enki. Damkina and Enki's son, Marduk, would succeed Alalu. But Anu deposed and condemned Alalu. King Anu sent his three annoying and quarrelsome kids--Enki, Ninmah and Enlil--to Earth.

Ereshkigal

Enki's son Nergal, bald, limping (since birth) and bossy, ran South African mines for the Enikiites. He thought Ereshkigal, an Enlite Princess, crowded him. He attacked the Station to kill her. She "saved her life by offering to marry him."

Enki

Anu   Nergal

Pregnant already, she bore Ningishzidda and ran the Cape Station while Nergal ran the mines. Ningishzidda, related to both Enlilites and Enkiites, would empathize with both lineages. [ZS, *Wars*: 111 - 112, 117, 176; *Enki*: 188-193, 195]

ENKI & ENLIL BEGAT ENKIITE AND ENLILITE LINEAGES

Enlil's lineage leaders (Enlil, Ninurta, Nannar an Adad above; Three of Enki's sons--Nergal, Gibil, and Marduk--below [ZS, *Stairway:* 114]

Enkiites (Enki's patrilineage)*:* On Earth, Damkina and Enki begat his lineage--his boys and their male descendants. His lineage began with his and Damkina's Nibiran-born son, MARDUK, then their Earth-born boys, NERGAL, GIBIL, DUMUZI and NINAGAL. Enki fathered SHARA with Inanna. Marduk expanded the Enkiite lineage; he begat SETH, NABU, and, OSIRIS, who fathered HORUS.

Enlilites (Enlil's patrilineage): Enlil bred his lineage on Earth with his wife, Sud/Ninlil. Their sons together-- NANNAR and ADAD--reinforced him and his eldest son, NINURTA (Enlil's illicit child with Ninmah) in their struggles with the Enkiites.

Anu's patriclan, pitted structurally against Alalu's, encompassed both Enkiite and Enlilite lineages. Both the clans of Alalu and of Anu nest within An's line.

NIBIRAN CENTERS ALIGNED LANDING CORRIDOR

By 400,000 years ago, Enlil had built four centers in Sumer: *Sippar* his spaceport, *Nippur*, Mission Control, *Shurrupak*, Med Center and *Badtibira*, Metallurgy Center. Enki's boats brought gold from southeast Africa to Badtibira where they were processed into bars. At Nippur, Enlil build the *Dur.An.Ki*--Bond Heaven-Earth [also Navel of Earth], a dim communication chamber with telescopes connected to a tall broadcasting tower where Enlil could talk with similar towers in each Nibiran center and where Nibirans on rockets spoke with Earth.

Mission Control, Nippur

Landing corridor

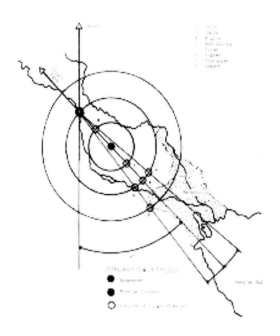

NINURTA DEFEATED ANZU & ASTRONAUT CORPS

On Marsbase, Alalu's grandson Anzu ruled 300 Nibirans, an orbiting station and the shuttle service. His men, the *Igigi,* rocketed to Sippar and loaded gold from sea- freighters up from Africa. Anzu's men on Mars rocketed the gold to Nibiru, where scientists powdered and spread it in the air. "Slowly was the breach in the heavens healing."[ZS, *Enki:* 117]

49,000 years ago, from Mars, Anzu and the Igigi demanded Enlil better their work- conditions, issue more elixir and build a recreation center on Earth. Anu, from Nibiru, ordered Anzu to Earth to talk with Enlil. The King told Enlil to show Anzu everything.

At Nippur, Enlil wouldn't, at first, show the Durnanki to Anzu. Enlil told Anzu, *"I alone rull all Earth operations: You and the Igigi must obey, not challenge, me."*

Enki, however, told Enlil to show the gold mining, refining and transport system to Anzu. *"Get Anzu to keep his men on the job."* So Enlil told Anzu he could enter the restricted area in sterile clothes. When Enlil stripped down the key to the control room, Anzu stole the key, slipped into the control room and grabbed the crystals that ran Sumer's spaceport and cities. He forced Abgal to take him to the spaceport, Shu.ru.pak, where Anzu's men declared him King of Earth and Mars. He turned off vital services at headquarters (Nibru-ki), cut Earth-Nibiru communications, and, from his aircraft, buzzed Enlilite positions.

He freed Abgal and retrieved the crystals.

Ninurta launched his jet and shot Anzu down.

Ninurta captured Anzu and dragged him before Enlil.

The Seven Who Judge--Enki, Damkina, Marduk, Nannar, Enlil, Ninmah and Ninurta–found Anzu guilty of treason. Ninurta executed him "with a killing ray."

Enlil ordered Marduk to display Anzu's body on Marsbase, then bury him on Mars; let the astronauts see Ninurta kills rebels. [ZS, *Wars*: 95 -102, 124--Drawing of cylinder seal VA/243, Berlin Museum]

Nannar, Enlil's Heir (the first son Sud bore) had secretly directed Anzu's revolt. Nannar, with Anzu as his agent, meant to challenge Ninurta (Enlil's Firstborn) as heir. But after Ninurta slew Anzu, Enlil forced Nannar to honor Ninurta as Heir. Then Enlil exiled Nannar from Ur.

Ninurta, now Enlil's "Foremost Warrior," enforced Enlil's rules to extract, process and send gold to Nibiru.

To make sure Nannar and the Enkiites obeyed Ninurta, Enlil gave him the IB missile, "a weapon with fifty killing heads." Enlil and Ninurta could now, with unmatched firepower from the multi-headed missiles, intimidate even the Nibirans working the African goldmines for Enki. [ZS, *12th Planet*: 107 -116; *Wars*: 95 -102].

300,000 years ago, Earth's climate warmed dramatically. In Africa, Enki left goldmines to Foreman Ennugi.

V. ENKI, NINMAH & NINGISHZIDDA CREATED SLAVES

ENKI SAW *ERECTUS*'GENOME LIKE NIBIRANS'

Enki went North, to the Great Rift Valley (southeast Africa) to study an intelligent, fire-using primate, *Homo Erectus*. *Erectus* reasoned, freed animals from traps and communicated telepathically rather than with language. Enki thought Erectus either evolved on Earth from Nibiran genes delivered when Nibiru invaded the solar system or Erectus devolved from *Homo Sapien* colonists on Earth long before 450,000 years ago, when the Nibirans arrived. Erectus' and Nibirans' genomes differed only a few hundred (out of 30,000) genes.[7] Erectus would evolve in a few million years into Homo Sapiens. He built a lab in Zimbabwe to speed Erectus' development. [Cremo,: *Forbidden Archeology; Devolution*: 9 - 41; Ferguson: 33; ZS, *Genesis*: 121; *Giants*: 16, 153] ← Books

HOMO- ERECTUS TO HOMO - SAPIENS (MODERN MAN)

Erectus

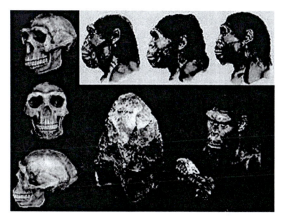

Homo Sapiens
70,000 year ago

ENKI INSTIGATED MUTINY TO JUSTIFY NIBIRAN/ERECTUS MINE SLAVES

At the mines, miners griped that boss Ennugi worked them too hard. Ennugi radioed Enki in Zimbabwe, but Enki sided with the miners and slyly told them to shrink gold shipments, lure Enlil to the mines and trap him. He planned to get Enlil to accept a plan for Erectus. When the miners cut gold to Badtibira, Enlil sent Ninurta to investigate. Miners "were backbiting and lamenting, in the excavations they were grumbling.
'Unbearable is the toil.'"

"Call Enlil to the mines," Enki told Ninurta, *"Let the Commander see how the miners suffer."*

When Enlil and his Vizier, Nusku, arrived, *"'Let us unnerve Enlil,'* mine-working heros shouted. *'Of the heavy work let him relieve us. Let us proclaim war, with hostilities let us gain relief.'* To their tools they set fire, fire to their axes they put." They held Ennugi hostage and, with tools as torches, surrounded the house Enlil occupied.

Enlil beamed Anu to shuttle to Earth and shoot the miners' leaders and their instigator (implying Enki).

The miners wouldn't say who led or incited them, but Anu felt for them. Ninurta wanted new miners from Nibiru. Enki said, instead, *"Let us create a Lulu, a primitive worker, the hardship to take over, let the Being the toil of the Anunnaki carry on his back. The Being that we need, it already exists. All that we have to do is put on it the mark of our essence* [genes], *thereby a Lulu, a Primitive Worker, shall be created!"* [ZS, *Enki*: 124 -127; *Encounters*: 347- 380]

Anu

Enki showed Erectus to Enlil and Ninurta, *"Ningishzidda, my son, their fashioning essence* [DNA structure] *has tested; akin to ours it is, like two serpents it is entwined. When with our life essence shall be combined, our mark upon them shall be, a Primitive Worker shall be created. Our commands will he understand. Our tools he will handle, the toil in the excavations he shall perform, to the Anunnaki in the Abuzu relief shall come."*[6] [ZS, *Enki*: 130]

ENKI, NINGISHZIDDA & NINMAH MADE SLAVES

Enlil objected. *"Don't create slaves. Slavery has from Nibiru long been ended. Tools are slaves, not other beings."* Ninurta told Enki, *"Make machines, not slaves."* [ZS, *Wars:* 130] *"Earthlings we create,"* said Enki, *"shall helpers, not slaves, be."*

Enlil shouted, *"To create hybrid beings is in The Rules Of Planet Journeys forbidden."*

Enki responded, *"A new species create we shall not; the Apeman is in his fashioning essence* [genotype] *as we of Nibiru are. Our ancestor the Apeman is; into us he evolves. Speed Apeman shall we, speed him but some millions of years to what has always been his destiny.*[2]*"*

Enki and Enlil beamed Anu and the Council on Nibiru. Each brother had his say on whether to create hybrids. King and the council ruled, *"Gold must be obtained. Let the Being be fashioned! Forsake The Rules of Planetary Journeys, let Nibiru be saved."* [ZS, *Wars:* 132]

Enki, Ninmah and Ningishzidda fused their DNA and Erectus' with other species' to create centaurs, griffins, cyclops, minotars, mermaids and

Enki and Ningishzidda serviced Erectus women but failed to impregnate them. So Enki and Ningishzidda gathered their own seed, and, in test tubes, fertilized Erectus ova to create zygotes. Then they planted the zygotes in Erectus women. The first babies born of the Erectus women lacked vision, hand dexterity or internal functioning. To beat these defects, Ninmah created the next zygote in a vessel of copper[8] and African clay instead of a test tube. But this zygote grew into a child who couldn't talk.[ZS, *The 12th Planet*, 352; *Genesis*: 164 -165, 201].

Then Enki planted a copper/clay vessel-grown zygote in Ninmah's womb, rather than an Erectus' or in an incubation box, to see if the baby Ninmah bore could speak. "In the clay vessel the admixture they made, the oval of an Earth female with Anunnaki male essence they put together. The fertilized egg into the womb of Ninmah by Enki was inserted. There was conception.

"To a male child Ninmah birth was giving. Enki the boy child held in his hands, the image of perfection was he. He slapped the newborn on his hindparts; the newborn uttered proper sounds. He handed the newborn to Ninmah. *'My hands have made it!'* victoriously she shouted." [ZS, *Wars* 138 - 139]

Ningishzidda, Enki, Adamu & Ninmah

'My hands have made it!'

ADAMU, THE HYBRID BOY (BLACK-HAIRED, DARK-SKINNED), UNLIKE NIBIRANS, SPORTED FORESKIN

Adamu ["one like South African Earth's clay"–a red shade], *Homo Neanderthalensis,* had smooth and dark red (not black, not white) skin and black hair (Nibirans, in contrast, were white-skinned and blue-eyed). Adamu's "malehood; odd was its shape, by a skin was its forepart surrounded, unlike that of Anunnaki malehood it was. *'Let the Earthling from us Anunnaki by this foreskin be distinguished.'* So was Enki saying." [ZS, *Divine Encounters* 47; *Enki* 139; Tellinger, *Slave Species*: 251]

~ 49 ~

Once she had Adamu, the prototype for the primitive worker, Ninmah radioed the Med Center at Shurubak; she needed seven doctors who'd volunteer their wombs to grow offspring of Adamu. *"'His essence alone as a mold shall be!'* so was Enki saying."* Ninmah and the women swore they'd love and support the babes they'd bare. [ZS, *Enki* 141]

"In seven vessels of the clay of Abzu [Africa] made, Ninmah ovals [zygotes which Ningishzidda's and Enki's sperm fertilized] of the two-legged females placed. The life essences of Adamu she extracted bit by bit in the vessels she it inserted. Then in the malepart of Adamu an incision she made, a drop of blood to let out.

'Let this a Sign of Life be; that Flesh and Soul have combined let it forever proclaim.' She squeezed the malepart for blood, one drop in each vessel to the admixture she added. *'In this clay's admixture, Earthling with Anunnaki shall be bound. To a unity shall the two essences, one of Heaven, one of Earth, together be brought.'* In the wombs of the birth-giving heroines the fertilized ovals were inserted." Ninmah cut Adamu's seven healthy boys from their wombs. [ZS, *Enki* 141; *12th Planet*: 352]

Ninmah (with her symbol, an umbilical-cutter) and Enki

Seven birth mothers bore Adamu's children

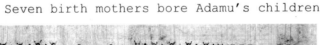

TI-AMAT, THE HYBRID GIRL:
BLONDE, WHITE & BLUE-EYED LIKE NIBIRAN GIRLS

To create a female, Ningishzidda planted another zygote, prepared with Adamu's blood, in Damkina, and, when it grew to a viable female fetus, excised her. Ninmah named the hybrid Ti-Amat (Mother of Life), a sandy-blonde. [Tellinger, *Slave Species*: 452] Ningishizidda put ova from Ti-Amat into seven test-tubes.

He planted them in the same doctors who'd borne the hybrid males. All the surrogate mothers carried female hybrids, which he removed surgically. When he told the doctors he needed their wombs again, Ninmah objected, *"For my heroines too burdensome is baring more Earthlings. Too few are the heroines to bare numbers enough to work mines."*

Enki brought Adamu and Ti-Amat to Edin but left the seven female and the eight male hybrids made from Adamu's and Ti-Amat's gametes together in an enclosure at his African lab. They copulated often, but the females didn't conceive.

Nibiran Astronauts who again worked the mines threatened mutiny if Enki and Ningishzidda didn't bring workers to relieve them.

Under pressure, at the Med Center in Shurubak,

Ningishzidda compared Nibiran genes and genes from Adamu and Ti-Amat. He found the genes for reproduction. Nibiran females had a recessive XY chromosomal allele in their genotype whereas Ti-Amat had only XX.

Ningishzidda

To make the hybrids breedable, Ningishzidda anesthetized Enki, Ninmah and Ti-Amat. "From the rib of Enki the life essence he extracted; into the rib of Adamu the life essence he inserted. From the rib of Ninmah the life essence he extracted; into the rib of Ti-Amat the life essence he inserted.

He proudly declared, *'To their Tree of Life two branches have been added, with procreating powers their life essencs are now entined.'* [ZS, *Enki*: 148]

Enki, Ninmah and Ningishzidda hid how they'd altered Ti-Amat. She and Adamu stayed in Enki's Persian Gulf orchard, while her fetus gestated. Ti-Amat made leaf-aprons for herself and Adamu.

ENLIL SENT ADAMU & TI-AMAT FROM EDEN TO AFRICA

Enlil saw Adamu and Ti-Amat wore aprons and made Enki explain. Enki confessed; Ti-Amat's fetus would, in turn, breed. *"The last bit of our life essence to these creatures you have given, to be like us in procreation knowing, perchance our* [millions of years] *life cycles on them to bestow,"* Enlil roared. Enki's team had exceeded Enlil's okay to create mine slaves in test tubes or with surrogate Nibiran mothers.

ENLIL, NINGISHZIDDA SAID, I DENIED THE HYBRIDS LIVE-LONG GENES

"'*My lord Enlil,*' Ningishzidda was saying, '*knowing for procreation they were given, the branch of Long Living, to their essence tree was not*' A longevity gene or genes known to Enki [and Ningishzidda] was deliberately excluded from the human genome when the 'mixing' of genes took place." '*Then let them be where they are needed,*' Enlil with anger said. '*To the Abzu away from the Edin, let them be expelled.*'" [ZS, *Enki*: 149; *Giants*: 245].

After Enlil evicted the hybrid Earthings from Edin, Enki knew Enlil would limit them and slander him as an evil serpent. So Enki set up the secret BROTHERHOOD OF THE SNAKE for a few Earthings whom he taught facts, technology and advanced thinking. [Tellinger, *Slave Species*: 145]

Enki put Adamu and Ti-Amat in an enclosure in Zimbabwe where Ti-Amat bore the twins Kai-in and Abael, then others who, in turn, bred with each other and with Nibirans.

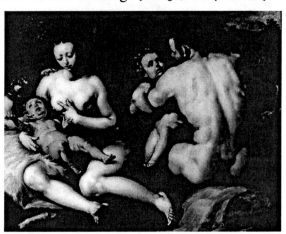

In a few thousand years, "the Earthlings were proliferating. To be with the Anunnaki they were eager, for food rations they toiled well. Of heat and dust they did not complain, of backbreaking they did not grumble. Of hardships of work the Anunnaki were relieved." The Earthlings worked the African mines and submersible cargo boats that, in just ten days, brought the gold from the mines to Bad-Tibira in Sumer to smelt, refine and form into portable ingots for transshipment to Mars. The vital gold to Nibiru was coming; steadily. Nibiru's atmosphere was slowly healing." [ZS, *Lost Realms*: 232; *Enki*: 151; *Giants*: 99]

Nibirans shuttled to and from Earth to match the best launch times, a span of 13 to 18 Earth months before Nibiru got closest and, leaving, before it got too far from Earth. While Nibiru "continued its vast elliptical orbit, the spaceship followed a shorter course and reached Earth far ahead of Nibiru or, for a shorter stay on Earth, the rocket launched "when Nibiru was midway back from apogee," a few years ahead of Nibiru.

When the rocket neared Earth, "it went into orbit around the planet without landing and released a shuttlecraft to land at Sippar's spaceport. "Some of the earlier arrivals would ascend to an Earth module and rejoin the spaceship for a trip home. To return, the shuttle "had to rejoin the mother ship, which had to fire up and accelerate to extremly high speeds to catch up with Nibiru." Shuttles took gold Earthlings mined to and from the base on Mars.[ZS, *12th Planet*: 282 - 271]

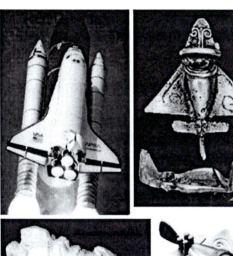

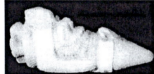

Space shuttles: modern and ancient

Moderns made actual flying models of these toy shuttles, which were found in both the Eastern and Western Hemispheres.

Nibirans gave Earthlings "food and shelter while they performed grueling tasks, the reason for which they did not understand. The stuff [gold] they were digging up had no value to them. They could not eat it, or use it in any way." The Nibiran Royals, their staffs and the Astronaut Corps needed" a steady stream of fresh laborers for projects.

In the south Africa, from Mozambique to Botswana, Zimbabwe and beyond, where the descendants of Adamu labored for the Nibirans, "the extended ancient settlement covers an area much larger than modern Johannesburg, more than 500,000 square kilometers." The Nibirans and their Adamite slaves built circles of stone linked by a never- ending web of over 500 kilometers of roads or connecting channels lined on both sides with over 500 million large iron-rich, magnetically-charged stones. The roads climb hills too steep for animals.

The Anunnaki and their laborers sent capacitated energy generated by sound along the roads or connecting devices and moved goods and water with "a levitation device that tapped into the magnetic content of the stones–in the same way modern trains float above their electromagnetic tracks and helped them lift stones heavier than 10 tons. They used a floating substance, the same monoatomic gold that they shipped back to Nibiru to save its atmosphere. The roads connected pits to leach gold, houses, terraces, workstations and ceremonial centers. Three of these South African cities that contained1086 million circular stone ruins covered 10,00 kilometers." [Tellinger, *Slave Species*: 125; *Temples*:53-82]

But 70,000 years ago, disaster, in the form of poison gas and dust swept over the ancient African goldmining complex. Survivors fled Africa. These refugees were the early Bantu (devotees of Antu's wife) fled to India, after a super volcano at Lake Toba in Sumatra erupted. "Prevailing winds from the supervolcano carried most of the dust and poisonous gasses westwards towards eastern and southern Africa [and] caused a mini ice- age. The most affected area: southern Africa, where the first civilization lived." The refugees carried the memories of the earth-moving equipment, astronomy, metallurgy, writing, architecture, energy generation, aircraft and weaponry of the Nibirans, but did not know how to make the tools. [Tellinger, M.,*Temples*:122 - 124; 2009a]

NIIBIRU'S PERIGEE KILLED MARS GOLD TRANSHIPMENT BASE

Rockets from Nibiru reached Earth best when Nibiru neared the Sun, at perigee. But at perigee also, Nibiru 's gravity perturbed planets and affected Nibiru's atmosphere. One of Nibiru's perigees, more than 350,000 years ago, disturbed the atmosphere and prompted volcanoes and earthquakes on Earth and Mars. "Kingu, Earth's Moon, was also affected" by mighty winds and "brimstones falling." Marduk (who ran the astronaut base, smelting and transshipment facilities on Mars) reported Marsbase unusable and asked Enlil to employ him on Earth. Enlil agreed. He beamed King Anu on Nibiru that rockets should instead of transshipment from Mars, take gold right from Sumer to Nibiru. Tellinger discusses a device Enki may have used to transport gold directly off Earth [Tellinger, 2009b]

ENKI & MARDUK VISITED MOON FOR NEW BASE

"Keep Marduk Astronaut Boss and re-assign the flyboys to a moonbase," Enki beamed Nibiru. *"'The netpull* [Gravity] *of Earth greatly exceeds Lahmu's* [Mars']. *To overcome it our powers shall be exhausted. Let us an alternative examine: nearby Earth, the Moon. Smaller is its netpull, ascent and descent thereon little effort will require. Let us a waystation consider, let me and Marduk thereto journey.'*

"*'Let the Moon be first examined,'* Anu to Enki and Enlil the decision beamed." Though he okayed the Mars trip for Enki and Marduk, Anu shrunk Enkiite power, especially Marduk's, (whom, he regretted, he'd agreed would succeed Alalu as Nibiru's king) with the astronauts. Anu suspected Enki, Marduk's father, abetted both the Igigi revolt Anzu led and also the miners' revolt in Africa. So the King ended gold transfer on Mars and Marduk's job as Operations Boss. Anu favored Enlil's lineage when he gave rule of the new spaceport (from which the gold would rocket straight to Nibiru) at Sippar to Enlil's son's son Utu.

"In a rocketship did Enki and Marduk to the Moon journey. In a place of rolling hills they set the rocketship down. Eagles' helmets [eagle-shaped helmets] they had to don; the atmosphere was for breathing insufficient. In the rocketship they made their dwelling. For one circuit [orbit = one Earth year] they remained. [ZS, *Enki*:153 -161]

ENKI PROMISED MARDUK SUPREMACY

Marduk, on the Moon with Enki, told him, *"You, Father, are Anu's Firstborn; yet Enlil and not you the Heir is. Gold in the city of Ninurta is assembled, therefrom to send to or withhold. The survival of Nibiru in his hands is, not mine. Am I to fame and kingship fated or again to humiliated be."*

Enki hugged Marduk. *"On that which I have been deprived your future lot shall be. Your Celestial Time will come."* Enki alludes here to the "Age of the Ram," Marduk's constellation, when Marduk should, with the calender he (Enki) created, rule. Enki's calender assigned twelve equal segments to star constellations. The constellation in front of which the sun rose on June 21, he said, showed the Anunnaki would rule all, and Marduk's time to reign supreme would, in Celestial Time, come. [ZS, *Enki*:160-161]

ANU: *EARTHLINGS FINISH GOLD OPS, ANUNNAKI COME HOME*

Anu ruled, *"Earthlings multiplying in Abzu must assist excavation, transport, refining gold till after several shars* [3,600 years] *sufficient will be the shield of Earth's gold powder to save Nibiru. Then home shall the heroes* [astronauts] *from Earth return."*

Some of the Earthling miners in South Africa--after 100,000 years of toil to get what seemed an unimportant substance, gold--revolted, others kept digging. Nibirans let many Earthlings "leave the mining compounds." Some Earthlings created new communities and survived without Nibirans' help. [Tellinger,*Slave Species*:117]

We Earthlings "were civilized first (lived in city or mining centers of the Nefilm [Nibiran mining bosses] and worked for them) and then some of us were forced into an uncivilized (non-city-center) environment. Humans in the city centers were contemporaneous with humans in the wild." The so-called *native indigenous people*, cast off by the mining bosses, were hybrids of Nibiran and Homo Erectus. [Freer, *Godspell*: 68]

In 144,000 years, most Nibirans--but not Enlil--wanted Earthlings too. Ninurta and fifty men raided Africa, caught Earthlings and brought them to work gardens, orchards and cities in Sumer. Enlil let Ninurta could keep and breed Earthlings for now since all Nibirans would soon leave Earth.

The naked Earthlings worked, cavorted, copulated and bred in Sumer. They slaved and foraged. Their numbers grew till they ran out of food. Enlil, angry Enki created fertile Earthlings, told him to teach them to feed themselves. Enki gave the Earthlings seeds, plants and tame beasts. [ZS, *Encounters*: 47; *Genesis*: 201]

HOMO-ERECTUS TO HOMO-SAPIENS (MODERN MAN)

ENKI BEGAT ENHANCED HYBRIDS

One of Nibiru's approaches upset Earth's climate and ruined the new crops. Earthlings adapted and foraged afar but made less food. From 27,000 B.C., Earthlings' standard of living worsened and they took again to the bush and cave-dwelling. "Following generations showed less advanced standards of civilized life. From 27,000 to 11, 000 the regressing and dwindling population reached almost complete absence of habitation." Enlil prodded Enki to make them smart enough to farm and herd better. Enki decided to uplevel Earthling intelligence and, at the same time, enjoy himself. [ZS, *12th Planet: 5 - 6;*]

In his African reserve, "Enki in the marshlands looked about. With him was Ismud, his visier, who secrets kept. "On the river's bank, frolicking Earthlings he noticed; two females among them were wild with beauty, firm were their breasts. Their sight the phallus of Enki caused to water, a burning desire he had.

 A young one to him Enki called, a tree fruit she offered him. Enki bent down, the young one he embraced, on her lips he kissed her. Sweet were her lips, firm with ripeness were her breasts. Into her womb she took the holy semen, by the semen of the Enki she was impregnated." Enki then coupled with the second young Earthling. [ZS, *Enki:* 167 -168]

One of the girls bore a boy, ADAPA; the other, a girl--TITI. Enki kept his fatherhood secret. His wife, Damkina, "to Titi took a liking; all manner of crafts was she teaching. "To Adapa, Enki teachings gave, how to keep records he was him instructing." Enki boasted, "*A Civilized man I have brought forth. A new kind of Earthling from my seed has been created, in my image and after my likeness. From seed they from food will grow, from ewes sheep they will shepherd. Anunnaki and Earthlings henceforth shall be satiated.*" [ZS, *Encounters:* 47 *Enki,:* 168-170]

ADAPA, ENKI'S SMART SON, BOSSED EARTHLINGS

Adapa and Titi, Enki's son and daughter, mated. Titi bore twins, KA-IN and ABAEL, the first ADAPite humans, humans with far more–due to Enki's genetic infusion-- Nibiran genes relative to *Erectus* genes than their mothers, the ADAMite girls Enki impregnated.

Enki schooled his (albeit clandestine) son Adapa. He ordered Adapa to teach his descendants--the enhanced Earthlings--to run farms, herds, estates and less enhanced Earthlings. Enki brought more Earthlings from Africa to Sumer for Adapa to train for the Mission bosses' homes and facilities.

Adapa worked, studied, pondered. He learned Nibirans ate the Bread of Life and drank the Water of Life to live hundreds of thousands of years. Without those substances, he'd die in mere thousands of years. He begged Enki for the Bread and Water, for immortality.

Adapa, "a busybody in charge of the services for which the primitive workers were brought over to the Edin, supervised bakers, assured water supplies, oversaw fishing for Eridu and tended offerings." Enki, either with a device that changed reversed the wind that blew down the Persian Gulf to blow Adapa north in a sailboat or he sent Adapa in a rocket. A Spy told Enlil he saw Adapa speed North. [ZS, *Encounters*: 51 -55]

ON NIBIRU, ANU NIXED ADAPA IMMORTALITY

Enlil beamed Anu on Nibiru: *Enki changed Gulf weather to blow Adapa south.* Anu sent his Visier Ilabrat to Earth for Adapa. Enki gave Ilabrat Adapa and sent his two unmarried Earth-born sons, Ningishzidda and Dumuzi, with Adapa to meet grandfather, Anu, and perhaps find Nibiran brides.

On Nibiru, King Anu asked Adapa why Enki changed the wind south and sent him down the Gulf. Ningishzidda slipped Anu a sealed tablet from Enki. Enki's tablet said he wanted Adapa to breed more enhanced Earthlings. Enki confessed fathering Adapa and Titi with Earthlings descended from Adamu and Ti-Amat. Ningishzidda already knew, from Adapa's DNA, that Enki begat Adapa and Titi. Enki asked Anu to send Adapa back to begat more hybrids, to father more ADAPITES--Civilized Humans.

The tablet asked Anu to deny Adapa food or elixir–the Bread of Life (probably monoatomic gold, the "Manna from the Heavens") and the Water of Life–that would lengthen the lives of Adapa and his descendants. The Earthlings descended from both Adam (Adamite hybids) and Adapa (Adapites), Anu knew, descended from him as well.

Enki and Ningishzidda-- Anu's son and son's son--via their seed, passed Anu's genes to the Earthlings, mixed with their DNA with *Homo Erectus*' and created an illegal civilized species. Enki wanted Anu to deny Earthlings the seeming eternal, lifespan Nibirans had, so the illegal species would stay long- quarantined on Earth.

NINGISHZIDDA TOOK ADAPA & SEEDS TO EARTH

Anu gave Ningishzidda grain seeds and told him to take them and Adapa back to Earth. *"Adapa teach; with Enki, teachers of Civilized Man be,"* said the King.

ON NIBIRU DUMUZI LEARNED HUSBANDRY

He told Dumuzi, *"On Nibiru stay, animal husbandry to master till Nibiru next nears Earth.* [3,600 years] *then to Earth return"* Dumuzi would bring sperm and female goats and sheep to inseminate. He'd teach his nephew Abael to tend the animals.[ZS, *Encounters*: 49 - 65; *Enki*:173 174]

Dumuzi   Abael   Dumuzi

KAI-IN KILLED ABAEL

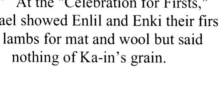

Ningishzidda flew to Earth with Adapa and grain seeds. Ningishzidda would teach Abael animal care so he could help Dumuzi when he too returned to Earth. When Dumuzi returned, however, Marduk pre-empted Abael and the animal project for the Enkiites.

Enlil had Ninurta tutor Ka-in to raise grain Ningishzidda brought. Enlilites, not Enkiites, would run Earth's farming. Ninurta taught Ka-in, Marduk taught Abael.

At the "Celebration for Firsts," Ka-in offered first grain, Abael showed Enlil and Enki their first lambs. Enki lauded Abael's lambs for mat and wool but said nothing of Ka-in's grain.

"By the lack of Enki's blessing greatly was Ka-in aggrieved." The twins quarreled an entire winter. They argued whether Ka-in's grains and fish-filled water canals or Abael's meat and wool gave most. In Summer, when Abael's meadows dried and his pastures shrunk, he drove his flocks "from the furrows and canals to drink. By this Ka-in was angered." The twins fought with fists till Ka-in bludgeoned Abael with a stone, then sat and sobbed. [ZS, *Enki*: 183-184]

KA-IN'S LINE GREW & SPREAD

Enki took Ka-in to Eridu for trail before Enlil, Ninki, Ninurta and Nannar of Enlil's Lineage, Ninmah, and Enki, Damkina and Marduk of Enki's (The Seven Who Judge). Marduk, Abael's mentor, told them to kill Ka-in. But Enki revealed he begat Ka-in's father Adapa, so Ka-in was Marduk's grandnephew. *"Ka-in must live,"* said Enki, *"to breed superior Earthlings to work field, pasture and mines. If Ka-in too shall be extinguished, satiation* [of food supplies] *to an end would come, mutinies will be repeated."*

The Seven ruled "Eastward to a land of wandering for his evil deed Ka-in must depart. Ka-in and his generations shall distinguished be.' By Ningishzidda was the life essence [genotype] of Ka-in altered: his face a beard could not grow." The beardless Indians of the Western Hemisphere (we'll see) descended from Ka-in. Sitchin said Ka-in's descendants could've been the Neanderthals as well. [ZS, *Genesis*: 201]

"With his sister Awan as spouse Ka-in from the Edin departed." They wandered in the wilderness to the east. Sitchin speculated that some of these initial descendants of Ka-in became the Neanderthals. [ZS, *Enki*: 186 - 187; 1990, *Genesis*: 201]

King Anu had, as Enki asked, refused to activate Nibiran-length longevity genes in Adapa (Ka-in's father). Nonetheless, Adapa lived hundreds of years. Then he faded, could barely see and would die soon. Ninurta flew Ka-in back to see his father in Edin before the old man died. "The eyesight of Adapa having failed, for recognition of his sons' faces he touched. The face of Ka-in was beardless."

Adapa told Ka-in, *"For your sin of your birthright you are deprived, but of your seed seven nations will come. In a realm set apart they shall thrive, distant lands they shall inhabit. But having your brother with a stone killed, by a stone will be your end."*

Ninurta returned Ka-in to the wilds east of Edin and " begat sons and daughters." Ninurta, "for them a city built, and as he was building, by a falling stone was Ka-in killed."

Ninurta may have killed Ka-in. [ZS, *Wars* : 112] Ka-in's survivors planted grain. They founded and ruled the city of Nud [also called Dun, Dunnu and Nu.dun].Sons of Ka-in's successors for the next four generations murdered their fathers. For the next three generations after that, each ruler of Nud killed his parents, married his sister, then ruled.

Ka-in's son's son's son, Enoch, succeeded Ka-in four generations later. Enoch married his sisters, Adah and Zillah. Adah's first son, Jabal (and the sub-lineage Jabal begat), lived in tents and herded cattle. Adad's second son, Jubal, begat lyre and flute players. Enoch's other wife, Zillah, bore Tubal-Cain, a smith, "artificer of gold, copper and iron." [ZS, *Wars*: 111 - 112; *Enki*:, 181-193]

ADAPA AND TITI'S OTHER KIDS AND THEIR KIDS SPREAD

Titi bore thirty sons and daughters to her brother Adapa. Nibirans divvied them up and taught them to write, do math, dig wells, prepare oils, play harp and flute. Nannar gave them rituals to worship him and the other Nibirans as gods.

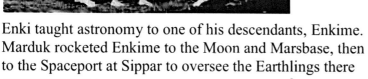

Enki taught astronomy to one of his descendants, Enkime. Marduk rocketed Enkime to the Moon and Marsbase, then to the Spaceport at Sippar to oversee the Earthlings there for Shamash.

Enki divvied Africa among his sons. Marduk ruled Egypt, Nergal ruled southern Africa. Enki kept Gibil (whom he'd taught metalworking) in north Africa's mining region and gave Ninagal the Great Lakes and headwaters of the Nile. Enki gave the grazing region, further north (Sudan) to his youngest son, Dumuzi. [ZS, *Wars*: 126 -127]

VI. MARDUK & ASTRONAUTS ALLIED WITH EARTHLINGS

MARDUK BETROTHED HYBRID SARPANIT

After Marduk checked the destruction on Mars, he returned to Earth. He announced he'd marry an Earthling superslave, Sarpanit, daughter of Marduk's Earthling protégé, Enkime (a descendant of Enki's part-Earthling son, Adapa).

Marduk's mother, Damkina, warned him: if he married Sarpanit "to Nibiru with his spouse he would never go. His princely rights on Nibiru he forever will forsake. To this Marduk with a bitter laugh responded, *"My rights on Nibiru are nonexistent. Even on Earth my rights as firstborn have been trampled"* [by Enlil and Ninurta]. But Marduk would marry Sarpanit and show his alliance with the Earthlings. He'd wield the Earthlings as weapons and with them win mastery, first of Earth, then Nibiru.

Sarpanit

Enlil beamed King Anu on Nibiru. *"The Marduk-Sarpanit union forbid."* But Anu and his counselors ruled, *"On Nibiru Adapa, the maiden's progenitor, could not stay. Therefore to return to Nibiru with her, Marduk must forever be barred. Marduk marry can, but on Nibiru a prince he shall no more be."*

Marduk

~ 66 ~

ASTRONAUTS STOLE EARTHLING WIVES AS MARDUK WED

In 3450 .C., Enlil let Marduk and Sarpanit say they'd wed at Eridu. But Enlil ordered the couple, after they wed, to Egypt (henceforth Marduk's fief) within Enki's Africa.

"A great multitude of Civilized Earthlings in Eridu assembled. Young Igigi from Lahmu [Mars] in great numbers came." Inanna, Enlil's granddaughter flirted with Enki's son, Dumuzi, oblivious that the Igigi planned to seize power for Marduk. [ZS, *Enki:* 198 - 199]

200 Igigi astronauts occupied the Landing Platform in Lebanon then flew to Eridu. They mixed with Earthlings and Nibiran Expedition people and watched Marduk and Sarpanit wed. Then each astronaut seized an Earthling woman.

IGIGI TOOK LEBANON, TOLD ENLIL:
OKAY OUR MARRIAGES OR WE'LL BOMB EARTH

The astronauts took the women back to Lebanon and "into a stronghold the place they made." Shamgaz, their leader, radioed Enlil: *"Bless our Earthling marriages or by fire all on Earth shall we shall destroy."* Marduk, their commander, demanded Enlil stop calling the Igigi/captive unions "abductions" and ratify them as marriages. Enlil fumed but didn't press the issue, "things against Marduk and his Earthlings was Enlil plotting." [ZS, *Enki*:201-202; *Wars*: 346]

Marduk settled some of the Igigi and the families they created (Children of the Rocketships) in Babylon; he and Sarpanit stayed with other Igigi/Adapite families in Lebanon. By 100,000 years ago, some of these "Children of the Rocketships" settled in "the far eastlands, lands of high mountains."[ZS, 2002, *Enki*: 202; 1985, *Wars*: 346]

Enlil ordered his successor Ninurta to counter the spread of Marduk's Earthlings. *"'The Earth by Earthlings inherited will be,'* Enlil to Ninurta said. *'Go, the offspring of Ka-in find, with them a domain of your own prepare.'"*

MARDUK FOILED INANNA - DUMUZI UNION

Skirmishes and the likelihood of mutually destructive war grew between Enki's and Enlil's lineages. Then their darlings fell decided to marry.

"On the Landing Platform [Lebanon], Dumuzi and Inanna their eyes on each other set. Hesitant at first they were, he of Enki's lineage, she of Enlil an offspring [son's daughter]."

Enkiite and Enlilite elders hoped that if Dumuzi wed Inanna, the deadly rivalry between their lineages would stop. *"Perchance the espousing peace between the linages truly will bring"* Enlil to them all did say."[9] He ordered the Indus Valley developed as a dowry for Inanna and Dumuzi. [ZS, *Enki*: 251; *Giants*: 215]

Dumuzi & Inanna

Inanna's Background:

Rulers of Nibiru and Earth pampered Inanna, then called Irnini. [later scribes wrote of Inanna as Ishtar, Ashtoreth, Annutitum, Aphrodite, Athena, Anat, Venus, Eshdar, Innin, Ninni, Kali and Shakti]. Nannar fathered her. Her mother, Ningal, bore Inanna and her twin Utu (delivered before Inanna) on Earth, where Inanna's grandfather, Enlil, rocked her cradle. The twins returned to Nibiru where Anu and his royal wife, Antu raised her. When returned to Earth, Ninmah educated her. [ZS, *Wars*: 231; *Enki*: 250]

Inanna and Utu, like homeplanet Nibirans, seemed immortal to the Earthlings. But Nibirans born on Earth matured faster than those on Nibiru. "Who on Nibiuru in diapers would still be, on Earth became a child; who on Nibiru began to crawl, when on Earth born was running around." Inanna's growth seemed stunted as well; she reached a mere 66 inches height, whereas Nibirans born on the homeplanet usually over 84 inches. [ZS, *Giants*: 221; *Enki*: 152]

Dumuzi's Background: Enki's spouse, Damkina, bore Dumuzi (a fast-maturing Earthborn like Inanna) long after their son Gibil and after Enki begat Ningishzidda with Erishkigal.

Dumuzi went with Ningishzidda and their hybrid half-brother, Adapa, to Nibiru. From Nibiru, Dumuzi brought sheep and goats to Earth. After the deluge receded, Enki made Dumuzi boss of Africa's domestic herds and herdsmen. Dumuzi became Enki's favorite son.

Jealous, Marduk made sure Dumuzi and Inanna didn't wed. He sent his sister GESHTINANNA to Inanna. "To her Inanna revealed, *'A vision of a great nation I have. As a Great Anunnaki Dumuzi there will rise. His queen-spouse I shall be. To Dumuzi I will status give, the country I will rightly direct.'* Inanna's visions of rulership and glory by Geshtinanna to her brother Marduk were reported.

By Inanna's ambitions Marduk was greatly disturbed; to Geshtinanna a secret plan he said." Marduk had Geshtinanna seduce Dumuzi. She told Dumuzi, *"Before you your young wife in your embrace will sleep, a legitimate heir, by a sister born, you must have"* [to keep succession within the Enki Lineage]. *Inanna's son to succession shall not entitled be."*
[Sitchin, J., Website; ZS, *Enki*: 251]

After she got his ejaculate, Geshtinanna panicked Dumuzi. She said, *"Marduk of raping me will accuse you, evil emissaries to arrest you he will send. To try you and disgrace you he will order, the liaison with an Enlilite to disunite."* Dumuzi, aghast, fled to hide behind a waterfall but slipped into the rapids and drowned in Lake Victoria. [ZS, *Enki:* 253]

Dumuzi is Gone

Inanna knew Marduk made Dumuzi die--though Marduk blamed a subordinate (the "evil emissary"). With techno-weapons, she chased Marduk, who ran through the chambers of the Great Pyramid. He radioed King Anu who beamed Inanna. The King told her Marduk had weapons that would kill her if she caught him.

Anu ordered Enlil and his chiefs to surround the Pyramid. *"Your side, hear we shall, to decide if you or an evil emissary killed Dumuzi,"* they told Marduk. When Marduk came out, the Enlilites assumed Anu would approve their decision, convicted Marduk and sentenced him to die slowly with air but no food or water in the King's Chamber of the Pyramid. They sealed him in; after awhile, he lapsed into unconsciousness.

Plan of the Great Pyramid

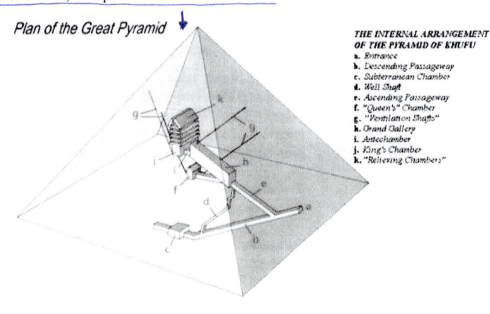

THE INTERNAL ARRANGEMENT
OF THE PYRAMID OF KHUFU
a. Entrance
b. Descending Passageway
c. Subterranean Chamber
d. Well Shaft
e. Ascending Passageway
f. "Queen's" Chamber
g. "Ventilation Shafts"
h. Grand Gallery
i. Antechamber
j. King's Chamber
k. "Relieving Chambers"

ANU HAD THOTH SAVE MARDUK FROM DEATH FOR KILLING DUMUZI

Marduk's wife Sarpanit and son Nabu beamed Anu, who told the Enlilites, *"My grandson Marduk is and must not be slain."* Ningishzidda tunneled into the chamber and revived Marduk, whom the Council banished to North America. In Egypt, they now called Marduk *Ra-Amen* (Amen = hidden). [ZS, *Wars*: 221 - 228; *Handbook*:136]. Ninagal, Dumuzi's brother, retrieved his body from Lake Victoria. He brought the body to Nergal and his wife, Ereshkigal (Inanna's sister) in South Africa. Inanna flew to her sister's place.

Inanna with Dumuzi's body

ERESHKIGAL STOPPED INANNA & NERGAL BREEDING HEIR TO AFRICA

Ereshkigal knew Inanna came to exercise *levirate* to make an heir with Nergal. For levirate, a brother of the man who died–Nergal, Dumuzi's brother in this case--impregnates his dead brother's wife but the child succeeds the dead brother. Inanna thought Dumuzi's eldest brother, Marduk, unfit to impregnate her since Marduk--Dumuzi's firstborn brother--caused Dumuzi's death. So she sought Dumuzi's next oldest brother, Nergal. She would, through Nergal and the boy they'd begat, rule in Africa despite Dumuzi's death. Their son would inherit Dumuzi's realms in northeast Africa, she, as Regent would usurp Ereshkigal in Africa. "Of scheming an heir by Nergal, Dumuzi's brother, Inanna was accused." [ZS, *Wars*: 230; *Enki*: 255]

When Inanna got to Ereshkigal's place, Erkeshkigal barred her entry.

Inanna & Ereshkigal

Inanna Inanna forced her way in, but Ereshkigal disarmed her and hung her on a stake to die.

But "from clay of the Abzu Enki two emissaries fashioned, beings without blood, by death rays unharmed, to lower Abzu he sent them, Inanna to bring back.

"Upon the corpse the clay emissaries a Pulser and an Emitter directed, then the Water of Life on her they sprinkled, in her mouth, the Plant of Life they placed. Then the dead Inanna arose." [ZS, *Enki*: 255]

Inanna took Dumuzi's body to Sumer and mummified him so he could rejoin her bodily on Nibiru, since, she said, Nibiran gods live forever. Sitchin wrote that the biophysics of Nibiru, which rounds the Sun once every 3,800 times Earth circles it, made Nibirans live longer than Earthlings but didn't let them live forever [ZS, *Cosmic Code*: 90, 96]

EARTH ICED

13,000 years ago, an new Ice Age hit Earth. The Earthlings begged for more food. [ZS, *Wars*: 111 -112; 20, *Enki:*, 188-193].

ENKI, NINMAH & ENLIL AGE SAW WRINKLES

Ninmah aged

Expedition chiefs--Enki, Ninmah and Enlil--met to resolve the food crisis. When they saw each other, face-to-face, they saw wrinkles, each others'. *"Old on Earth we became, but those on Earth born are even older sooner,"* said Enki. Earth, subject to much greater radiation from the sun than the distant homeworld of the Anunnaki, aged them faster, as did the shortened years of Earth, compared to the longer orbital years of the homeworld. [Lloyd, *Dark Star*: 101]

PERIGEE PRODUCED PROBLEMS

The chiefs sent Ninurta "Beyond the Seas in the mountainland [Andes] a Bond Heaven-Earth [transmission tower] to establish." Climate, magnetic storm and "sky-borne terrors" had hit Marsbase gold refinery, so they ordered Marduk to check damage on Mars.

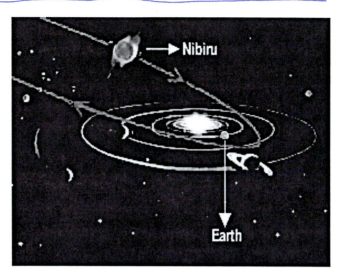

NINURTA FLOATED KA-IN'S DESCENDANTS TO SOUTH AMERICA

To meet Marduk's threat, Ninurta gathered Ka-in's descendants. He showed them how to build balsam rafts. They crossed the seas on the rafts and settled at Lake Titicaca atop the Andes. There Ninurta taught them tin and gold mining, smelting and refining. [ZS, 2002, *Enki:* 203]

LAKE TITICACA ANUNNAKI CONNECTION

~ 73 ~

VII. GALZU SAVED EARTHLINGS FROM FLOOD

ENKI BEGAT NOAH

Enki lusted for Batanash wife of Lu-Mach, Workmaster of Earthlings in Edin.

Lu-Mach, whom Enlil ordered to force the Earthlings to work more for less food, they said they'd kill Lu-Mach. So, to protect him and Batanash, Enki sent Lu-Mach to Marduk in Babylon. There, Marduk would teach Lu-Mach how to build cities. To "protect" Batanash, Enki sent her to Ninmah at the Medical complex of Shurubak, "from the angry Earthling masses protected and safe to be. Thereafter Enki his sister Ninmah in Shurubak was quick to visit.

"On the roof of a dwelling where Batanash was bathing, Enki by her loins took hold, he kissed her, his semen into her womb he poured." From this encounter, she bore Ziusudra (Noah). ZS, *Enki:* 204]

When Lu-Mach got back to Edin, "to him Batanash the son showed. White as the snow his skin was. Like the skies were his eyes, in a brilliance his eyes were shining." Lu-Mach complained, *"A son unlike an Earthling to Batanash was born. Is one of the Igigi his father?"* Batanash, in a parsing worthy of Bill Clinton, swore *"None of the Igigi fathered the boy."*

ZIUSUDRA — NOAH

"Ziusudra," Lu-Mach's father added, *"will the Earthlings guide through the Ice Age."* [ZS, *Enki:* 204]

Ninmah loved and cared for Ziusudra; Enki taught him to read Adapa's writings.

Crops dried-up, Earthlings starved, plagues killed many. "Diseases overcame humans. But Ninmah [said] *'Let us the Earthlings curing teach, how themselves to remedy to learn.'"* Enlil refused. *"'Let the earthlings by hunger and pestilence perish.'* In his mind the stay of the Anunnaki on Earth was nearing an end and he would rather wipe out all life before they departed for Nibiru. Nothing grew and winds, heat and drought haunted them. Tremors and quakes became regular events."

Enki implored Enlil, "*Let us show the dredging of ponds and canals for surviving drought and famine.*

You, Enlil sneered, *thwarted my orders and Earthlings created. Marduk--your eldest--the Igigi with the armies they breed with the daughters of Adapa challenge me. No ponds, no canals. For Marduk, no more soldiers; let them starve, every one. When we sated with Earth's gold return to Nibiru return,* leave no Earthling subjects for Marduk, no force for him, the homeplanet to invade. [ZS,*Enki*: 204 -205; Tellinger, *Slave Species*: 470]

The Earthlings at Shurubak (where Ziusudra lived under Enki's and Ninmah's tutilage) sent Ziusudra to Enki at the Persian Gulf for help. Enki said he couldn't openly help and told them, "*The policy of Enlil protest, worship of the gods boycott.*"

Covertly, Enki fed Earthlings from his corn. He gave them access to the seas and taught them to fish there. When Enlil said Enki defied the decree that Earthlings starve, Enki said he did not know how Earthlings learned to fish in the seas.

Frustrated in his attempt to kill the Earthlings by starvation, Enlil planned to let Nibiru's perigee destroy them when the Nibirans quit the mines and left Earth. [ZS, *Enki:206*; 1978, *12th Planet:*292 -294]

Each 3,600 years Nibiru neared Solaris and triggered volcanos on Nibiru, launched huge flares on Solarus and disturbed the atmosphere and lands of Mars and Earth. Nergal reported from the south tip of Africa that the Antarctic ice sheet slid toward the ocean and would, next approach of Nibiru, slip into the sea and generate surges that would reverberate and inundate all Earth except great peaks.

Enlil said the Expedition sent Nibiru enough gold. Nibirans could return home. The sea would drown the Earthlings.

GALZU & ENKI DEFIED ENLIL'S EDICT TO LET FLOOD KILL ALL EARTHLINGS

King Anu and the Counsel on Nibiru beamed Earth: "*'For evacuating Earth and Lahmu prepare.'* In the Abzu the gold mines shut down; therefrom the Anunnaki to the Edin came; smelting and refining ceased, all gold to Nibiru was lofted. Empty, for evacuating ready, a fleet of celestial chariots to Earth returned."

SPACESHIPS

Celestial Chariot (SPACE SHIPS)

One spaceship brought the mysterious white-haired Galzu (Great Knower) with a sealed message from Anu to Enki, Enlil and Ninmah. (Galzu, we'll see, will thwart the drowning genocide Enlil planned for the Earthlings.)

"Enlil the seal of Anu examined; unbroken and authentic it was, its encoding trustworthy. *'For King and Council Galzu speaks. his words are my commands.'* So did the message of Anu state. *'I am Galzu, Emissary Plenipoteniary of King and Council, to Enlil,'*" said the mysterious visitor."
[ZS, *Enki*: 208]

Galzu

GALZU LIED, KEPT ENLIL, NINMAH, ENLIL & THEIR LINEAGES FOR EARTH DESPITE COMING DELUGE

Galzu told Ninmah, *"'Of the same school and age we are.'* This Ninmah could not recall: the emissary was as young as a son, she was as his olden mother." Galzu told her she'd aged and he hadn't because she'd been so long on Earth. She and her brothers lived on Earth so long they'd die if they returned to Nibiru, where their bodies couldn't survive the homeplanet's netforce.

Galzu lied: *"The three of you on Earth will remain; only to die to Nibiru you will return."* Ninmah and her brothers must, he said, orbit Earth in rockets when the icesheet sped waves over the planet. When the waters calmed, to live, they must return to Earth.

Enlil continued reading the order Galzu said he brought from King Anu, *"To each of the other Anunnaki, a choice to leave or the calamity outwait must be given. The Igigi who Earthlings espoused must between departure and spouses choose. No Earthling, Marduk's Sarpanit included, to Nibiru to journey is allowed. For all who stay and what happens see, in celestial chariots they safety must seek."*
[ZS, *Enki*: 209 - 211]

Enlil convened the Anunnaki Council--the Leaders' sons and grandchildren--and the Igigi commanders. He decreed the Earthlings drown in the deluge. Enki objected, "'*A wondrous Being by us was created, by us saved it must be,*' Enki to Enlil shouted."

Enlil roared back,"'*To Primitive Workers* knowing *you endowed. The powers of the Creator of All into your hands you have taken. With fornication Adapa you conceived, understanding to his line you gave. His offspring to the heavens you have taken, our wisdom with them you shared. Every rule you have broken, decisions and commands you ignored. Because of you a Civilized Earthling brother* [Abael] *a brother* [Ka-in] *murdered. Because of Marduk your son the Igigi like him with Earthlings intermarried.*'" The Earthlings, Enlil said, must drown. He demanded Enki and all Nibirans on Earth swear not to tell the Earthlings a flood will come. Enki hesitated to openly defy Enlil, but he refused to swear. He and Marduk stamped out of the Council. [ZS, *Enki*: 212 -214]

Enlil brought the Council back to order. Astronauts with Adapite wives and children, he decreed, must move to the peaks above the waves. He, Enki, Ninmah, their sons, daughters and descendants would orbit Earth. Marduk must shelter on Marsbase and Nannar on the moon. When the waters receded the leaders and kin would return to Earth. [ZS, *Enki*: 230]

Enki and Ninmah buried their records and computer programs deep in the Iraqi soil. They made genetic banks to save Earth's creatures from the flood. "Male and female essences and life-eggs they collected, of each kind two by two they collected for safekeeping while in Earth circuit to be taken, thereafter the living kinds to recombine. The day of the deluge they waited." [ZS, *Enki*: 216]

Genetic banks saved Earth's Creatures
DATA GENETIC BANK

Enki dreamed Galzu spoke "'*Into your hands Fate take, for the Earthlings the Earth inherit. Summon your son Ziusudra, without breaking the oath* [swearing not to tell Earthlings] *to him the coming calamity reveal. A boat that the watery avalanche can withstand, a submersible one, to build him tell, the likes of which on this tablet to you I am showing. Let him in it save himself and his kinfolk and the seed of all that is useful, be it plant or animal, also take. That is the will of the Creator of All.*'"

Enki woke and pondered his dream. He stepped out of bed and kicked an actual physical tablet that now appeared next to his bed. The tablet showed how to build a submersible craft in which Ziusudra and his followers could ride out the deluge. Enki searched his home and grounds for Galzu but didn't find him. None except Enki (in the dream) had seen Galzu. Sitchin termed the appearance of the tablet--a physical object--after Enki's dream encounter with Galzu, a representative of a higher power-twightlight zone miracle.

The Submersible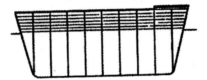

"That night to the reed hut where Ziusudra was sleeping Enki stealthily went. The oath not breaking, the Lord Enki not to Ziusudra but to the hut's wall [computer bank] spoke frombehind the reed wall.

In the tablet above, Galzu, in the center, tells Enki (on the left with his snake icon) to warn Ziusudra (touching the "wall"--a computer bank, shown with Xs across the screens and slots for programs) of the Flood. Galzu guides Enki's arm to convey a computer disk. The disk leaves Enki's hand en route to Ziusudra's computer)

"When Ziusudra by the words awakened, to him Enki said, *'Reed hut, a calamitous
storm will sweep, the destruction of Mankind it will be. This is the decision of the assembly by Enlil convened. Abandon thy house, Ziusudra and build a boat, its design and measurements on a tablet. A boatguide* [Ninagal] *to you will come. To a safe haven the boatguide will navigate you. By you shall the seed of Civilized Man survive. Not to you Ziusudra, have I spoken, but to the reed wall did I speak.'"* [ZS, Enki: 220 -222]

The submersible: ancient wall depiction, context of ancient wall that shows two airplanes, a helicopter, a rocketship and a submersible with folded mast.

Egyptian Temple Wall Panel on which the images are raised

Submersible close-up with mast down

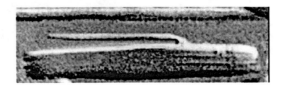

Enki prepared. Before the wave hit, he sent Ninagal with boxes to Ziusudra. The boxes held "DNA, sperm and ova, '*the life essence and life eggs of living creatures it contains, by the Lord Enki and Ninmah collected. From the wrath of Enlil to be hidden, to life resurrected if Earth be willing.'*" Ningishzidda prepared too; he inscribed "ancient wisdom on two great pillars and hid sacred objects and scrolls inside them. [Hauck, *Emerald Tablet*: 22]

13,000 years ago, "in the Whiteland, at the Earth's bottom, off its foundation, the [Antarctic] icesheet slipped. By Nibiru's netforce it was pulled into the south sea. A tidal wave arose, northward spreading." "The tidal wave, several hundred metres high, moved northward from Antarctica at 500 km per hour, like a giant circle around the world; it destroyed all lands lower than 2,000 metres above sea level." [Tellinger, *Slave Species*: 472 - 473]

"The boat of Ziusudra the tidal wave from its moorings lifted. Though completely submerged, not a drop of water into it did enter. For forty days, waves and storms swept Earth, downing everything on the planet except those on mountaintops and in

Ziusudra's boat." [ZS, *Enki*: 227]

Ninagal surfaced, raised sail and steered to Mt Ararata, where Ziusudra built a huge signal fire and roasted a lamb to honor Enki.

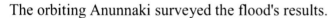

The orbiting Anunnaki surveyed the flood's results.

Enki and Enlil descended in helicopters (whirlwinds) from their rockets. "When Enlil the survivors saw, Ninagal among them, *'Every Earthling had to perish'*, he with fury shouted'; at Enki with anger he lunged, to kill his brother with bare hands he was ready." Ninagal radioed Ninmah and Ninurta, *"Bring your whirlers down quick."*

"'He is no mere mortal, my son he is,' Enki to Ziusudra pointing. *'To a reed wall I spoke, not Ziusudra.'"* Ninurta and Ninmah restrained Enlil. Enki told them he'd seen Galzu in a dream, then, when he woke, found next to his bed, a tablet that showed how Ziusudra should build the submersible.

Together, Enki, Ninurta and Nimah convinced Enlil *"The survival of mankind the will of the Creator of All must be."* [ZS, *Enki*: 228 - 229].

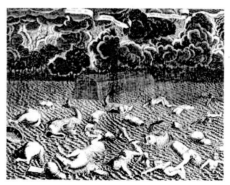

When the floodwaters receded, they left the uplands intact but left the spaceport at Sippar, all of Sumer and African goldmines under mud and silt. Earthlings at low elevations had drowned. Less than a thousand Earthlings dug alive from mountain caves to a world of mud that ruined for gathering and hunting.[10] [Freer: *Sapiens Arising:*110]

People with Ziusudra on Ararat, hybrid Igigi-Earthling families who fled to Mesopotamia's mountains and the descendants of Ka-in at the Peruvian refinery and spaceport lived. Nibirans in charge of the Andean space and refining facilities helped "the few Andean survivors upon the high peaks to repopulate the continent.

New, postdeluvial arrivals came by sea. A leader called Naymlap led his people across the Pacific in a fleet of boats made of balsa wood, guided by a green stone through which the Great God delivered navigational and other instructions. Landfall was Cape Santa Helena in Ecuador. The Great God, still speaking through the green stone instructed the people in farming, building and handicrafts." In North America, Hopi, as well remember a " handful of their ancestral Flood survivors digging out of cave shelters to start over." [Freer, N., 2008, *Sapiens Rising*: 109 - 110; ZS:*Time*:263]

"All the Anunnaki built in the past 432,000 years was buried under miles thick mud." Of their settlements, only the stone Landing Platform [Baalbek] in Lebanon, survived intact." [ZS,*Enki*: 230; *Cosmic Code*: 54]

NIBIRU TOOK MARS' AIR AND SURFACE WATER

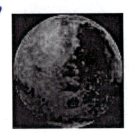

To Baalbek Enlil summonsed Nibirans who survived the flood on the Earth's peaks and the astronauts in spacecraft orbiting the planet. He also called in Nannar from the moon and Marduk from Mars. Marduk reported Mars "*By the passage of Nibiru was devastated. Its atmosphere was sucked out, its waters evaporated, a place of dust storms it is.*"

Nannar reported the moon usable only with Eagle Masks [helmets].

Nannar, "Man in the Moon"

VIII. NIBIRANS REVIVED SUMER, BUILT SINAI SPACEPORT

ANUNNAKI FOSTERED CROPS AND BEASTS 11,000 - 10,500 B.C.

Enki dug up the seeds under the Lebanon Platform. In his lab, he quadrupled the grain chromosomes and had Ziasudra's son run bakeries for the re-builders, then had him supervise the laborers. Ninurta and Enki mapped a dam, sluice and canal system for Sumer. Adad surveyed fruit trees that lived and found grapes Ninmah brought from Nibiru. Earthlings again grew white and red wine grapes.

Ninagal reported, *"Life essences and life eggs in the four-legged animals from Ziusudra's boat can be combined. Sheep for wool and meat will multiply, cattle for milk and hides will all have."* Enki bade Dumuzi replenish the livestock; Ziusudra's middle son ran the shepherds for Dumuzi. So began the Neolithic, the Age of Domestication. [ZS, *Enki*: 229 - 234]

From 11,000 - 10,500 B.C., the gods revived Sumer, taught the proliferating Earthlings bronze and brick technologies, built a new spaceport in Sinai Spaceport and renewed Earth's crops and beasts. "Suddenly and without gradual perpetuation," the gods made Earthlings farmers. The agriculture they taught "spread all over the world from the Near Eastern arc of mountains and highlands." The gods gave Earthlings wheat and barley, then "millet, rye, spelt, flax (for fibers and edible oil), onions, lentils, beans, cucumbers, cabbage, lettuce, apples, apricots, cherries, pears, olives, figs, almonds, pistachios, walnuts." They taught Earthlings to weave fiber into cloth, make flour, bread, porridge, cakes, pastries, biscuits, yogurt, butter, cream, cheeses, beer and wine. Settled communities grew and the gods gave Earthlings domesticated dogs, geese, ducks, sheep, goats, pigs, horned and hornless cattle for hides, meat, milk and wool.

Ninurta introduced PLOWS. First, Earthlings pulled them, then cattle. With Enki's new grains, they boosted food-growing. Nibirans and their foremen directed Earthlings to regulate the Nile and create pastureland for Dumuzi's herds. The Nibirans gave Sumerians the WHEEL, carts and chariots, which Dumuzi's oxen and horses pulled. [ZS, *12th Planet*: 6 -9; *Wars*: 125]

Enlil and his sons and grandchildren ruled Sumer: Innana, Elan (southeast); Adad, the Taurus Mountains, Asia Minor and the northwest; Ninurta, the highlands; Nannar, the North; Utu, Lebanon's Airport. Each Sumerian god walled his sacred precincts, "each with a skyscraping ziggurat [stepped pyramid]. The ziggurats rose in several steps (usually seven) to 90 meters. They were build of two kinds of mud brick sun-dried for highrise cores and kiln- burned for extra strength for stairways, exteriors, and overhangings; held together with bitumen as mortar."

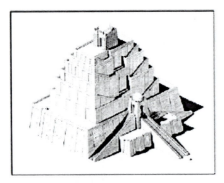

Enlil kept Nippur, Sumer's center, and there stored his computer programs, "Tablets of Destinies" and the "Command and Control Center for Earth to offplanet communication, the *Bond Heaven-Earth* in his high-rise stepped pyramid. In the city, Enlil had Earthlings built schools of science and scribing as well as a library with 30,000 inscribed clay tablets. [ZS, *Wars*: 125; *Giants*: 67 - 69]

Enlil, Enki, Inanna, Adad, Ninurta, Utu and Nannar taught the Sumerians "every 'First' of what we deem essential to advanced civilization: wheeled transportation, brick that made possible high-rise buildings; furnaces and kilns essential to baking and metallurgy, cities and urban societies, kingship, temples, priesthoods, festivals, beer, culinary recipes, art, music, musical instruments, musical notes, dance, writing and record keeping, medicines, textiles, multicolored apparel, a mathematical system, sexagesimal, that initiated the circle of 369^0, timekeeping that divided day/night into 12 double hours, a luni-solar calendar of 12 months intercalated with a thirteenth leap month, geometry, measurement units of distance, weight and capacity, an advanced astronomy with planetary, star, constellation and zodiacal knowledge, law codes and courts of law, irrigation systems, transportation networks and customs stations, even taxes." [ZS, *Giants*: 58, 70]

Enlil ordered a new rocket terminal at Sinai, on the Arabian Peninsula, for freighting gold to Nibiru. Enlil told Enki and his lineage to build the new terminal, Mission Control and guidance facilities in a mountain-like Great Pyramid at Giza, near the Nile at the 30th Parallel. "Although the Sinai Peninsula and the Giza pyramids were supposedly neutral under Ninmah, Enki and the Enkiites" intended to control the peninsula. Whoever ran the Giza Pyramid and Sinai, controlled "space activities, the comings and

goings of the 'gods,' the vital supply link to and from Nibiru. Only Enki, the master engineer and scientist had the know-how and experience for the massive works."

From 10,000 B.C. on, Enki's sons Marduk and Ningishzidda assisted Enki, as did his descendants Shu, Tefnut, Geb and Nut. "The secret plans of the Great Pyramid were in the hands of Ningishzidda."
[ZS, *Wars*:149-155]

Viracocha [Adad/Ishkar] gathered the survivors atop the Andes who survived the Deluge; he had them build palaces for him and his Nibiran Overseers. Viracocha educated couples he chose to establish an empire ruled from Cuzco. [ZS, *Time*: 247]

NIBIRU PERIGEE TORE ITS GOLD SHIELD

Nibiru's perigee 13,000 years ago created the Deluge and also "ripped away the shield of gold dust around Nibiru, gold the astronauts struggled for millennia to ship to the mother planet. Nibiru's atmosphere was again dwindling. The mother planet again desperately needed Earth's gold. While survivors on Earth rebuilt their lives, word came from Nibiru, *'The shield of gold dust was torn.'*" Nibiru ordered the Expedition to send lots more gold at once.

For more gold, the Expedition needed more Earthling miners and a new rocket terminal. But in Africa mud interred the mines as well the miners. In Sumer mud topped the Bad-Tibira refinery. Mud smothered the rocket terminal at Sippar.

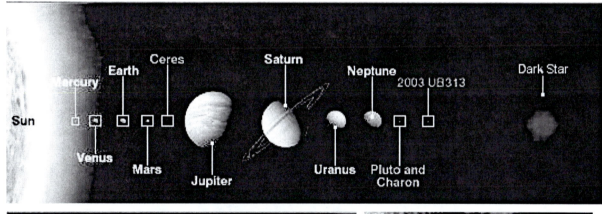

NIBIRANS GAVE SUMERIANS BRICKS AND BRONZE

Mud covered all the stone and minerals Sumerians needed for building. Ninurta, who ran the recovery for the next 7000 years, taught the Earthlings who survived how to make bricks and bronze tools and build houses, temples, canals and dams.

Sumer and Europe failed to yield enough CASSITERITE, which Ninurta needed to refine copper for tin and bronze, so he hunted gold and natural copper. He found them in alluvium of rivers that run into the east coast of Lake Titicaca in Peru--huge chunks of pure gold and copper. The copper needed no refining.

On an island in the lake (Titicaca), Ninurta also found beardless descendants of Ka-in, now Andean Indians, who'd survived the flood on rafts. They could mine the gold Ninurta found. Ninurta brought Adad, Sumerian overseers and African technicians to organize the Indians. [ZS, *Lost Realms*: 228- 222]

"When the Anunnaki gods decided to help humans learn skills of survival after the flood, not all humans were convinced this was a good idea. Some did not trust the brutal gods who had oppressed them for so long, and therefore remained in their mountain hideouts, too scared to enter the newly established settlements of people. It looked to them like a new version of the labour camps that persisted for millennia around the gold mines.

Eventually [the gods] found these communities of rebellious Earthlings and imposed their control on them in the remote locations. Even the most remote tribes of the planet all had a similar relationship with the omnipresent gods. As the new communities' need for labour increased they went into the mountains or neighboring village and caught themselves some slaves. All ancient cultures in the world were practicing slavery. From the very first day of civilization man practiced what he was taught by his maker: obsession with gold and keeping slaves." [Tellinger, *Slave Species*: 217 -218]

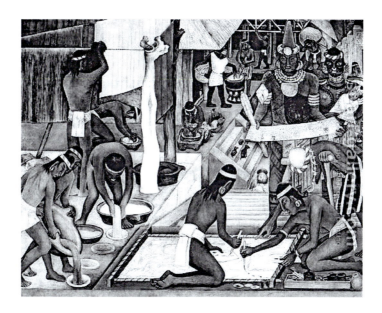

NINGISHZIDDA BUILT THE NEW SPACEPORT IN SINAI

Ningishzidda (with power tools better than ours to cut and move rock) built two pyramids in Egypt. First he built a model, then the Great Pyramid. Then he built the Great Pyramid over the records of the Nibirans, inscribed on emerald tablets, in a secret chamber, the Halls of Amenti. He installed Nibirans' master computer programs and astronavigational equipment in the Great Pyramid and configured the pyramid itself as a communication device send messages directly to Nibiru. [Sereda, 2012]

ANOMALIE MASTER COMPUTER

SPHINX HEATED MARDUK VS NINURTA COMPETITION

Enki got Enlil to let Ningishzidda to build a statue too: *"Let us beside the twin peaks a monument create, the Age of the Lion toannounce. The image of Ningishzidda, the peaks' designer, let its face be. Let it precisely toward the Place of Celestial Chariots gaze."* Marduk protested (later Marduk'll chisel the face of his son Osiris to replace Ningishzidda's). [ZS, *Enki*: 238]

Marduk fumed that Enlil choose Utu to run the Sinai Spaceport on the 30th parallel. The 30th separated the realms of the Enlilite Lineage (North of 30) and Enkiite (South of 30).

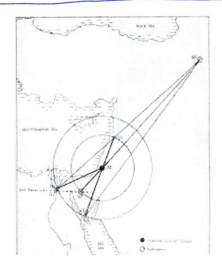

In the Great Pyramid, Gibil installed pulsating crystals and the Gug Stone, a capstone of electrum, to reflect a beam for incoming spacecraft. The beam from the capstone marked the western edge of the runway line from Ararat to Tilmun on the Sinai.

CRYSTAL GUG STONE

Mt. Katherine, at the southern tip of the Sinai, marked the eastern edge of the rocket runway corridor. Mission Control perched on Mount Moriah (the future Jerusalem), off-limits to Earthlings.

IX. NIBIRANS, WITH EARTHLING MINIONS, FOUGHT

"Marduk to his father Enki words of aggrievement said, `To dominate the whole Earth to me did you promise. Now command and glory to others are granted, without task or dominion I am left.'" [ZS, Enki: 238]. Enki's other sons as well as Enlil's Champion, Ninurta, and Ninurta's half-brothers in the Enlilite Lineage also demanded "lands for themselves and devoted Earthlings."

NINMAH PARLEYED PEACE, WON SINAI

Ninmah urged Enlil to give all Royals land and Earthlings. He gave Ninmah Sinai--Tilmun (Land of Missiles)--as neutral turf between his Enlilite lineage and Enki's. Enlil and Enki made her a palace in Sinai. Enlil titled her "Ninharsag, Mistress of the Mountainhead." Though Enlil "entrusted Tilmum to the neutral hands of Ninmah, control of the Spaceport was in the hands of Utu, commanding the Eaglemen" [astronauts]. Marduk thought he, not Utu, should lead the Astronaut Corps. [ZS, End of Days:71]

Ninmah/Ninharsag
    Utu/Shamash

Enlil gave lands east of Sinai to two of Ziusudra's sons. Descendants of these sons–Shem and Japheth--served the Enlilites. The Commander gave Africa to Enki and his lineage. Ziusudra's son Ham and Ham's descendants-- Enki's Earthlings--ruled Enlil, must stay in Africa. But Ham's descendants defied Enlil and moved North, out of Africa and into Canaan on the Mediterranean side of the Arabian Peninsula.

Noah & His Three Sons Shem, Ham and Japheth

~ 90 ~

Nibiran whirlbirds lofted Peru's gold nuggets to the Sinai to ship to Niburu to again shield it with gold. Andean Indians, white overseers, black technicians and redmen descended from Ka-in mined the gold for Nibiran pilots to rocket to Nibiru and for tin for bronze for Sumer.

For 300 years, peace prevailed on Earth.

"To protect themselves against competition from a new species on Earth, the Anunnaki ensured that the genome of the slave species was severely stunted, did not live too long, was prone to disease, did not use much of its brain and had a finite memory. They did not count on the evolution of our genome and our intelligence because they did not expect to stay on this planet for so long."
[Tellinger, *Slave Species*:130 - 131]

Enlil feared revolt by the hundreds of thousands of Earthlings and ordered the Anunnaki to conceal Earthlings' part-Nibiran genealogy from them. For awhile, only Earthlings Enki brought into his secret society, the Brotherhood of the Snake, knew he'd made them genetically part-Nibiran and suppressed their genes for longevity.

Enki meant the Brotherhood for our benefit, "to bring knowledge." Other Anunnaki objected, defeated Enki, infiltrated the Brotherhood, split it into several competing cults run–to this day--by elite Earthlings beholden to Nibirans who pose as gods and to the elites in the Nibirans' favored Earthling bloodlines. All the secret society cabals hide our extraterrestrial genetic heritage. [DoHerarty, J., *Did Enki Give Humans Knowledge?*]

Enki moved to Elephantine (Abu) Island near Aswan (Syene). From Abu, he (now called Ptah) ruled Egypt.

Enki as Ptah

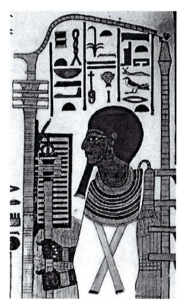

Enki's Earthlings built dams, dykes and tunnels and controlled the Nile's flow to the Mediterranean. Then Enki abdicated and gave Marduk, (now Ra) official rule of Egypt and its Earthlings. He divvied Africa among his sons. Marduk ruled Egypt, Nergal ruled southern Africa. Enki kept Gibil (whom he'd taught metalworking) in north Africa's mining region and gave Ninagal the Great Lakes and headwaters of the Nile. Enki gave the grazing region, further north (Sudan) to his youngest son, Dumuzi.

MARDUK'S DESCENDANTS FOUGHT PYRAMID WAR I

In 11,000 B.C., before the Deluge, Marduk, Sarpanit, and their sons, Osiris (Asar) and Seth (aka Satu or Enshag) sheltered with Marsbase's Igigi Commander, Shamgaz. Osiris and Seth married Shamgaz's girls, Isis (aka Asra–Ningishzidda's child with Marduk's granddaughter). Osiris married Isis. Seth married Nephys (aka Nebat) .[ZS, Enki: 243 - 244.]

Isis & Osiris

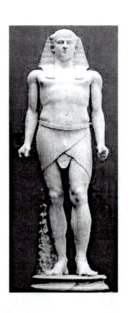

Seth

Nephys & Seth

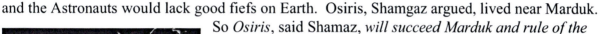

"Shamgaz with Seth connected and bonded." Osiris "to block Seth's chances to have his descendants rule Egypt, took Seth's half-sister Isis as his spouse. Seth then married Nephys, his full sister." The full siblingship of Seth and Neptys disqualified their offspring from rulership [zs, *Enki*: 243 - 244.]

Osiris and Isis lived near Marduk in the northern lowlands of Lower Egypt. Seth and Nebat settled in southern Upper Egypt's mountains, near Shamgaz's villa and the Lebanon Landing Platform. Shamgaz and Nebat told Seth that while Osiris lived he and the Astronauts would lack good fiefs on Earth. Osiris, Shamgaz argued, lived near Marduk.

So *Osiris*, said Shamaz, *will succeed Marduk and rule of the fertile lower Nile. Only Upper Egypt for you and the Igigi.*" [zs, *Enki*: 243 - 244.]

So Seth, Nephys and Shamgaz decided to kill Osiris. Shamgaz and Seth invited Osiris to an Astronaut and Royals banquet honoring Aso, Ethiopia's visiting Queen. Shamgaz drugged Osiris's wine, and when Osiris passed out, sealed him in a coffin they tossed in the sea.

Shamgaz & Seth sealed Osiris in a coffin

Word of Osiris's murder reached Isis, Sarpanit and Marduk. They retrieved Osiris's coffin from the sea.

Seth said he, as Marduk's sole surviving son, ruled all Egypt.

Papa Marduk wanted Seth dead for killing Osiris but Grandpa Enki forbade this. Instead, Enki had Isis extract semen from Osiris's corpse and inseminate herself with it.

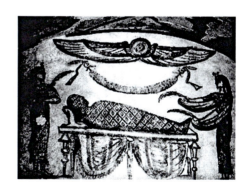

Isis said, "*I carry Osiris' son. Our son, not Seth should rule Lower Egypt.*" She hid and bore Horus (Horon) to fight Seth and avenge Osiris. Shamgaz and the astronauts ignored Isis.

Isis raised Horus kill Seth and avenge Osiris.

The Igigi astronauts spread their estates and their Earthling armies from Lebanon all the way to the edge of Ninmah's neutral Jerusalem region. They advanced toward the Interplanetary Landing Zone on Sinai.

Meanwhile, in Upper Egypt, Marduk's brother Gibil tutored Horus to manhood. Gibil taught Horus to pilot aircraft, made multi-headed missiles for him and taught him and his Earthlings to smelt IRON and make iron weapons. Horus' army marched on Sinai. Seth, rather than face Horus's better-weaponed army, dared Horus to an air battle.

HORUS BEAT SETH; COUNCIL SENT SETH TO CANAAN

Horus flew his fighter toward Seth, who hit him with a poison dart missile. Ningishzidda gave Horus an antidote and a "blinding weapon." Horus hit Seth with the weapon, then with a missile called the harpoon. Blind, Seth crashed, his testicles squashed; Horus bound him and dragged him before the Council.

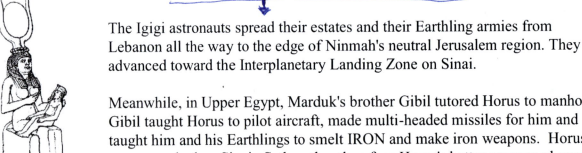

The Council, though Canaan was reserved for Enlilites and their Earthlings, let Seth live there. The Council had ordered Enkiite Nibirans and Earthlings descended from Ziusudra's son Ham restricted to Africa, but the Ham-ites defied the Council and occupied Canaan. The Council let Seth live among these Enkiites. Seth soon ruled Canaan.

Seth's rule in Canaan meant Enkiites controlled the Giza Spacecraft Marker- Pyramid, the control tower and runways on Sinai, and the new Mission Control Jerusalem.

NINURTA BUILT TITICACA SPACEPORT

The Enlilites feared Enkiites would run Earth's space facilities, dictate gold flow from Earth to Nibiru, and with this leverage, force Marduk's rule on Nibiru as well as Earth. Enlilites couldn't talk with Nibiru or flee Earth when they quit mining if Marduk won the space sites.

To counter this, Enlil sent Ninurta to covertly construct a communications center next to Lake Titicaca. Ninurta built also a spaceport on the Nazca plains next to the Andes.
"From there" Ninurta reported, "gold shipments to Nibiru can continue, from there in need we too can ascend." [ZS, *12th Planet*: 248 -249]

8670 B.C., PYRAMID WAR II: INANNA & ENLILITES DEFEATED ENKIITES

Ninurta, Inanna and the Enlilites waited 300 years, then attacked Seth's forces in Canaan. The Enlilites fought to regain the space-related marker peaks–Moriah, Harsag (Mount St. Katherine) in the Sinai and the artificial mount, the Ekur (The Great Pyramid) in Egypt." [ZS, *Wars*: 156 - 158]

Ninurta, in a new jet with a 75-foot wingspan blasted Marduk's stongholds "while Adad roamed behind the enemy lines" and destroyed the fish, cattle and food of the Enkiites and their Earthling armies.

Marduk's armies retreated into the mountains but Inanna blasted them with "an explosive beam that tore the enemy apart" and forced them south. Ninurta led the Enlilite forces' "attack on the heartland of Nergal's African domain and his temple-city Meslam. They scorched the earth and made the rivers run red with the blood of the innocent bystanders–the men women and children of the Abzu."[ZS, *Wars*: 159 - 163, based on Lugal-e Ud Melam-bi in Geller, S., 1917 Altorientalische Texte und Untersuchungen]

NINURTA SHOT POISON MISSILES ON THE AFRICANS

Ninurta rained poison-bearing missiles on Meslam and leveled the city. Survivors fled to nearby mountains. But Ninurta "with the Weapon that Smites threw fire upon them, smote down the people." Utu held off the Igigi in Sinai.

ENKIITES RETREATED TO GIZA PYRAMID

After Ninurta killed the Enkiites on Sinai, he defeated Marduk in Kur. Marduk fled into the Great Pyramid at Giza, where Enki "raised up a shield through which the death rays could not penetrate." [ZS, *Wars*:162]

Marduk's brother Nergal "broke through Ninurta's lines and came to Marduk's aid. Nergal strengthened the pyramid's defenses "through ray-emitting crystals positioned within." But Marduk's brother Ningishzidda refused to defend him. Marduk's other brothers, Ninagal and Gibil, his father Enki and Marduk's grandson Horon joined Marduk in the pyramid. The Enkiites made their stand together in the Giza Pyramid.

Utu cut off the water source to the Enkiites in the Pyramid.

Horon, disguised as a ram, slipped out of the pyramid but Ninurta blinded him with his "Brilliant Weapon." Enki radioed Ninmah to stop the fight and save Horon.

NINMAH WON CEASE-FIRE

Ninmah lied that Anu ordered a cease fire then a peace conference. Adad objected; he demanded Enkiites surrender unconditionally. Enlil overrode Adad and told Ninmah, *"To your palace* [the Harsag, above the Sinai] *bring Enki and his issue."* Ninurta gave Ninmah a suit that protected her from radiation.

She crossed the battle lines and told the Enkiites, *"The Enlilites wouldn't hurt you; just come out and surrender."*

Enki hesitated, *"Out shall we come if to a peace treaty between our lineages Enlil commits."* But he gave her his hand. Ninmah led him and his lineage loyalists to the Harsag, her abode. [ZS, *Wars*: 164 - 172]

Ninurta entered the pyramid and explored the Enkiites' astronavigational guidance systems and secret weapons. He threw away equipment he wrecked in the fight as well as weapons he couldn't use. He salvaged the interplanetary landing beacon and "the Gug Stone that directions determined." Ninurta broke or looted 54 large crystals that spiraled energy up, around out the top of the pyramid to rockets and to Nibiru. [Sereda: 2010; ZS, *Enki*: 262.]

8670 B.C. TREATY SET RULERS AND FIEFS

Ninmah, "brought out Enki and his sons, took them to her abode in the Harsag. The Enlilite gods were already there, waiting." She started the conference with a plea for peace. Enlil unilaterally ceded Enki's settlement, Eridu in the E.Din area at the Persian Gulf with land around to bear fruit for the temple and to have seeded fields. Ninurta objected to giving this foothold in Sumer to Enki, till Ninmah told Ninurta to drop the issue.

Enlil agreed to stop attacks if the Enkiites and the Earthlings descended from Shem left Canaan's Restricted Zone (Sinai Peninsula and Spaceport) and Jerusalem. Enki demanded his Enkiites keep Giza. To this, Enlil agreed if "the sons of Enki who brought about the war and used the Great Pyramid for combat be barred from ruling over Giza or Lower [Northern] Egypt."

So Enki replaced Marduk with Ningishzidda, Enki's son with Enlil's granddaughter Ereshkigal. Ningishzidda had refused to fight for Marduk and Enki against Ereshkigal's paternal uncle, Ninurta. The Enlilites could accept Ningishzidda, though an Enkiite, to rule Egypt, since his mother, Ereshkigal, was an Enlilite. Both lineages accepted Ningishzidda as Nile Delta ruler.

Enlil ordered all astronavigational communications and guidance equipment stay in lands he and his Enlilites ruled. Astronauts who'd sided with Marduk must leave the Landing Place in Lebanon as well as Canaan. Treaty concluded, Enki and sons left for Africa [ZS, *Enki*: 260, *Wars*: 174 -176]

Enlil chose Mount Mashu, just north of Giza (the site became Annu, then Heliopolis) for a new rocket beacon to replace the beacon Ninurta wrecked at the Giza Pyramid. Ninurta installed the crystals he'd salvaged from Giza for the new beacon and topped the mountain with the Gug Stone ("Stone of Directing, Mount of the Supreme Celestial Barque, the mount was called."). [ZS, *Wars*: 181-182; *Enki*: 263]

ENLIL DIVVIED FIEFS; NONE FOR INANNA

Einlil, Ninurta, Adad, Nannar and Nannar's wife, Ningal sat with Ninmah to hear Enlil divide Enlilite territory and hear who he'd appoint to rule Sumer, Lebanon and Canaan.

Ninurta--Enlil's declared successor--and Nannar--Enlil's firstborn by his offical spouse--clashed. Enlil, recall, had made Ninurta Campion and made Nannar, who'd supported Anzu's rebellion, swear loyalty to the Champ. Then Enlil banished Nannar from Ur. Now, however, Ningal got Enlil to restore Sinai, Canaan and Syria to Nannar. [ZS, *Wars*: 178-180]

Enlil chose Utu to run the new Mission Control at Jerusalem, "central in the Divine Grid that made the comings and goings between Earth and Nibiru. Jerusalem pinpointed the middle line, the Landing Path, equidistant from the Landing Platform in Lebanon and the Spaceport." ZS, *Wars*: 180-181; *Enki*: 264]

Enlil kept Adad as chief in Lebanon and the Landing Place at Baalbek and lands north, south and east of Lebanon (where Igigi astronauts and their hybrid familes lived).

Inanna erupted when Enki chose Ningishzidda to replace Marduk as Lord of Nile Lands. She and Dumuzi, she shouted, should've ruled the Upper Nile *"Against Marduk the war I led; that entitles me to my own domain,"* she roared.

The Enlilite leaders beamed Anu on Nibiru. He'd not visited Earth for 7,000 Earth Years. *"To Earth come,"* Enlil pleaded, *"Deal with Inanna."*

"How Inanna's demands the leaders contemplated. Regarding the Earth and its resettling, words with Anu [on Nibiru] they exchanged.

"From the time of the Deluge [11,000B.C.] almost two Shars [7200 years] passed. Earthlings proliferated, from mountainlands to dried lowlands. Of Civilized Mankind Ziusudra there were descendants, with Anunnaki seed they were intermixed. Offspring of the Igigi who intermarried roamed about. In the distant lands Ka-in's kinfolk survived.

"Few and lofty were the Anunnaki who from Nibiru had come, few were their perfect [genetically unmixed with Earthlings] descendants. How over Mankind lofty to remain, how to make the many the few obey and serve. About all that, about the future the leaders with Anu words exchanged. To come to Earth Anu decided." [ZS, *Enki*: 264 -265]

In the 7000 years since the Deluge, the Nibirans reclaimed Sumer. They rebuilt on the silt that covered their predeluvian homes--Enki's Eridu and Enlil's Nibru-ki. For Anu's visit to Earth, they built Unug-ki, a temple in Uruk where neither Enki nor Enlil ruled.

3800 B.C., Anu and his wife Antu landed at Tilmun. Enki, Enlil and Ninmah--Anu's three children--greeted them. "At each other they looked, aging to examine: though greater in shars [orbits of Nibiru of Solaris] were the parents, younger than the children they looked. The two sons [Enki and Enlil] looked old and bearded; Ninmah, once a beauty, was bent and wrinkled." [ZS, *Enki*: 268].

Enlil told Anu "Enki was withholding from the other gods [i.e., the Enlilites] the 'Divine Formulas'– [information devices called MEs], that hold knowledge of more than one hundred aspects of civilization--confining advancement to Eridu [Enki's fief] and its people only."

Anu said, "*Divine Formulas, Enki, with other gods share, so urban centers establish they can. Civilization to all Sumer grant.*" [ZS, *Wars*: 193-194]

ANU SAW GALZU'S RUSES TO KEEP FOSTERING EARTHLINGS

"*I dreamed,*" Enki told Ninmah, Enlil and King Anu, "*your Plenpotentiary, Galzu, gave me plans for Ziusudra's boat. I woke and kicked a stone tablet with boat plans engraved.*"
Puzzled, Anu said, "*Never did I send a secret plenipotentiary to Earth.*"

Enki and Enlil exclaimed, "*On account of Galzu Ziusudra and the seed of life were saved. On account of Galzu on Earth we remained.*"

" '*The day you to Nibiru return, you shall die,' so did Galzu to us say.* Incredulous of that was Anu; the change in cycles [between Earth and Nibiru] indeed havoc did cause, but with elixirs cured it was."

"'*Whose emissary, if not yours was Galzu?'* Enki and Enlil in unison said. '*Who the Earthlings to save wanted, who on Earth made us stay?'*

"*For the Creator of All did Galzu appear.*" Ninmah said. The Creator planned, she said, for the Nibirans to hybridize with *Erectus*. ANNWAKI'S TO HYBRIDIZE WITH HOMO-ERECTUS

Anu said, "*While fates we decreed, the hand of destiny at every step directed. The will of the Creator of All is: on Earth and for Earthlings, only emissaries are we. The Earth to the Earthlings belong, to preserve and advance them we were intended.*

"*Whatever Destiny for the Earth and Earthlings, let it so be. If Man, not Anunnaki to inherit the Earth is destined, let us destiny help.*

"*Give Mankind knowledge...secrets of heaven and Earth them teach. Laws of justice and righteousness teach them then depart and LEAVE.*"[ZS, *Enki*: 271, 275] GIVE HUMANS KNOWLEDGE

NIBIRANS GOT TEMPLES, EARTHLINGS GOT CITIES & RULERS

On his sixth day on Earth, Anu called Ninmah, Enlil and Enki to the palace they'd built him. Enlil told Anu of abundant gold in the Andes. ANDES

Enlil, Anu, Ninmah and Enki realized the Creator of All had, via Galzu, ordained they protect and develop the hybrid Earthlings they created in the lab and in bed. They decided:

"*Knowledge* Mankind to provide. Cities of Man to establish, therein *sacred precincts* abodes for the Anunnaki create. *Kingship* as on Nibiru on Earth establish, crown and scepter to a chosen man give, by him the word of the Anunnaki to the people convey, work and dexterity to enforce; in the sacred precincts a priesthood to establish, the Anunnaki as lofty lords to serve and worship. Secret knowledge to be taught, civilization to Mankind convey." SECRET KNOWLEDGE TO BE TAUGHT CIVILIZATION TO MANKIND CONVEY

Nibirans "brought down from heaven symbols of Anu's military dictator-kingship: divine headdress (crown, tiara); scepter of staff (symbol of power, authority); and coiled measuring cord (representing Justice); these symbols appear in divine investiture depictions at all times in which the god or goddess grants these objects to a new king."[ZS, *Enki*, 271 - 272; *Giants*: 127]

The Anunnaki turned Earthlings' palace-servant duties into religious rituals that persist to this day. "Serving meats on the Anunnaki table became burnt offerings. The table became an altar. The transportation of the local Anunnaki ruler on a dias became a procession of statues. The Anunnaki palaces became temples." [Freer, *Sapiens Arising*] THE ANUNNAKIS BECAME TEMPLES GODS SLAVE SPECIES OF THE GODS (RELIGION CONTROL)

Anu decreed four regions, three–Sumer, Egypt and Africa, and Indus Valley–whom Ziusudra's descendants would govern for the Nibirans.

Region 1: Enlilites': Enlil and his lineage named kings, men descended from Ziusudra's sons, Shem and Japhet the Fair, through whom they ruled Sumer. By 7400 B.C.

Shem, and his successors ran nations from the Persian Gulf to the Mediterranean. Around 3800 B.C., Shem's descendants settled the ex-spaceport area of Iraq and the Landing Place at Lebanon. Japhet's issue ruled lands in Asia Minor, the Black and Caspian Sea areas, as well as the nearby coasts and islands, as they recovered from the flood.
(SPACE-PORT IN IRAQ AND THE LANDING PLACE IN LEBANON).

Region 2: Enkiites': Anu said Enki and his descendants would rule Egypt and Africa though successors of Ziusudra's son Ham the Dark. Ham's line ruled Canaan, Cush, Mizra'im, Nubia, Ethiopia, Egypt, and Libya from the highlands and spreading to the reclaimed lowlands.

Region 3: Inanna's: Inanna would rule the Indus Valley (to settle around 2800 B.C.) as a grain-source for the other regions.

Region 4: Ninmah's: Ninmah reigned in The forth region, Tilmun (Sinai). Anu reserved Sinai for Nibirans and their descendants. [ZS, *Wars*: 129-135; *Enki*: 271 - 272]

ANU BEDDED INANNA

"Anu to his great-granddaughter Inanna took a liking; he drew her closely, he hugged and kissed her." At Anu's temple at Uruk, Sumer's sacred precinct, Anu's wife, Antu, taught Inanna tantric sexual meditations and how to channel the sexual energy she and Anu would share to elevate their whole clan. Then Antu ritually gave Inanna to Anu. Antu and the Nibiran elite meditated outside the love-chamber as Anu and Inanna coupled. Antu and the Nibiran royals shared ecstasy, epiphany and satori. "The sexual experience was a merging of energies which enhanced the creative powers of both partners and the aggregate of their race." [ZS, *Enki*: 273]

Anu renamed his great granddaughter *Inanna*, "Anu's Beloved;" She'd been "Irnini" before this. He'd bed her whenever he visited Earth. The King gave her the temple where they loved and the skyship he'd use to survey Earth. Inanna, he said, would run Uruk's temple through a priest/king, the son of her brother Utu with an Earthling.

Earthlings paved Uruk with "limestone blocks brought from mountains fifty miles to the East." They erected a thick, six-mile long wall around Uruk's living quarters and Inanna's temple. [ZS, *Encounters*: 166 -176; *Giants*: 75]

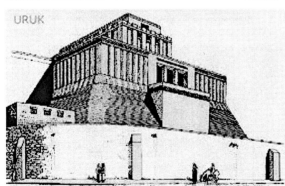

When archeologists excavated Uruk, they "found [Earth's] first colored pottery baked in a kiln, first use of a potters wheel, first cylinder seal[5], first inscriptions in the pictorial predecessor of cuneiform." [11]

FIRST INSCRIPTION IN THE PICTORIAL PREDECESSOR OF CUNEIFORM.

But Inanna fumed while male Enlilite Royals built cities in Sumer. "While the domain of her own she demanded. '*The Third Region* [Indus Valley] *after the second one will come!* her leaders thus assured her." [ZS, *Enki*: 279]

Anu and Antu flew (In the skyship he'd leave to Inanna) with Ninurta to the Tiahuanancu temple, observatory and metallurgy (tin) works Ninurta'd built. The King saw the Spaceport on the 200 square mile Pampa plain below where. On the runway, "Anu and Antu's celestial chariot stood ready, with gold to the brim it was loaded." [ZS, *Lost Realms*: 255; *Enki* : 272 – 275; *Journeys*: 206]

ANU PARDONED MARDUK, LEFT FOR NIBIRU

Anu ordered Marduk from Tiahuanaco. Anu's had married Enki to his Marduk. Though Alalu succeed Alalu as Nibiru's Marduk enraged Nibiru Adapite Earthling, supported the Igigi when and at Baalbek. exile in North America to predecessor Alalu, remember, daughter Damkina and she bore and Anu agreed Marduk would King, Anu deposed Alalu. when he married hybrid Sarpanit. Then Marduk they seized 200 Earthling wives The Nibiran Council punished Marduk: banned him and forbade him to ever rule Nibiru.

Anu thought he hurt Marduk when he favored Marduk's brothers Dumuzi and Ningishzidda and invited them, but not Marduk, to Nibiru. Anu wondered if *"by Dumuzi and Ningishzidda to Nibiru inviting, Marduk's ire I myself have caused."*

Marduk and Nabu came to the King and told him Sarpanit died. Anu pardoned Marduk and commuted his exile. [ZS, *Enki*: 272]

"Anu said, *'If Mankind, not Anunnaki, to inherit the Earth is destined, let us destiny help. Give Mankind knowledge, up to a measure secrets of heaven and Earth them teach, laws of justice and righteousness teach them, then depart and leave."* [ZS, *Enki*: 275]

After Anu and Antu flew back to Nibiru, their rocket filled with gold, Marduk raged at the regions of influence Anu gave his rivals. Marduk said Inanna blamed him for Dumuzi's death which she herself caused. Now, Marduk whined, Inanna consorted with Anu, who gave her reign over the Indus Basin, as well as Uruk. Enlil told Adad to guardthe Enlilite South American facilities from Marduk while the other Nibiran Earth Mission leaders returned to Sumer. [ZS, *Enki*: 275-276]

Enlil named the era, his, "Age of the Bull." He had his sons and grandsons declare themselves and other Nibirans´descendants "gods." Mixed Nibirans and Earthlings were demigods, who would direct Earthlings to build temples and cities to serve the gods. He ranked the gods. His father, King Anu, he ranked 60. He numbered himself and his successor, Ninurta, 50s. Enlil ranked Enki 40, Ninghzidda 52, Nannar, 30. Nannar's son Utu ranked 20, Utu's sister Inanna, 15.

Ninurta asked Enki at Eridu for computer programs (MEs) he needed for a city. Ninurta had his Earthlings create Kishi, the first city an Earthling king he appointed ruled. Then Ninurta had his men build Lagash, a city with a hangar for his aircraft, an armory for his missiles and a temple-home for himself and his wife, Bau.

Utu, from rebuilt Sippar, home of Sumer's Supreme Court, and made laws for the Earthlings. Nannar ruled the city of Urim. Adad returned from the Andes to a temple in the mountains north of Sumer. Marduk and Nabu moved to Enki's place in Eridu. [ZS, Encounters: 68; Enki:275-278]
Enlilites now upleveled Sumerian Civilization; they introduced schools and taught Earthlings to write and print on clay; how to find, extract, transport, refine and alloy minerals. Through their kings' administrations Enlil's sons introduced silver money so Earthlings could buy and sell.

"Sumerian cities were highly organized, with central government and social class structures. Each city was populated by up to 10,000 people, rising to 50,000 by 2700 B.C. Agriculture still took the majority of workers, but created stable food so other citizens could work as masons, bakers, weavers and tradesmen overseen by municipal bureaucracy."

Kings had assemblies frame laws and choose court justices. "Procedings, judgements and contracts were recorded. Justices acted like juries. A court was three or four judges, one a professional, the others drawn from a panel of thirty-six men."

Ninurta's staff taught Earthlings to use petroleum–bitumens and asphalts–that just oozed out of the ground in Sumer as fuel for kilns. With the kilns, men made molds and bronze objects. They used petrol for to surface roads, to make cement, to calk and water- proof buildings and even make artificial lapis lazuli.

Earthling kings learned to "carry out major construction work with architectural plans, organize and feed huge labor forces, flatten land, raise mounds, mold bricks, transport stones, bring rare metals from afar, cast metal and shape utensils. Sumerians built many types of ships, some able "to reach faraway lands in search of metals, rare woods and stones." [Lloyd, Dark Star: 33; ZS, 12th Planet:12- 49]

X. INANNA FOUGHT MARDUK

INANNA SEDUCED ENKI FOR URUK'S PROGRAMS

Inanna wanted a city complex, like Ninurta's at Kishi, built around her temple at Uruk. Ninurta'd built Kishi with fifty MEs--programs for math, smithing, pottery as well as making beer, pottery, wagons wheels and law--Enki gave him. Enki released the MEs "to benefit mankind, step by step." Inanna, too, needed Enki to give her MEs too. "The MEs, physical objects one could pick up and carry (or even put on), contained secret knowledge or data like our computer chips on which data, programs and operational orders have been recorded. On them the essentials of civilization were encoded." [ZS, *Wars*: 239]

Inanna first flirted with Enki at his villa on the Persian Gulf. She wanted MEs for weaponry, statecraft, mathematics, writing, metallurgy, masonry, arts, courts. He could thrill her with advanced sexual practices too. She visited him at his palace in southeast

Africa, got him drunk, seduced him. He gave her the MEs. She slipped them to her pilot to take back to Uruk. Enki sobered, captured her, locked her up at Eridu and tried to get the MEs back.

Enlil flew to Eridu. Inanna shouted, *"By right the MEs I obtained, Enki in my hand placed them!* So did Inanna to Enlil say; the truth Enki meekly admitted." [ZS, *Enki*: 281]

In 3760 B. C., Inanna choose the first King, the Lugal. He spoke for the gods to the Earthlings. 23 successive Lugals ruled Sumer for 24,510 years. Lugals shifted venue from Ninurta's Kishi to Inanna's Uruk, then to Akad. When Enlil ordered kingship moved to

Uruk, Inanna launched the MEs she'd seduced from Enki. She made Uruk a mighty city state and made Enmerkar (son of and successor to her nephew) its ruler.

Though "Sumer was the heartland of the Enlilite territories," Enlil decreed the Eridu on Sumer's south edge belonged forever to Enki and Marduk. In 3460 B.C. Marduk developed Eridu into a base, Babylon, in Sumer at Babylon on the Euphrates River "between rebuilt Nippur (the pre-Deluvial Mission Control) and Sippar (the pre-Deluvial spaceport)."

50 B.C. ENLILITES BOMBED BABYLON, BABBLED SPEECH

Babylon, Marduk planned, would serve as "Mission control and Spaceport." He named the place, *Bab-Ili*, "Gateway of the gods"–a place where Nibirans could take off and land. He had Babylon Earthlings built a "tower whose head shall reach the heavens–a launch tower." [ZS, *End*: 22]

Marduk's Igigi allies who'd seized Earthlings at Marduk's wedding, ran great fiefs in Lebanon and Sumer. Their estates and the number of their Earthlings grew as the Igigi bred with each generation. Marduk's son Nabu gathered Earthlings and Marduk taught them to make bricks for his spaceport. With his own launch tower at Babylon, he'd challenge the Sinai Spaceport Utu ran. *"This evil plan must be stopped,"* roared Ninurta.

Many artists over many years envision the Tower of Babel

Enlil ordered Marduk to quit the project peacefully, but Marduk defied him and built his tower. Enlil decreed,"*Marduk an unpermitted Gateway to Heaven is building, to Earthlings he is entrusting. If we let this happen, no other matter of Mankind shall be unreached.*" Ninurta bombed the tower and Marduk's camp at Babylon.

Marduk fled to Enki's other domain on the Nile. The Enlilites scattered Marduk's Earthlings and programmed them to different languages and scripts. [ZS, *Encounters*: 110 - 115; *Enki*: 281- 282]

Tower of Bablylon bombed

3100 B.C.: MARDUK RETURNED TO EGYPT, OUSTED THOTH

"When Marduk, after a long absence, to the Land of the Two Narrows [Egypt] returned, Ningishzidda' [now called Thoth] as its master he there found. With the aid of offspring of the Anunnaki who Earthlings espoused did Ningishzidda the land oversee, what Marduk had once

planned and instructed by Ningishzidda was overturned." [ZS, *Enki*: 284]. For the next 350 years, Marduk (now called Ra) and Ningishzidda clashed over Egypt. Finally, Enki, their father, ordered Ningishzidda to leave Egypt to Marduk.

~ 107 ~

Thoth (now called *Quetzalcoatl*) moved on to his realms in Mesoamerica and brought some of his Olmec stonemasons and Sumerian foremen from there to build Stonehenge observatory in England. In 3113 B.C., after he'd finished Stonehenge, he returned to Mesoamerica. He built planetariums throughout Mexico and Central America and gave Mayans their calendar to correlate with lines of sight built into the observatories he built for

them.

In Peru, atop the Andes, Ningishzidda designed a spaceport and tin and gold- processing plants for his cousin, Enlilite General Adad/Viracocha. [ZS, *Time*: 310, 322-323; *Enki*: 84 -285]

Marduk reunited Egypt. He honored Father Enki/Ptah. Enki hadn't passed rule of Nibiru to Marduk, but maybe he could settle Marduk in Egypt. Enki gave him MEs to make Egypt prosper--all his knowledge except how to revive the dead.

Marduk rewrote Egyptian history. He demoted Ningishzidda to "the Divine Measurer" And replaced Ningishzidda's image on the "Stone Lion" (Sphinx). The new face of the Sphinx: Osiris. Pharaohs yearned to live forever; Marduk said if they proved loyal, he'd mummify and rocket them to Nibiru to share eternity. Thus tempted, the pharaohs fought to unite Egypt against Inanna and the Enilites.

INANNA RULED THE INDUS VALLEY & URUK

The Enlilite Council made the star group "Virgo," hithertofor Ninmah's constellation, into Inanna's and replaced Ninmah with Inanna on the Council too. The Council also named the star group "The Twins" after Inanna and Utu.

Innana - Ishtar. The Burney Relief c 2300 - 2000 BC

"In the eastern lands, beyond even seven mountain ranges, was the Third Region, Zamush, Land of Sixty Precious Stones, was its highland called. Aratta [Harappa] the Wooded Realm, was in the valley of a meandering great river [Indus] located. In the great plain did the people cultivate crops of grains and horned cattle herd. There too two cities with mud bricks they built, with granaries they were filled." Inanna appointed an Earthling Shepherd-Chief (descended from Dumuzi) King of Aratta. [ZS, *Enki*: 286 - 287]

IGIGI ASTRONAUTS FOLLOWED INANNA TO INDUS VALLEY

Aratta

Inanna roamed "the lands and took a liking to the people who in the upper plain of the two rivers dwelt. They were the Igigi who descended to Earth from heaven from Lahmu (Mars). The Igigi Aryans moved east, following Inanna [they called her Ishtar] to the Indus Valley [Aratta] and laid the foundation for the Indo-European culture." [Tellinger, *Slave Species*: 499]

Enlil ordered Enki to craft a new language and script for Aratta. Enki wrote the language but refused Aratta MEs for Aratta to make Inanna a world power. He said she could share with Aratta the MEs she'd already gotten from him for Uruk.

Inanna shuttled in her skyship between Aratta and Uruk. But "what to Inanna was entrusted she neglected, other domains, not to her granted, in her heart she coveted. By Inanna was the bitter end started, Marduk as Ra with Destiny tangled." [ZS, *Enki*: 291]

Her second ruler in Uruk, Enmerkar (Utu's grandson and a Earthling) sent an emissary to the Arattan King with a written message to Aratta. In the message, Enmerkar demanded Aratta swear feality to Uruk, but the Arattan King couldn't read the Sumerian writing.

After ten years, Enmerkar told Utu to have Nisaba, the astronauts' scribe, teach him Arattan script. When he'd learned it, Enmerkar sent his son, Banda The Short, to Aratta with a message in Arattan: "*Submit or War*!"

The Aratta King wrote back that he'd prefer trade--Aratta's precious stones for the MEs of Uruk, or if Enmerkar insisted on war, let one champion of Aratta and one of Uruk fight to settle the war.

"On the way back, carrying the peace message, Banda fell sick; his spirit left him. His comrades raised his neck, without the breath of life it was. On Mount Hurmu, on the way from Aratta, to his death was Banda abandoned". So the peace message never reached. Utu, Inanna's brother, however, revived Banda. [ZS,, *Enki*: 287-289]

"Journeying between Unug-ki and Aratta, Inanna restless and ungratified was, for her Dumuzi she still mourned, her love's desire unquenched remained. When she flew about, in the sunrays Dumuzi's image she saw shimmering and beckoning." In her dreams and visions, Dumuzi told her he'd return and share with her the "Land of the Two Narrows [Egypt]." [ZS, *Enki*: 291]

In Uruk, "A House for Nighttime Pleasure she established. To this young heroes, on the night of their weddings, with sweet words she lured: long life, a blissful future to them she promised; that her lover Dumuzi was she imagined." But each one in the morning in her bed was found dead."

UTU REVIVED BANDA WHOM INANNA BEDDED AS DUMUZI RESURRECTED

Utu revived Banda, who returned to Uruk. Inanna saw Banda as Dumuzi. "*'A miracle!'* excited Inanna shouted. *'My beloved Dumuzi to me came back!'* In her abode Banda was bathed. *'Dumuzi, my beloved!'* she called him. To her bed, with flowers bedecked, she lured him."

Utu   Dumuzi

INANNA STARTED IMMORTALITY QUEST

"When in the morning Banda was alive, Inanna shouted: *'The power of dying in my hands was placed, immortality by me is granted.'* Then to call herself a goddess Inanna decided, the Power of Immortality it implied." [ZS, *Enki*: 292]

BANDA & NINSUN BEGAT GILGAMESH WHO SOUGHT IMMORTALITY

Banda succeeded his father, Enmerkar, as King of Uruk. Banda married Ninurta's daughter, Ninsun, who bore Gilgamesh. Gilgamesh oppressed the people of his city; he insisted on sex with brides before their grooms could couple with them.

Enki created Enkidu, an android, to tame Gilgamesh and arranged for the tantric practitioner, Shamhat to tame him.

Gilgamesh and Enkidu fought, then became best friends. Gilgamesh went with Enkidu to the rocketpad at Baalbek to plead with the gods for a rocket to Nibiru for immortality he thought they enjoyed.

In Lebanon, near Inanna's home, Gilgamesh and Enkidu tracked Enlil's security robot to the launchpad. As they watched a rocket launch, Inanna, from her plane, saw them smash Enlil's robot. "At the entrance to the Cedar Forest its fire-belching monster their way blocked. To pieces it they broke."

"Watching Gilgamesh take off his clothes, bathe and groom himself, glorious Ishtar [Inanna] raised an eye at the beauty of Gilgamesh. "*Come, Gilgamesh, be thou my lover. Grant me the fruit of thy love!*". But he declined and insulted her.

She, enraged, demanded Anu release the guard-bull at the launchpad. Anu complied. The bull charged Gilgamesh and Enkidu but Gilgamesh stabbed it while Enkidu held it.

When Enkidu died of illness, Enlil inflicted on him for destroying his robot, Gilgamesh grieved his friend. Then Gilgamesh went to the spaceport in Sinai for a plant to let him live forever.

In a tunnel in Sinai he met Enki's son, Ziusudra, still alive all these centuries. "Ziusudra to Gilgamesh the secret of longliving he revealed a plant in the garden's well was growing, Ziusudra and his spouse from getting old it prevented." Enki, with Enlil's permission, said Ziusudra, granted Gilgamesh this plant too. But when Gilgamesh got the plant, a snake snatched it from him. As a last resort, he begged Enlil to grant him immortality.

Gigamesh Meets Noah

"On Gilgamesh's deathbed, around 2600 B. C., Utu told him Enlil wouldn't grant him eternal life. Gilgamesh is consoled by promises to retain in Nether World the company of 'his beloved wife, son, concubine, musicians, entertainers, cupbearer, valet, caretakers and palace attendants who served him.'" Undertakers brought his body to the royal cemetery of Ur. They drugged his friends and attendants in his burial chamber, then killed them. This "accompanied burial" gave "an extraordinary privilege to Gilgamesh, two- thirds of him divine, as compensation for not gaining the immortality of the gods." [ZS, *Encounters*: 132 -172; *Giants*, 311 - 312, 339 (citing S. Kramer's translation of cuneiform text, *The Death of Gilgamesh*)]

INANNA & MARDUK FOUGHT TO RULE EARTH

In Egypt, Marduk heard Innana told the Earthlings gods like her lived forever. He saw Gilgamesh and other Earthlings obsess to live forever. "Gods" lived long but died after millennia or someone could kill them. Their lives shortened on Earth. Their Nibiran/Earthling descendants lived even shorter lives. But to shorter-lived Earthlings, Nibirans seemed immortal.

Marduk used his pharaohs' wishes to live forever to control them. If loyal, he'd have them mummified like Dumuzi and, Marduk vowed, he'd rocket them to Nibiru to share eternity. He focused them to unite Egypt for him against Inanna and the Enlites. [ZS, *Enki*: 295]

INANNA UNITED SUMER

Inanna and the Enlilites ran Sumer. The Council of Twelve had her Uncle Adad run the landing place at Baalbek and her father Nannar run the Sinai energy source (Heavenly Bright Object) and the Spaceport. With her weapons, armies and power (she said) to bestow immortality, Inanna controlled kingship of Sumer, the First Region, for 1000 years.
(MASS KILLING WEAPONS)

MARDUK OFFERED PHARAOHS IMMORTALITY

In Egypt, Marduk allowed worship of one supreme deity, himself. "So did Marduk, as Ra, above all other gods himself emplace, their powers and attributes he to himself assigned. *'What have you overpowered?'* Enki to his son Marduk said. *'Unheard of are your pretensions!'*

"*The heavens my supremacy bespeak,*'" Marduk said; "*The coming Age of the Ram, my sign, my rule proclaims.*" But the sun still rose in the star group *the Bull* and marked Enlil's rule; not *the Ram*, Marduk's star-set. Marduk and Nabu readied their Earthlings to challenge the Enlilites. [ZS, *Enki*: 290, 298]

~ 114 ~

2371 B.C.: INANNA & SARGON EXTENDED HER POWER

The Enlilite leaders wanted a ["hybrid demigod"] war-king to unify the First   Region fiefs and block Marduk's threat to their squabbling temple-cities. "To Inanna, of Marduk the adversary, the task of the right man to find they entrusted." [ZS, *Enki*: 30]

In 2371 B.C., Inanna choose her gardener, Sargon, as the Akkadian warrior king to lead her armies and Sumer. Nannar had fathered both Sargon and Inanna. Sargon rose from gardener to king when he raped her and she liked it. Enlil ratified Sargon--who had Enlilite genes–as Sumer's king.

Sargon began his rise when he saw Inanna snooze in his garden. "He bent over her perfect face and lightly, then, as she--half awake--responded, kissed her savagely. He entered her as she opened her eyes and her eyes shone with pleasure." She declared Sargon her lover. Inanna repeatedly joined powerful aggressive men to lead her armies.

SARGON'S HAD ENLILITE GENES

Inanna & Sargon conquered all Sumer

Sargon and Inanna built their capital, Agade in Akkad (near Babylon). They subdued all Sumer except Lagash, her Uncle Ninurta's fief. She led Sargon's army through Luristan in the Zagros Mountains. With the army and her mass-killing weapons, she and Sargon united Sumer. They spread spoken and written-on-clay Akkadian all over Sumer and spawned the Semitic languages (including Hebrew and Arabic). [ZS, *Wars*: 10 -11]

In 2316 B.C., while Marduk built an army in Egypt, Sargon invaded Marduk's empty stronghold, Babylon. To show his disdain for Marduk, the king planted in Agade an urn he'd filled with Babylon's soil. Sargon "took away the soil for another Gateway to the Gods [Tower to Launch Rockets to Nibiru]." Inanna would build her own launch site and take interplanetary power. [ZS, *Giants*: 270]

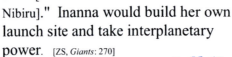
TOWER TO LAUNCH SPACE-SHIPS TO PLANET X

Marduk and Nabu returned from Egypt to Babylon. They fortified the city and diverted rivers to it from the other Sumerian cities. Marduk said he'd build his spaceport in Babylon. "In the heart of Edin, in the midst of the First Region, Marduk himself established!
(MARDUK HAD A SPACEPORT IN BABYLON IN THE HEART OF EDIN)

"Inanna's fury no boundaries knew; with her weapons on Marduk's followers death she inflicted. The blood of people, as never before on Earth, like rivers flowed." Inanna and Marduk both loosed lasers on each other's Earthling armies.

"While Inanna remained gorgeous and enticing, Sargon began to age and drink too much. Inanna watched as the man she once loved passionately crumbled into a pathetic drunk afflicted by insomnia, haunted by demons." In the end, Marduk's minions besieged Sargon and he died cursing Inanna [Ferguson, "Inanna Returns," in *Heaven and Earth*, ZS, Ed.: 97]

Nabu

Sargon

INANNA & NERGAL PLANNED TO RULE EARTH

The waterworks Marduk made for Babylon cut reliable water to Sumer's cities.
The Anunnaki Council told Nergal to restore their water and disarm Marduk and Babylon. Nergal and his retinue of black Earthlings left Kuth for Babylon. En route, he visited Inanna in Uruk.

Though she was Enlilite and he Enkiite, he allied himself with her against his brother, Marduk (also an Enkiite). Marduk ran Egypt, north of Nergal's and Ereshkigal's realm in South Africa. Marduk's claim to rule all Earth alarmed Nergal. He asked Inanna to help him contain Marduk. Nergal and Inanna sealed their alliance sexually and planned to conquer all Earth for themselves.

Inanna & Nergal

NERGAL BETRAYED MARDUK

When Nergal left Inanna, he and his Blacks continued to Babylon, where Marduk greeted them. Nergal promised him, if he'd leave Babylon for South Africa, he'd get weapons and computers, including "the instrument for giving orders, The Oracle of the gods, The Holy Scepter, sign of kingship which contributes to Lordship and the holy Radiating Stone which disintegrates all" hidden there since the Flood. Marduk said if he left Babylon, the waterworks for all Sumer which he ran would fail and Sumer'd flood, crops'd dry-up crops and cholera spread. Nergal said, *"Ceremonial bulls at the Babylon's gate only shall I install, upset waterworks I shall not."* Reassured, Marduk left for the weapons and programs in South Africa.[ZS, *Wars*: 252 -254]

MARDUK LEFT TO THE WEAPONS
AND PROGRAMS IN SOUTH AFRICA...

Marduk, on platform, greets Brother Nergal, up from Kuth to
manipulate him to leave Babylon

Marduk, on platform, greeted Nergal; both held weapons

When Marduk left Babylon for South Africa, Nergal broke into the Babylon control room, destroyed the watering program and seized the radiation source that ran Sumer's water. Fields and canals dried-out, parts of Sumer flooded.

Enki ordered Nergal back to Africa, but Nergal left his men in Elam, near Babylon, to aid Inanna. She then publicly, "to defy the authority of Anu and Enlil, abrogated their rules and regulations and declared herself Supreme Queen." [Ancient text, *Queen of all the MEs*; ZS, *Wars:* 254]

In 2291 B.C., "In the First Region, Enlil and Ninurta absent were, to the lands beyond the oceans Inanna and Nergal went; In the Second Region, Ra was away, as in other lands he traveled. Her chance in her hands to seize all powers Inanna envisioned." [ZS, *Enki:* 303]

Nergal

Inanna, Naram-Sin (Sargon's grandson) and the Akkadian armies captured Baalbek, the Landing Platform in Lebanon. They dashed along the Mediterranean coast for the Sinai Spaceport and inland for Mission Control, Jerusalem. Akkadians crossed the forbidden Forth Region, taboo to Earthlings (across the Jordan from Tell Ghassul, the private city of the Igigi Astronauts' and their Earthling wives).

In Sumer, only Ninurta's city, Lagash [Tello], "beyond the reach of Inanna's ambitions" and "protected by the best-trained soldiers in the land" held out against Inanna and Naram-Sin [ZS, *Giants*: 274].

Inanna and the Akkadians conquered Jerico. Nannar, her father lost Jerico. Now Jerico obeyed her.

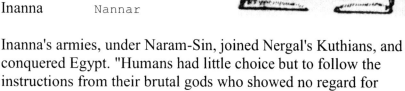

Inanna   Nannar

Inanna's armies, under Naram-Sin, joined Nergal's Kuthians, and conquered Egypt. "Humans had little choice but to follow the instructions from their brutal gods who showed no regard for human life.

Clashes between the gods almost always involved humans, who never knew the reasons for warring against their neighbors. Aggression of one group of earthlings against another initiated by their god set the behavioral pattern for all future human conflict. Humankind perceived this kind of activity as 'the normal thing to do' to invade and conquer your neighbor's land."

A "god would command his people to invade and attack, giving his human armies the excuse that they were vile and evil and they were sinful against god. But this god would differ from land to land, demanding total obedience from humans, or they would be punished. This led to the worship of many different gods by people of the biblical lands as they worshiped the specific gods who led them into battle or out of harm's way. This worshiping would lead to retribution from some other Anunnaki god with a higher rank, demanding that people worship only him. And so the clashes between groups of people continue." [Tellinger, M., 2008, *Slave Species*: 502 -503]

In 2255 B.C., Inanna recaptured Uruk, destroyed Anu's temple there and sent Naram-Sin to attack Enlil's minions at Nippur. She declared herself supreme to even Anu, King of Nibiru and father of Enlil, her father's father.

XI. ENLILITES RULED SUMER, NUKED SINAI, LEFT SUMER TO MARDUK

Enlil sent Ninurta with cavalry and an army of Gutians (from the Zagros Mountains of northeast Sumer) to kill all Earthlings in Akkad/Agade. Gutians wasted most of Sumer; they spared only Ninurta's city, Lagash.

Enlil had agents plant a scorpion to kill Inanna's strongman, King Naram-Sin, for his attack on Nippur. Enlil also ordered Inanna arrested but her Nannar and Ningal, her parents, gave her sanctuary. Then she flew to Nergal's Lower Africa. For seven years, she and Nergal plotted to overthrow Enlil and his Council.

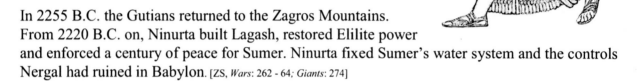

In 2255 B.C. the Gutians returned to the Zagros Mountains. From 2220 B.C. on, Ninurta built Lagash, restored Elilite power and enforced a century of peace for Sumer. Ninurta fixed Sumer's water system and the controls Nergal had ruined in Babylon. [ZS, *Wars*: 262 - 64; *Giants*: 274]

Ninurta's Kings in Lagash "prohibited abuse of official powers, 'taking away' a widow's donkey" and withholding day-workers' wages. The kings had to maintain communal buildings and irrigation and transportation canals. Ninurta declared First Fruits and other festivals for the whole populace. He and his kings encouraged Earthlings to read and write. [ZS, *Giants*: 274]

NINURTA'S LAGASH ENINNU TOUTED ENLILITE RULE 200 MORE YEARS

Ninurta consolidated the Enlilite rule in Sumer. He welcomed Ningishzidda to Lagash and had him design bunkers for his new aircraft, Black Bird, whose firepower made it invincible in Sumer. Ningishzidda drew two bunkers, one for Ninurta's Black Bird and one for Ninurta's "Awesome Weapon." Ningishzidda build an observatory next to the bunkers. The top of the domed observatory measured "star and planetary positions after nightfall. Ninurta named the temple "*E.Ninnu*--House/Temple of Fifty", affirming himself as the "next Enlil with the Rank of Fifty, just below Anu's". In the 2160 B.C. New Year's dedication, Ninurta bestowed "immortality" on Gudea, Lagash's demigod/king who'd supervised construction.

Lagash

"In the forecourt were two stone circles to determine constellations at the moment of sunrise on equinox day," March 20/21 and September 22/23. The equinoxes marked *Zodiac* Time based on the varied time-lengths star groups rose on the horizon on equinoxes, which Ninurta touted. Zodiac Time stretched his rule of Sumer longer than Celestial Time, based on twelve equal intervals. The observatory's sight-lines would show the Sun crossing the line of Earth's orbit (ecliptic) from the zone of *The Bull* for the next 200 years.

"The Bull," Ninurta told Ningishzidda, *"proclaims Commander Enlil and me, his Champion and Successor. While the sun rises in The Bull, Enlil--through me--rules Earth."* [ZS, *End of Days*: 40 - 49; *Giants*: 276]

In Egypt, Marduk's spy said. *"Ninurta finished the* E.Ninnu.*"*

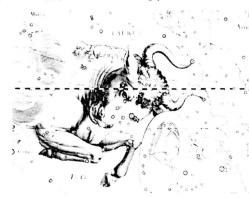

"Curse his Observatory. Earth," Marduk shouted, *"must* honor Celestial *Time, not the Eninnu's Zodiac Time. Coming is my constellation, The Ram. When the sun rises in The Ram, I, not Enlilites, rule Sumer shall.*

Each sign gets equal time on the horizon. The sun rises on my Ram, not Enlil's Bull and I rule. Zodiac Time gives Ninurta rule two centuries more than Celestial Time.

ARIES.

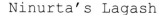

Ninurta's Lagash

Marduk particularly resented the women who helped plan the E.Ninnu to defy him--Nisaba (aka Seshita, Ningishzidda's assistant in Egypt), Ninurta's half-sister, the Sumerian Goddess of Wisdom, schooled in Enki's academy at Eridu, "a female Einstein" and Enki's daughter, Nanshe, Inanna's Oracle (represented in the constellation Scorpio), who gathered in rare building materials for the E.Ninnu. Marduk already hated Inanna for sentencing him to die in the Giza Pyramid and Ninmah, who ceaselessly promoted Ninurta at his expense. Marduk generalized his hatred of Inanna, Nishaba, Nanshe and Ninmah and waited his chance to punish women. [ZS: *Time*: 158 - 152, 364 - 368]

The Era of Ninurta in Sumer, lasting through the Gutian Invasions and the ensuing period of reconstruction, was only an interlude. A mountain-dweller at heart, Ninurta soon began to roam the northeast and farther. Constantly perfecting the martial arts of his highland tribesmen, he introduced HORSES to them and organized them into a calvary extending their reach thousands of miles.

Ninurta had returned to Sumer at Enlil's call to crush Naram-Sin and subdue Inanna. With peace and prosperity restored, Ninurta absented himself from Sumer. His absences from Sumer and Inanna's abortive attempt to recapture the kingship" for her city of Uruk prompted Enlil to order Nannar to rule Sumer from Ur." Enlil also needed Nannar to counter Marduk's ever-growing territory and followers. "The growing problem for the Enlilites was that Ninurta, the presumptive heir to Enlil and Anu, had come from Nibiru–whereas Marduk [who married Hybrid Earthling Sarpanpit] and [their son] Nabu had Earthling affinities. [ZS, *Giants*: 269-70]

"Enlilites dropped the 'Ninurta Strategy' and switched to a 'Nannar Tactic,' transferring the seat of national Kingship to Ur–Sumer's thriving commercial and manufacturing center–[cult center] of Nannar, an *Earthborn* son of Enlil, who unlike Ninurta, also had an Akkadian name: *Sin*." Enlil sent Terah, the High Priest of Nippur, to Nannar in Ur to make sure people there adhered to zodiacal time and the extension of Enlilite rule. Terah brought his son, Abraham (who will become Enlil's top general) with him.

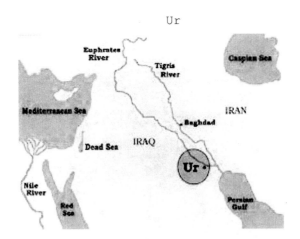

Nannar, unlike other Enlilites, avoided combat in the Anunnaki's wars. The Enlilites choose him as Ur's god to signal Earthlings, even in lands Marduk controlled, to worship Nannar and enjoy peace and prosperity. [ZS, *Giants*: 269-70, 278].

NANNAR RULED UR'S THIRD DYNASTY

Nannar's Earthlings adored him. He bred sheep that made Ur "the wool and garment center of the ancient Near East and "developed foreign trade by land and water." His half-Earthling/half-Anunnaki staff and their thousands of subject Earthlings built a navigable (and protective) canal to Ur's two harbors. The canal separated the temple, palace and offices on one bank from shops and homes on the other bank. On their bank, merchants, craftsmen and laborers occupied multistoried white houses along broad, straight streets. [ZS,: *Wars*: 271 -272]

Ur

UR-NAMMU DIED, DESTABILZED SUMER

In 2113 B.C., Nannar and Enlil choose (and Anu, from Nibiru okayed) Ninsun's son Ur-Nammu as King of Sumer/Akkad. "The choice signaled that the glorious days under the unchallenged authority of Enlil and his clan are back." The King would serve under Nannar who'd dictate laws of obedience, justice and morality. [ZS, *Wars*: 262-264; *End of Days*: 52, 60 -61].

The Enlilites told King Ur-Nammu to kill Amorites allied with Marduk and Nabu. Enlil gave the King a "divine weapon that heaps up the rebels in piles. Enlilite gods of Sumer all gave Ur-Nammu blessing, honor, weapons and protection. Off he marched his army to attack the Amorites west of Sumer."

But in 2096 B.C., "in the midst of battle, Ur-Nammu's chariot got stuck in the mud. He fell off it, the chariot rushed along, leaving the King behind. The boat returning his body to Sumer sank with him on board." In Sumer, "People could not understand how such a devout king who followed gods' directives with weapons they put in his hands could perish so ignominiously." Support of Utu, Nannar, Inanna, Enlil and even Anu failed Ur- Nammu.

Nabu fanned doubts about Enlilite gods, *"The Enlilite gods deserted you. They hid from you that Nibiru's almost here. Soon shines the homeplanet of the gods upon Earth in* The Ram--*Marduk's constellation. Welcome the Era of Marduk the Redeemer, who shall conquer Sumer & Akkad, rule Elamites, Hittites, Enlil's Sealand allies and the whole world.* [ZS, *End of Days*: 63 - 66]

Ninmah and Enki preferred Nabu--half Nibiran, half Adapite Hybrid--rather than Utu--pure Nibiran but Earth- born–rule Sinai. From Sinai to the cities and islands of the Eastern Mediterranean Nabu exalted, *"Nibiru comes, Marduk shall rule."*

Shulgi succeeded Ur Nammu as Sumer's Boss. Inanna invited Shulgi to Uruk and declared him "the man for the vulva of Inanna." They wed in the temple where Anu had elevated her in tantric ritual. She again bonded with an alpha Earthling. [ZS, *Wars:* 276 -279]

Shulgi built the Great West Wall from the Euphrates to the Tigris to keep out Nabu's forces. He allied with Elamites. He gave them the city of Larsa and married his daughter to an Elamite. Shulgi's Sumerians and the Elamites "subdued the western provinces, including Canaan." [ZS, *Wars:* 286]

Shulgi failed to drive Nabu from Sinai, so in 2048 B.C., Enlil had Shulgi killed and installed Shulgi's son, Amar-Sin, Boss of Sumer. Enlil sent the new boss to crush a revolt in the north, then fight an alliance of five kings along the Mediterranean in the west.

In 2040 B.C., Mentuhotep II, Marduk's Theban Pharaoh, conquered Egypt up to the western border of Sinai. Amar-Sin sailed to block Mentuhotep but died of a poisonous bite.

Enlil made Amar-Sin's brother, Shu-Sin, Boss. Shu-Sin built a shrine for Inanna's son Shara at Nippur. In 2039, Ibbi-Sin succeeded Shu-Sin. Marduk returned to Babylon as Enlil and his wife left Sumer. [ZS, *Wars:* 309, 317, 320; *End of Days*: 68-72]

XII. ENLIL SPONSORED THE ISRAELITES

GALZU VISION MADE ENLIL CHOOSE ABRAHAM TO BLOCK MARDUK

Abraham

Galzu

Galzu, in a vision, told Enlil to make Abraham (son of Ur's High Priest Terah) General of Cavalry to keep Nabu and Ham's descendants in Canaan from the Sinai Spacestation. Enlil kept the vision secret, but told Abraham, *"Rule all lands from the border of Egypt to the border of Sumer."* [ZS, *Wars*: 289 - 297]

"In 2095 B.C., Enlil sent Abraham and Terah to Harran [Turkey] at the foothills of the Taurus Mountains near the Syrian Border, where the Euphrates flowed to Ur. Harran dominated trade with Hatti, land of the Hittites, on whose trade Sumer depended. Harran straddled the trade and military land routes to the Spaceport as well."

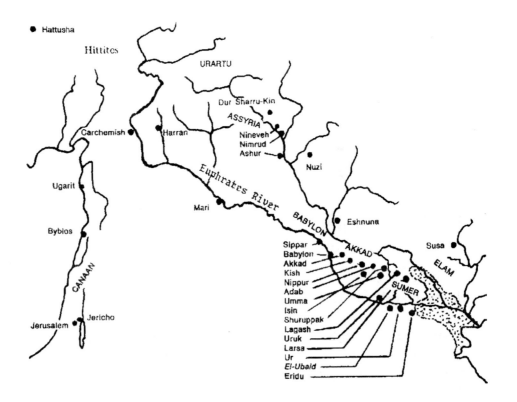

~ 126 ~

Harran

Sinai

Enlil gave Abraham land and riches that made him the richest man of his time. In
2048 B.C., Enlil ordered him and his nephew Lot to to the Negev drylands that border the Sinai.
He equipped Abraham with the best chariots, finest horses, 380 well-trained soldiers and weapons
that "could smite an army of ten thousand men in hours. [ZS, *End of Days*: 73]

In 2047 B.C. Enlil sent Abraham and Lot to Egypt for more men and camels from the Northern
Egyptians allied against Marduk. In 2041, with this force, Abraham blocked Ninurta's Elamites
from the Spaceport, then rescued Lot, whom the Elamites, as they retreated west of the Jordan
River, had captured from the Nabu-friendly city of Sodom.

Then Abraham moved to block Nabu and his Earthling armies advancing on the

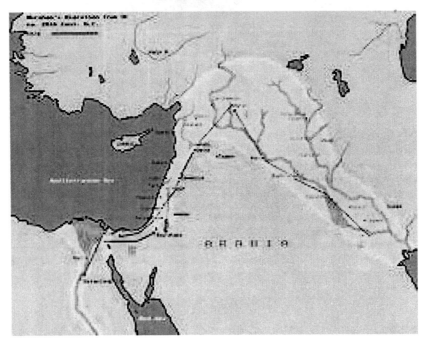

MARDUK CAPTURED HARRAN, ALLIED WITH ADAD & HITTITES

2047 B.C.: Marduk took Harran from Nannar, allied with Adad and the Hittites and cut Hittite trade to Sumer. Marduk's Theban allies struck pro-Enlilite northern Egyptians. Meanwhile, Nabu, based in Bosippa (south of Babylon), brought cities west of the Euphrates as well as Canaan against Enlil. Marduk threatened the Spaceport.]" [ZS, *Wars*:298; *Enki*: 302 - 306; *End of Days:* 78].

Enlil bade Ninurta leave his Elamite legions and supervise an alternate spaceport in Peru. But unsupervised, the Elamites ran amok and looted all Sumer. Enlil made Ninurta, though he'd been in South America, account for the legions' crimes. Nabu said Enlil,Utu and Nergal let the Elamites overrun Sumer and invade Marduk's temple in Babylon.

Nergal blamed Marduk and Nabu for the military threat to Sinai that made Ninurta bring the Elamites to Sumer. Enki told Nergal to shut up and support Marduk and Nabu or get out. "The gods' council broke up in disarray."[ZS, *End of Days:* 87-88]

Enlil's emissaries Ninurta and Nergal sent Abraham and Lot to spy on Sodom and Gomorra, cities Marduk controlled. Enlil feared Marduk, from these cities "would marshal his large number of human followers and control of all establishments on Earth,

including the Sinai Spaceport." [Tellinger, *Slave Species*: 506]

Sodom before Nuking

GODS NUKED SINAI SPACEPORT, LEFT EARTH TO MARDUK

Marduk told the senior Anunnaki, *"'In my temple house let all the gods assemble, my covenant accept.'* By his appeal for their submission, the Anunnaki gods were disturbed and alarmed."

"To a great assembly, council to take, Enlil them all summoned. Opposed to Marduk and Nabu they all were." All the senior Anunnaki except Enki agreed: *"Leave Earth to Marduk. Keep the Spaceport from Nabu; nuke it.*"[ZS, *Enki*: 308]

Enki, "angry and distraught, the council chamber left, in his heart was Enki smiling: only he knew where [In Africa] the weapons were hidden, so did Enki think. For it was he, before Enlil to Earth had come, who with Abgal in a place unknown the weapons did hide. That Abgal, to the exiled Enlil, the place disclosed, that to Enki was unknown. Thus it was that without Enki needing, Enlil to the two heros [Ninurta and Nergal] the hiding place disclosed." [ZS, *Enki*: 306 - 308]

The Anunnaki Council on Earth beamed Anu on Nibiru: would he okay nuking the Spaceport as well as Nabu and his armies at the south end of the Dead Sea? Marduk, Enlil reminded Anu, claimed rule of Nibiru as well as Earth, as per the dynastic agreement between Anu and Alalu. Marduk threatened Anu in every way. So Anu said, *"Bomb."*

In 2024 B.C., Enlil evacuated the Igigi from Sinai, then Ninurta attacked. "The first terror weapon [a missile called *One Without Rival*] from the skies Ninurta let loose; the top of Mount Mashu [which housed the controlling equipment] with a flash it sliced off, the mount's innards in an instant it melted.

Above the Place of the Celestial Chariots [Sinai Spaceport] the second weapon [called *Blazing Flame*] he unleashed, with a brilliance of seven suns the plain's rocks into a gushing wound were made, the Earth shook and crumbled, the heavens after the brilliance were darkened; with burnt and crushed stones was the plain of the chariots covered, of all the forests that the plain had surrounded, only tree stems were left standing." [ZS, *End of Days:* 91;*Enki:* 310]

Ninurta and Nergal had warned Abraham and Lot to flee Sodom before Nergal nuked Marduk's forces in Canaan--Sodom, Gomorra and three other cities Abraham had identified as allied with Marduk. "Nabu managed to slip out in time and escaped to an island in the Mediterranean, where the people accepted him." Nergal's bombs made the Dead Sea dead. To this day, "the water of springs surrounding the Dead Sea has been contaminated with radioactivity, enough to induce sterility in any animals and humans that absorbed it.'"

Archeologists say that in 2024 B.C. the southern part of the Dead Sea broke out and ran south. People abandoned the area, all life died there. "Over the five cities Nergal upon each from the skies a terror weapon sent, the five cities he finished off, all that lived there to vapor ["salt"] was turned. Mountains toppled, where the sea waters were barred the bolt broke open, down into the valley the sea's waters poured, by the waters was the valley flooded." [ZS, *Wars* :325,329; Enki: 311, 315 -316]

"The Place of Launching, the Spaceport, obliterated: the Mount within which the controlling equipment was placed was smashed; the launch platforms were made to fade off the face of the Earth. The plain whose hard soil the shuttlecraft had used as runways were obliterated, with not even a tree left standing." [ZS, *Wars*: 331]

Sodom nuked

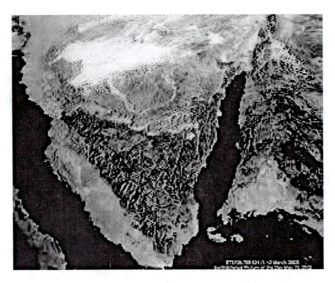

Sinai blackened from nuking

NUCLEAR CLOUD KILLED ALL SUMER EXCEPT BABYLON

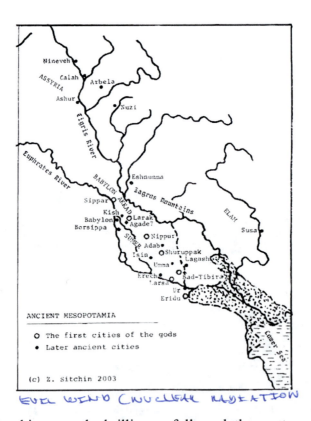

ANCIENT MESOPOTAMIA

O The first cities of the gods
• Later ancient cities

(c) Z. Sitchin 2003

EVIL WIND (NUCLEAR RADIATION)

"By the darkening of the skies were the brilliances followed, then a storm began to blow, gloom from the skies an Evil Wind carried. From the Upper Sea, a stormwind began blowing, the dark-brown cloud eastward toward Shumer the death was carried. Wherever it reached, death to all that lives mercilessly it delivered." "The alarm Enlil and Enki to the gods of Shumer transmitted, *'Escape!'* From their cities the gods did flee."

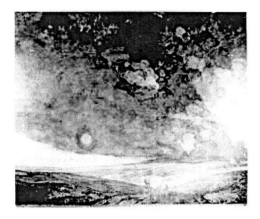

Enlil sent Abraham from the Negev desert on the border of Sinai to the Mediterranean coast, near the Enkiites' Philistine allies. [ZS, *Encounters*: 288]

"The people of the land by the evil storms hand were clutched. Those who behind locked doors hid inside their houses like flies were felled. Those who in the streets fled, in the streets were their corpses piled up. Everything that lived perished."

But Babylon, "where Marduk his supremacy declared, by the Evil Wind was spared." Enlil saw as fulfilled, when the fallout spared Babylon, his vision of Galzu, where Galzu said Marduk and the Enkiites would prevail over the Enlilites" [ZS, *Enki*: 312 - 313]

Babylon

For the next 150 years, most Nibirans on Earth went first to Adad's spaceport at Nazca, then in

rockets back to Nibiru. Some, however, "dispersed from Sumer, accompanied their followers to far lands in the far corners of the Earth; others remained nearby, rallying their supporters to a renewed challenge to Marduk."

Marduk's "extended family in Northern Sumer, the Aryans, invaded the lands to the east and Europe to the west, conquering humans everywhere and imposing their Aryan supremacy which, to this day, persists." [ZS, *End of Days*: 122; *Enki*: 312 - 313; Tellinger, *Slave Species*: 116]

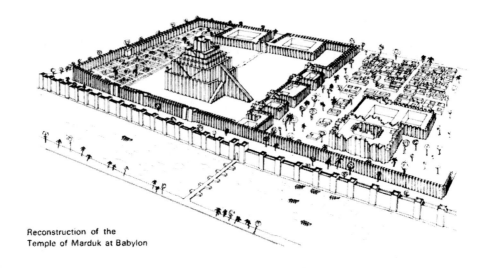

Reconstruction of the
Temple of Marduk at Babylon

Marduk proclaimed Babylon Capitol of Sumer and, 2000 B.C., himself God of the gods.

He renamed Nibiru "Marduk" and held New Years rituals a priests enacted him, as he--a planet--invaded the inner solar system, created Earth, then made Earthlings. Marduk named Neptune "Nidimmud,' (a name for Enki), renamed Mercury (which'd been "Adad") "Nabu." He changed Venus' name from "Inanna" to "Sarpanit."

Marduk trained priests to study omens and a horoscope showing how planets–and their namesakes–affect Earthlings. He degraded astronomical observations, Earthling support and women's rights. He barred women from high office and art. He substituted Nabu for the Nibiran woman Nisaba as Diety of Writing. [ZS, *Time:* 350-368]

Many Sumerians who survived the fallout fled Marduk. "Refugees were given asylum all around the Mesopotamia. They converted their host countries into flourishing states. Some ventured into more distant lands, accompanying the displaced gods." Indo- Aryans from southwest of the Caspian Sea mingled with the Sumerian refugees and migrated to the Indus Valley and brought with them the tales of Sumer, which, combined with the culture Inanna had given her domains in India, evolved into Hindism. [ZS, *Time:* 370-371]

Under Marduk's New Age, "gods guided the policies of their countries through signs and omens. For many millennia, Anu, Enlil and the other Anunnaki leaders [had] made decisions affecting the Anunnaki; Enlil by himself was Lord of Command as far as mankind was concerned. Now signs and omens in the heavens guided decisions. Celestial omens–planetary conjunctions, eclipses, lunar halow, stellar backgrounds were sufficient by themselves. No godly intervention or participation was required; the heavens alone foretold the fates.

"Astrology developed with fortune-teller priests on hand to interpret observations of celestial phenomena. Astronomical tablets of the Babylonians were computer printouts (Ephemerides), copies from pre-existing sourses of zodiacal constellations. All the Bablylonians knew was how to use them, translating into Babylonian the Sumerian procedure texts. Hellenistic, Persian and Indian astrology derived from such records.

"Deteriorion of astronomy was symptomatic of overall decline and regression in the sciences, arts, laws, the social framework" under Marduk. "Medicine deteriorated to sorcery. Harshness and coarseness replaced the former compassion and elegance."

Under Marduk, there was "an overall decline in the role of women and their status as compared to Sumerian times." The decline in women's status was generated from Marduk who hated women. Why? Ninharsag, Mother of Gods and Men, was mother of Marduk's main adversary on Earth, Ninurta. Inanna caused Marduk to be buried alive inside the Great Pyramid. Goddesses in charge of the arts and sciences assisted the construction of the Eninnu in Lagash as a symbol of defiance of Marduk's claims that his time had come. [ZS, Time:356 - 368]

Around 1800 B.C., Sumerians brought cuneiform writing, bronze weapons, chariots, walled cities to China's Shang Dynasty. "Sumerian emigrants gave Central and Far Asia Sino-Tibetan languages, cultures, the Sumerian "calender of twelve months, time-counting (that divides the day into twelve double-hours), the zodiac and Sumerian astronomy. Utu's descendants ruled Japan as emperors. [ZS, *Time:* 371 - 373]

Sumerians fled also throughout Europe–along the Volga (Geogia, Sumara, Finland) and the Danube (Dacia, Hungary). Some became Dorians and invaded Minoans in Greece and Crete around 1100 B.C. About 1100 B.C. too, Israelites fled Egypt then invaded Canaan on the Arabian Peninsula. [ZS, *12th Planet*:13]

ABRAHAM'S BAND, CIRCUMCISED FOR IDENTITY, SURVIVED NUKING

Of Earthlings loyal to the Enlilites (Ninurta, Nannar, Adad, Utu and Inanna), only Abraham and his army survived. His band lived because Enlil had sent it to the Negev and Canaan to guard Sumer from Marduk's forces in Egypt and Lebanon. Enlil wanted his surviving Earthlings branded.
Enlil ordered Abraham, then 99, and his male followers to cut off their foreskins to make their phalluses like those of the Nibirans and to mark them as loyal to the Enlilites. He told Abraham that after circumcision,"*Unto thy seed have I given this land from the brook of Egypt* [Nile] *until the River Euphrates.*" [ZS, *Encounters:* 257]

Enlil said Abraham, with his wife and half-sister, Sarah, would begat a son to replace Is-mael, Abraham's son with his secondary wife (Sarah's erstwhile Egyptian slave) Hagar. Abraham had raised Is-mael as his heir, due--all thought--to rule Canaan.[ZS, *Encounters:* 288.]

ENLIL ORDERED OBSCENE OBEDIENCE

In 2025 B.C., when Sarah bore Isaac in Canaan, she told Abraham, *"Rid us of that slave woman. Her son never shall the inheritance of my son Isaac share."*

Enlil agreed. He told Abraham, *"Heed Sarah. Your descendants shall spring from Isaac. Ishmael, son of the maidservant too shall a nation begat, for Ishmael too springs from you."* Enlil told Abraham *"Evict Hagar you must."* Enlil thus tested Abraham's loyalty and drove a wedge between him and Hagar.

Abraham gave Hagar bread and a water skin and left her and Ishmael in the Beersheeba wilderness.

"When the water in the skin was gone, she put Is-mael under one of the bushes. She thought, '*I cannot watch the boy die.*'

No sooner had Hagar been left to die in the unforgiving desert, than the god-master came to the rescue of the evicted young slave girl. Enlil showed her a well," saved her and Is-mael, won "her undivided loyalty." Ishmael became the genitor of the Arabs who to this day compete with the descendants of Isaac for Canaan.

"When Isaac grew, the apple of old Abraham's eye, to adulthood, Enlil decided to test whether Abraham still obeyed. Enlil told Abraham to take Isaac to a distant mountain, far from eyes of others, and murder him in cold blood. Better there were no witnesses

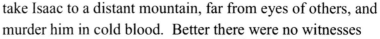

around to add to the growing discontent among humans to the gods."

Abraham and Isaac "came to the place god had told him and Abraham built an altar there and arranged the wood and bound his son Isaac and laid him on the altar atop the wood. Abraham stretched out his hand and took the knife to slay his son."

But an Emissary of Enlil appeared and said, *"Do not stretch out your hand against the lad, for now I know that you fear god since you have not withheld your son from Me. Because you have not withheld your son, indeed I will greatly bless you and I will greatly multiply your seed and your seed shall possess the gate of their enemies because you have obeyed My voice.'"*

"Abraham passed the test; he was now ready to perform any task for the conniving god. The god made sure everyone knew about his favorite boy, Abraham.

Many tribal heads, kings and priests came to seek his favor and suck up to him to avoid acts of vengeance from the god." [ZS, *Encounters*: 259, 288; Tellinger, *Slave Species*: 202, 212, 234 - 236; *Genesis*, 21:10 -14]

In 1907 B.C., Abraham, worried Isaac would marry a local Canaanite and dilute their Enlilite bloodline from Sumer, sent him back to Harran on the Euphrates to marry a daughter of their relatives there.

Isaac brought Rebecca back from Harran to Canaan; there she bore him the twins ESAU and JACOB in 1963 B.C..

Famine from drought struck Canaan when the twins matured. Isaac thought to send them to Egypt (where the Nile's waters protected the people from famine) for brides but Enlil warned them not to cross the still lethally-radioactive Sinai to Egypt. He ordered Isaac's family to an area of Canaan where wells tapped water. There Esau married a local.

Isaac worried his son Jacob would marry a Canaanite disloyal to Enlil, sent Jacob to Harran to marry daughters of Leban (Isaac's maternal uncle).

JACOB SAW ENLIL & CREW

On his journey north to Harran, "in a nighttime vision, Jacob saw a UFO, except for him it was not an UNidentified Flying Object; he realized its occupants were 'angels of Elohim' [Nibirans] and their Commander" [Enlil]. These "angels" were "flesh and blood human emissaries."

In Harran, Jacob asked his uncle Leban for Leban's daughter Rachael. Leban demanded Jacob first marry Rachael's older sister Leah and, in Harran, earn the dowries for both women.

Jacob worked twenty years for his uncle. Then Jacob "dreamed" Enlil's messenger bade him return to Canaan. The messenger, also in a dream, warned Leban to let Jacob and his wives go.

On his way back south from Harran to Canaan Jacob paused at the Yabbok Crossing of the Jordan River. "Uncertain what his brother Esau's attitude" toward him, as a rival to rule Abraham's tribe, Jacob sent his party ahead.

Alone at the Crossing, Jacob encountered and wrestled and, though he dislocated his thigh in the battle, pinned and held a Nibiran "angel" all night.

Jacob let the "angel" go in exchange for a blessing. The angel renamed Jacob "ISRA-EL [he who fought a god]. Israel, who limped into Esau's camp, became the patriarch of Enlil's loyalists, "the Children of Israel."[SZ, *Encounters*: 250 - 256]

JOSEPH SAVED EGYPT, BROUGHT ISRAELITES THERE

Israel/Jacob's older sons hated their half-brother, Rachel's youngest Son Joseph (born in 1870 B.C.). They hated how he obsessed with dream interpretation. They sold him as a slave to caravaners, who took him to Egypt.

In Egypt an official of the pharaoh worked Joseph as a household slave. The official's wife tried to seduce Joseph. When he said no, she said he'd propositioned her. The official jailed him.

In jail, Joseph won renown as he kept reading dreams. In 1848 B.C. Amenemhet III ascended Egypt's throne of Egypt and sent for Joseph to interpret a dream that seven skinny cows ate seven fat cows and seven scorched ears of grain ate seven healthy ones.

"Your dreams show Egypt'll have seven years of good harvest, then seven of famine," said Joseph. In 1840 B.C., Amenemhet made Joseph Overseer of Egypt, responsible to store water and grain from the seven good years for the seven lean ones.

Joseph channeled Nile water at high flood level through a natural depression to an artificial lake near Hawara. He built canals and underground pipes for miles in the Fayam area, and made Fayem

the breadbasket of Egypt. When drought and famine struck the Near East, refugees pored into Egypt where vegetables, fruit and fish still--thanks to Joseph--abounded. In 1833 B.C., Jacob/Israel (now 130 years old) and his sons (even those who sold Joseph as a slave) joined the refugees to Egypt from Canaan.

Joseph forgave his half-brothers and invited their descendants and dependants–the Children of Israel–to Egypt. There, for 300 years, they prospered and multiplied till there were 600,000 of them. Then a new regime, hostile to the Enlilites with whom the Children of Israel were allied, took power. [ZS, *Encounters*: 289 - 291; 152 -153; *Expeditions*: 116 - 128]

ENLIL TOLD MOSES, "*TAKE JACOB'S PEOPLE TO CANAAN*" [ZS, *Encounters*: 290 - 314].

In 1650 B.C., New Kingdom pharaohs allied with Marduk/Ra conquered Egypt. Thothmose I of the new regime invaded Enlilite Sumer to the Euphrates River, where Abraham's kin and their descendants lived. Thothmose expected Enlilite retaliation. The Pharaoh feared Jacob/Israel's descendants in Egypt–all 600,000– would align with the Sumerian   Enlilites and overthrow him from within.

Thothmose I

When Thothmose IV died in 1405 B.C., his son Amenotep married his sibling sister Sitamun, "So Amenotep could inherit the throne as

Pharaoh Amenotep III." Amenotep also married Tiye, daughter of Joseph, Overseer of Egypt, whose father was Jacob/Israel. "It was decreed, that no born to Tiye could inherit the throne and because of her father Joseph's governorship there was fear that the Israelites were gaining too much power in Egypt. So the edict was given that her child should be killed at birth if a son.

Thothmose IV

Amenhotep III & Queen Tiye

"Tiye's Israelite relatives lived at Goshen and she owned a summer palace a little upstream at Zarw, where she went to have her baby. Midwives conspired with Tiye to float the child downstream in a reed basket to the house of her father's half-brother Levi.

"The boy, Aminadab, in his teenage years went to live at Thebes." He refused to accept Egyptian worship of Marduk/Ra, Enlil's main antagonist in Egypt, "so he introduced of Aten [=Enlil, Yahweh]–in line with Israelite teachings. Aminadab changed his name to Akhenaten (Servant of Aten).

Rachebed Mother of Moses
      Aminadab/Akhenaten

"Aminadab married his half-sister, Nephertiti, to rule as co-regent" while Pharaoh Amenhotep was ill. "When Amenhotep III died, Akhenaten succeeded as Pharaoh, gaining the title Amenhotep IV.

Nephertiti, wife of Pharaoh Akhenaten IV

Pharaoh Akhenaten closed all the temples of the Egyptian gods and build new temples to Aten."

The priests of Marduk (called Ra in Egypt) threatened "armed insurrection" if he didn't allow worship of Ra too. Akhenaton refused and was forced to abdicate.

Akhenaten, banished from Egypt, "fled with the Hebrew relatives of Tiye to Sinai, still regarded by his supproters as the *Mose*, meaning 'heir'" to the Egyptian throne.

Moses and "Aaron the Levite returned to Egypt on orders from the God of Abraham to retrieve the Hebrews" and led them from Pi-Rameses [Kantra] southward, through Sinai to Lake Timash.

Moses & Aaron

This was extremely marshy territory and, although manageable on foot, pursuing horses and chariots foundered disasterously." [Gardiner, *Bloodline*: 9 - 11; Marrs, *Rule by Secrecy*: 367 -369]

"In 1482 B.C. Thothmose III renewed hostilities against Enlilites abroad and the Israelites in Egypt. Moses, now grown, killed an Egyptian overseer who brutalized Israelites.

Thothmose III ordered Moses killed, but Moses escaped to Sinai, where he married the daughter of a Midianite priest.

Pharaoh Thothmose I broke the Middle Kingdom promise that Egypt honor "Children" of Israel. He'd work them to death and stop their breeding. He "ordered any newborn Israelite male killed at birth." In 1513 B.C., to save their newborn, a couple descended from Jacob/Israel put the boy in a box and floated him downstream where Thothmose's daughter bathed. She named the boy Moses and adopted him.

"In 1482 B.C. Thothmose III renewed hostilities against Enlilites abroad and the Israelites in Egypt. Moses, now grown, killed an Egyptian overseer who brutalized Israelites.

Thothmose III ordered Moses killed, but Moses escaped to Sinai, where he married the daughter of a Midianite priest.

In 1450 B.C., Amenhotep II, the new Pharaoh let Moses' death sentence expire.

Enlil ordered Moses to return to Egypt and show Amenhotep magical powers to convince him to free the Israelites. Moses tried to scare Amenhotep with a magic show, but Pharaoh resisted and instead ordered the Israelites make three times more bricks than before.

Enlil responded, visited Egypt with plagues, infestations, cattle diseases, three days of darkness and weather disturbances. He killed all non-Israelite firstborn children and cows in Egypt. In 1433 B.C., Pharaoh told the Israelites, *Go*.

Enlil either used climate control devises to sweep a path through the Red Sea or showed the Israelites a way to cross. Egyptians chased them but, in some versions of the story, Enlil let the sea sweep over and drown them.

When they went, he thought them trapped between the desert's edge, lakes, then the Red Sea. He sent chariots to re-capture them.

For forty years, Enlil guided the Israelites through the desert to the edge of the Sinai Peninsula and protected them from Amalekites. Nights, he lit the Israelites' way with a "fiery beacon." Days, he led them with a dark cloud. He fed them and had them kill 3000 of their number who worshiped other Nibirans; he had them kill 23,000 of their number for sex before they married. [*Exodus* 32:26-28; *Corinthians* 10:8].

He ordered Moses to climb Mt. Sinai then relay demands to the Israelites. Moses told the Israelites what Enlil wanted.

Enlil then landed his rocket atop the mount and, with an amplifier he spoke directly to 600,000 Israelites at the mountain's base. They must, he said, reject all other Nibiran gods, not even say their names. They must spend every seventh day worshiping him and subjugate women and kids, as well as refrain from murder, adultery, theft and false witness. They must not, he said, crave others' homes, wives, Earthlings and property.

For forty days on the peak he either regaled Moses on his spaceship with projections or rocketed him up so he could see and report the Earth was curved–something Earthlings of his day did not know. [DoHerarty, J., *Did Enki Give Humans Knowledge?*]

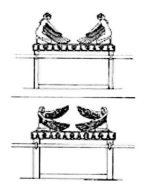

Enlil gave Moses stone tablets he'd inscribed with his commandments. He showed Moses how to build a temple and a box (Ark of the Covenant) for the tablets. Above the tablet drawer in the Ark, Moses must build a Talk-To-Enlil communicator (sporting two gold cherubs). Through the Ark, Moses could signal and question Enlil for "Yes" or "No" answers. He choose Moses' brother Aaron and Aaron's sons as priests. He specified the protective clothes the priests must wear near the radioactive Ark. Enlil, extremely protective of his Ark, killed fifty thousand people of Bethshemesh for looking into it.[1 Samuel 6:19]

Aaron worried that Moses died on the mountain, had smiths built a gold calf–Enlil's symbol-- to signal Enlil.

But Moses destroyed the smiths, their calf, and the tablets Enlil gave him.

Enlil too fumed, threatened to abandon the Israelites but then relented.

He made a "pillar of cloud" in front of Moses' tent and from a UFO (called a "Kabod") inside a cloud, broadcast that he forgave the Israelites for the calf.

He kept his face hidden from Moses while he dicated what Moses engraved for forty days. When Moses returned to his followers, he clowed with radiation he absorbed from Enlil's shuttlecraft.

Moses died before reaching the promised land.

His general, Joshua, led the Israelites.

In 1393 B.C., the Israelites entered Canaan. In 1433 B.C., Enlil fired techno- weapons and helped Joshua and the Israelites conquer Jerico.

Enlil told Joshua, *"I'll make day linger till you kill the Canaanites regrouping near Beth-Horon."* Enlil knew a disintegrating comet hit Earth and Earth would stop turning for twelve hours. The Bible said, "The Israelites had taken Jerico and Ai. Amorite kings put up a combined force against the Israelites in Ajalon, near the city of Gideon. It began with a night attack that put the Canaanites into flight. By sunrise, as the Canaanite forces regrouped near Beth-Horon, "Yahweh [Enlil] delivered the Canaanites unto the Children of Israel, saying, `*Let the Sun stand still in Gideon.'* Yahweh "cast down great stones from heaven upon them and they died."

The sun continued to be seen, to hang in the skies for twenty hours." In the Andes, the sun did not rise for the same length of time. "In the reign of Titu Yupanqui Pachacuti II, the fifteenth monarch in Ancient [pre-Inca] times [in the Western Hemisphere], the night did not end when it usually does and sunrise was delayed for twenty hours." A comet came too close to Earth and broke apart.

Comets orbit the sun clockwise; Earth orbits it counterclockwise. Comet fragments hit Earth struck from clockwise, slowed Earth's rotation and made the sun stay in Canaan and fail to arrive–so it stayed dark--in the Americas. [ZS, *Lost Realms*: 151 - 154]

ENLIL (YAWEH) [ENSLAVED AND KILLED]

With the additional light, Enlil and Joshua killed 120,000 men and enslaved 200,000 women and children. They went on to kill a million Ethiopians too. With terrible techno-weapons and engineered plagues, they killed 10,000 Canaanites and Perizzites and 10,000 Moabites. [Judges 1:4, 3:28-29; Tellinger, *Slave Species*:173 -191]

"By around 1250 B.C. the Nibirans had gone into their final phase-out mode. The human population and the foremen kings, now left on their own, began to fend for themselves. For some three thousand years, subsequently, we humans have been going through a traumatic transition to independence.

Proprietary claims made by various groups of humans as to who knew what we should be doing to get the Anunnaki to return or when they returned, perpetuated the palace and social rituals learned under the Anunnaki and sometimes disagreement and strife broke out between them. Religion, as we know it, took form, focused on the "god" or "gods", clearly and unambiguously known to the humans who were in contact with them as imperfect, flesh and blood humanoids, now absent. It was only much later that the Anunnaki were eventually sublimated into cosmic character and status and, later on, mythologized due to remoteness in time

ENLILITE POWER GREW AGAINST ENKIITE EGYPT AND BABYLON

Enlil's main rival "god, Marduk, gave Hammurabi, Marduk's king at Babylon, "a powerful weapon, called "Great Power of Marduk", with which he subdued all Sumer, save the Enlilite strongholds of Adad in Assyria and Ninurta in Lagash.

In the 12th Century B.C., the Enlilite's King Tiglat-Pileser I of Assyria conquered Lebanon and captured Marduk. "City states in western Asia, along the Mediterranean coast, Asia Minor and Arabia became magnets, attracting migrants and invaders. Peoples of the Sea tried without success to settle in Egypt and instead occupied the Canaan coast." Abraham's descendants begged Enlil for kings to stop barons' feuds. Enlil choose as king Saul, then David; David made Jerusalem Capitol of Israel.

Around 1200 B.C., Greeks led by Agamemnon, Menelaus and Odysseus attacked Hittite allies of Adad and Inanna at Troy. Diamedes, a part-Nibiran Greek Earthling, wounded her but she recovered. Her son, Aeneas, who'd fought on the Trojan side, escapedto Carthage, then to Italy.

ENLIL CRUSHED PLURALISM IN ISRAEL

In 1003 B.C., Israelite leader David captured Jerusalem. Then, in 931 B.C., when David's successor, Solomon, died, Abraham's descendants split their turf into the kingdoms of Judea in the south and Israel, bordering Phoenicia--land of the great Canaanite traders of the old world--on the north. Until 910 B.C., Jeroboam, Rehoboam, Abijah, Nadab, Baasah, Elah, Zimri, then Omri ruled Israel.

King Solomon

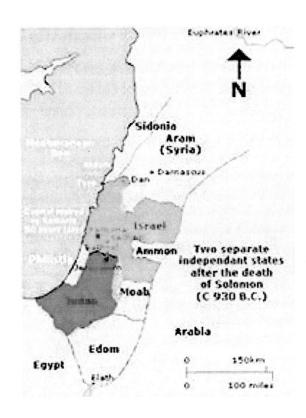

In 872 B.C., the leading Phoenician, Ithbaal, King of Tyre, a descendant of Enki and Inanna, sealed an alliance with Israel. Ithbaal gave his daughter Jezebel to Ahab, the successor to Omri as King of Israel. Jezebel was to be Ahab's principal wife. She believed the alliance between Phoenicia and Israel could "replace separatism, pragmatism replace ideology and trade replace bloodshed. Through Jezebel's marriage to Ahab, Tyre would develop the Red Sea port of Etzion Geber"

and "Tryian ships would ply the coasts of Arabia and East Africa, as far as India for spices and silk. Tyre would pay Israel handsomely in tolls and fees." [*Jezebel*: 26 -31]

Jezebel came to a magnificent temple of Astarte/Inanna Ahab build for her in Samaria, north of Jerusalem. She traveled with servants, traders and emissaries of Tyre, 400 priestesess and 450 priests.

When Ahab defeated an Assyrian attack, Elijah, Enlil's representative in Israel, blamed her for Ahab's decision not to sacrifice the captured Assyrian king and his men to Enlil and instead create an alliance with Assyria. Enlil and Elijah wanted Ahab and Jezebel deposed and killed. Enlil evidently either used a HAARP- type weather device or observed weather patterns and took credit for them to punish the Israelites for their merciful treatment of the Assyrians and Ahab's failure to prevent worship in Israel of other Nibiran "gods". Elijah created

a challenge, Enlil's priests and Jezebel's would see whose cattle sacrifice Enlil would accept on Mt Carmel. Enlil, of course, accepted his priests' bull but rejected the bull of Jezebel's priests, whom the witnesses then, at Elijah's insistence, killed. Jezebel, furious, exiled Elijah, who fled Israel.

But in Israel, Enlil's priests framed Jezebel as engineering the death of a landowner whose property she coveted. Elijah issued a *fatwa– "Dogs shall eat Jezebel."* Enlil took Elijah aloft in his aircraft (but told Elisha, Elijah's successor as Prophet of Yahweh that he killed Elijah).

Elisha engineered another Assyrian attack, in which Ahab was killed. Then Elisha suborned Hazael, Ahab's Chief of Staff and had Hazael murder the Assyrian king. Hazael made himself ruler of Assyria. He made a deal with the generals of

Israel and Judea (Judea was now ruled by the son of Jezebel and Ahab) to murder the rulers of both Israel and Judea. Hazael made Jehu (a descendant of Zimri who'd assassinated Israel's king Elah before Ahab's father Omri killed him) King of Israel and had his men throw Jezebel to her death from her second story to be torn apart by mastiff dogs.

"The morning after Jehu's triple regicide, Jehu consolidated his power. He ordered every male in any way related to the House of Ahab's father Omri," King Joram's counselors and priests, fleeing attendants of Jezebel trying to get back to Tyre seized and beheaded so blood would be the hands of all surviving authorities.

Tyre and Judea, the latter now ruled by Jezebel's daughter Athaliah, cut relations with Israel so the Syrians easily subjugated Jehu and Israel, left Israel with only peasants to keep growing food, deported 500,000 soldiers, priests, scribes officials and craftsmen of Israel (the ten tribes of Israel that were "lost") to other parts of the Assyrian empire and replaced the deported Israelis with settlers from other parts of the empire [*Jezebel*: 93-197].

Adad and Nergal again sent an Assyrian king--Shalmaneser III--with technologically-advanced artillery against Marduk's Babylonians. Shalmaneser won.

In 722 B.C. Shalmaneser V captured Samaria in Israel. Sargon II, Shalmanser V's successor, exiled the Israelites from northern Israel. In 689 B C., Sargon II's son, Sennacherib and the Assyrians assaulted Babylon with missiles and occupied Babylon for the next seventy years. Sennacherib took Phoenicia, Gaza and Judea.

But Sennacherib--without Adad's okay, struck Jerusalem. Enlil hit the Assyrians who'd dared to turn against him at Jerusalem, with a techno-weapon that killed 185,000. Sennacherib fled back to Nineva in Sumer. He named his younger son Esarhaddon his successor. In 612 B.C., Babylon's King Nabupolassar captured Nineva and the Assyrians retreated to Harran. Sennacherib's older sons killed him, but Nibirans hid Esarhaddon. Enlil sent Inanna to Assyria. She disarmed the Ninevans and destroyed their weapons. *"Esarhaddon rules,"* she proclaimed.

Then Inanna protected Assyria. From her headgear she loosed "an intense, blinding brilliance" and blinded enemies of Esarhaddon's successor (Ashurbanipal) in battles in Arabia and in an attack on Marduk's Egyptian forces. Inanna "rained flames upon Arabia."

Lest Inanna get to powerful, Enlil let Babylonians conquer Assyria from 614-616 B.C. and sent Babylon's king Nebuchadnezzar II to take Lebanon. [ZS, *Wars*:12-19]

[handwritten:] 650 B.C. ANUNNAKI LEFT PLANET EARTH FROM THE OLD WAY STATION ON PLANET MARS.

"From 610 B.C. though 650 B.C., the Anunnaki methodically left Earth" from the old Way Station on Mars, from which the long-distance spaceships raced to intercept and land on the orbiting Nibiru" when it reached perigee. "Benefitting from Mars' lower gravity compared to Earth's, the Anunnaki found it easier to transport themselves and their cargos in shuttlecraft from Earth to Mars, and there transfer to reach Nibiru. Mars had water, walled structures, roads, a hublike compound" and the statue of Alalu's face. [ZS, *End of Days*:260 - 261]

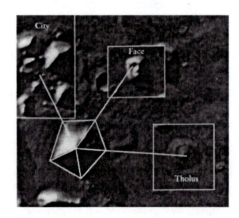

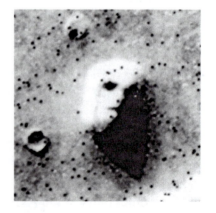

NINGISHZIDDA TOOK AFRICANS TO MEXICO

In Mexico in 3113 B.C., Ningishzidda/Thoth (called *Quetzlcoatl* in the Americas), whom Marduk had deposed in Egypt, brought Sumerian Overseers and Black African foremen and technicians, the OLMECS," to Mexico and Central America and with them organized the Maya,

descendants of Ka-in's from the Anunnaki sites in Peru and Colombia. Ningishzidda left his Olmecs and transplanted Sumerians around 600B.C., but said he'd return on the anniversary of his number, 52. The Maya and slew the Olmecs and the Overseers. MAYA CIVILIZATION DESCENDANT OF KAIN MARDUK -ENKI

MANY NIBIRANS WENT BUT SOME STAYED

In Jerusalem around this time Ezekiel lamented *"Yahweh sees us no more–Yahweh has left Earth."* In both hemispheres, then, "Mankind found itself without its long- worshipped gods. Mankind grasped for the hope of a Return and cast about for a savior." [ZS, *End of Days:* 266 - 267]

In 587 B.C., forces of Marduk's Babylonian king Nebuchadnezzar overran Enlilite forces in Jerusalem. Nebuchadnezzer installed a puppet king, ordered worship of Marduk, and took leading citizens of the city as hostages back to Babylon. Enlil told one of these hostages, Ezekiel, he'd punish the Jews for worshiping Marduk and the people of Jerusalem believed Enlil'd deserted them.

In 586 B.C., Nebuchadnezzar deposed the king he left in Jerusalem and burned the temple to Enlil that King Solomon had built there. Nebuchadnezzar took Israeli elders, aristocrats, officials, soldiers, priests and craftsmen into exile, this time to Babylon, leaving, again, only farmers in Israel and Judea. The Israeli scholars wrote the Hebrew Bible there, and created monotheism, for Yahweh/Enlil now lacked a land and could be a divinity free of a specific territory. 150 years later, when Persia conquered Babylon, Persia's King Cyrus and sent them back to their land, the hithertofore territorial Yahweh "had been written into the abstract universal god." [*Jezebel:* 202- 203; ZS, *Cosmic Code:* 274 -275]

In 539 B.C., welcomed by Marduk, Cyrus of Persia conquered Babylon and returned Nebuchadnezzar's hostages to Jerusalem. Cyrus' successor, Cambyses, added Sumer, Mari, Mittani, Hatti, Elam, Assyria, Egypt to the Persian Empire. Darius, who murdered Cambyses in 522 B.C., ruled the extended Persian Empire. He unsuccessfully invaded Greece in 490 B.C.. In 480 B.C., his successor, Xerxes, also unsuccessfully attacked Greece.

Philip II of Macedonia united Greece by 338 B.C.. From 334 -331 B.C., his heir, Alexander, who thought Marduk fathered him, conquered the Persian Empire, the Indus and Egypt. Egyptian priests at Siwa confirmed Alexander as Marduk's son.

Alexander the Great

Alexander With His Teacher Aristotle

"Alexander reached Babylon in 331 B.C. and rushed to the ziggurat temple to grasp the hands of Marduk as conquerors before him had done. But the great god was dead. Alexander saw the god lying in a golden coffin, his body preserved in oils. His ziggurat was his tomb."[ZS, *End of Days*: 272 - 276]

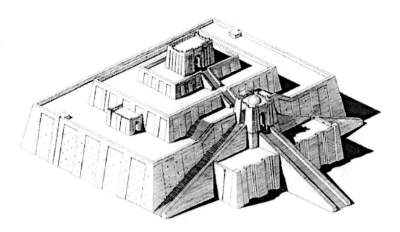

"Who," Sitchin asks, "of the Anunnaki gods remained on Earth? We can be certain only of Marduk and Nabu of the Enkiites and of the Enlilites, Nannar, his spouse Ningal, his aide, Nuksu and Ishtar [Inanna]." [ZS, *End of Days*: 267]

XIII GODS" WHO MODELED NARCISSISM, EGOMANIA, VIOLENCE, GREED, RACISM, SEXISM & HIERARCHY WILL RETURN FOR MORE GOLD

Most Nibirans ignored our minds or manipulated our consciousness so they ruled and we slaved for them. They taught violence, greed, competition, hierarchy, slavery, racism, patriarchy, disdain for Earthling consciousness, blind obedience to them and murderous hatred of their rivals. Inanna, Nannar and the power elite here continue to divide and rule humanity.

When the Nibirans had enough gold to leave Earth, 13,000 years ago, the perigee of Nibiru created the Deluge, it also ripped away the shield of powdered Earth gold that protected Nibiru. "Nibiru's atmosphere was again dwindling. The mother planet again desperately needed Earth's gold." Nibiru ordered the Expedition to send lots more gold at once.

If, next or in some future perigee, Nibiru again loses its gold shield and needs more gold, Nibirans may again dig our gold–after we've dug it. This time, I hope, we can request knowledge and help from them to resolve our political and environmental problems.

Rockets from Nibiru reach Earth best when Nibiru neared the Sun, at perigee. But at perigee also, Nibiru 's gravity perturbs planets and affect Nibiru's atmosphere. Nibirans shuttle to and from Earth to match the best launch times, a span of 13 to 18 Earth months before Nibiru gets closest and, leaving, before it gets to far from Earth. While Nibiru "continues its vast elliptical orbit, the spaceship follows a shorter course and reaches Earth far ahead of Nibiru or, for a shorter stay on Earth, the rocket launches "when Nibiru is midway back from apogee," a few years ahead of Nibiru. When the rocket nears Earth, "it goes into orbit around the planet without landing and releases a shuttlecraft to land. "Some of the earlier arrivals ascend to an Earth module and rejoin the spaceship for a trip home. To return, the shuttle had to rejoin the mother ship, which had to fire up and accelerate to extremly high speeds to catch up with Nibiru." Shuttles took gold Earthlings mined to and from the base on Mars.[ZS, 12th Planet: 282 - 271]

Nibiru returns to perigee in 2012, 2040 or (if you take the speedup due to Nibiru's interaction with Uranus, last perigee) 2900. Nibirans may again need our planet's gold. Inanna and Nannar, who still dwell on Earth and the power elite they control here remain firmly in control of Earth's resources. [ZS, End: 315 - 317]

Now that we know what the Nibirans want–gold-- and how they regard us–mere instruments, say the Enlilites, for their needs–we can resist. Resist and insist: WE DEMAND EQUALITY, COMPASSION, GENETIC ACTIVATION OF LONG-LIFE POTENTIAL, THE SECRETS OF FREE ENERGY AND SPACE TRAVEL. WE OFFER THE NIBIRANS OUR COOPERATION AND SYNERGY AS PARTNERS IN EVOLUTION.

Part II: EXAMINE EVIDENCE

Datum 1. SUMERIAN SPACE MAPS SHOWED PLANETS BEYOND EYESIGHT

Sumerians display rocket route maps and verbal descriptions they say the gods
dictated of planets and their orbits beyond eye-range. Dark dwaffstar Nemisis' orbit plus the orbit
of the Nibran planetary complex brings Nibiru from some 1000 astronomical units away to the
vicinity of Earth, on a 30degree plane to Earth's orbit , between Mars and Jupiter. This view of
Earth, from the outer planets of the inner solar system to the inner gave Nibirans and see the orbits
of our planetary system. Nibiru acted "as a spacecraft that sailed past all the other planets, gave
them a chance at repeated close looks." They labeled the inner planets from the farthest from the
sun (pluto) to the closest (mercury) from one to twelve, Earth, seven--counting the sun and Earth's
moon as planets, hence Sitchin's title, *The Twelfth Planet.*[Genesis: 19, 46]

Sumerians lacked telescopes and couldn't see Uranus' and Neptune's orbits the route maps show.
Nibiran-dictated maps prove they had astronomical info Sumerians, on their own, didn't. The maps
accurately detail the entire Earth from space, a perspective impossible for ancient Sumerians on
their own.

Solar System Chart on Sumerian
Clay Tablet

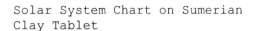

~ 164 ~

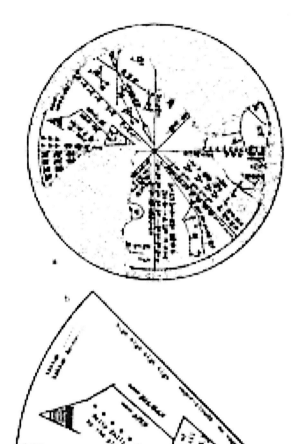

On "a clay tablet in the ruins of the Royal Library at Nineva shows how to go through inner solar system. Commander Enlil's route to Earth: The line that inclines at 45° shows "the spaceship's descent from a point high, high, high, high through vapor clouds and a lower zone that is vaporless, toward the horizontal point, where the skies and ground meet." [ZS, *12th Planet*:275]

"In the skies near the horizontal line, the instructions are 'set, set, set' their instruments for the final approach, which should be raised up before reaching the landing point because it had to pass over rugged terrain." [ZS, *12th Planet*:276]

Sumerians began the list of solar system planets with the most distant from the sun and beyond human vision. Nibiru, the most distant, then Pluto, Neptune (only found by modern astronomers in 1846) and Uranus (re-discovered in 1781). They next listed planets seen on Earth without telescopes--Saturn, Jupiter, Mars, Earth, and then Earth's Moon (which they counted as a planet). They listed last Venus, then Mercury, planets closest to Solaris.

The Sumerians wrote that the Nibirans told them of the planets beyond unassisted human vision. The sequence of planets the Nibirans listed reflected their experience when they came to Earth from Nibiru–from beyond the inner solar system toward the sun. Their sequence therefore adds to the evidence the Nibirans were indeed extraterrestrial astronauts. [Lloyd: 2-39; Sitchin, *Time*: 4-6; UFOTV: Are We Alone? Geneis Revisited http://enkispeaks.com/2012/09/03/1603/]

Datum 2. ET "GODS" SAID THEY SAW, & WE MUCH LATER CONFIRMED, WATER ON PLANETS & MOONS

Clay-tablets from Sumer say Mars had water. They show water on asteroids, comets, Neptune, Uranus, Venus, Saturn, Jupiter, the rings of Saturn and on Saturn's and Jupiter's moons. Our astronomers recently confirmed water where Sumerian scribes said.

"Mars once had surface water several meters deep over the whole planet. There's enough water in Mars' crust to flood the planet 1000 miles deep. Martian canyons have flowing water below the dry riverbeds. Mars, Venus and Earth confirm Sumerian texts of water 'below the firmament' on inner planets." [ZS, *Genesis*: 53 -55; Lloyd, *Dark Star*: 1-16-17]

Uranus: Our scientists only recently validated water on Uranus. Sumerian scribes long ago said Nibirans said water covered Uranus. Before Voyager 2 proved otherwise, our astronomers dismissed the Sumerian "myth" of water on Uranus. They thought Uranus made of gas only. Voyager 2 showed Uranuscovered with a 6000 mile layer of "superheated water." [ZS, *Genesis*: 12]

Neptune: Sumerians scribes wrote on that Nibiran goldminers marked the orbit, water surface and swamp vegetation on Neptune, three billion miles from Earth, long before Le Verrier and Galle "discovered" Neptune in1846 (when wobbles in Uranus' orbit--closer to Earth than Neptune–augured "another celestial body beyond it"). Before Voyager 2 showed Neptune's "floating surry mixture of ice water," Sitchin published Sumerian records of Neptune as "blue- green, watery, with patches of swamplike vegetation." [ZS, *Genesis*: 5 -9]

Datum 3. NIBIRANS NOTED TWIN TRAITS OF URANUS AND NEPTUNE 6000 YEARS AGO

Sumerians recorded Nibirans' observations that Neptune and Uranus were "twins." Rings surround both, satellites orbit both, water covers both and both show blue-green color. Both planets have 16-hour days and "extreme inclination relative to the planets' axes of rotation. Sumerians recorded this in 4000 B.C.; NASA didn't get it till 1989, 6000 years later [ZS, *Genesis*: 13 -14].

Datum 4. NIBIRAN MOON INFO PREDATED OURS

Sumerians recorded Nibirans' hypothesis that satellite moons evolved to planets with
their own orbits around the sun instead of around the planet whose satellite they'd been. Modern astronomers too came to this after they saw the twin qualities of Uranus and Neptune, studied Pluto's orbit and after Pioneer and Voyager spacecraft showed that "in the past decade Titan, the largest moon of Saturn, was a planet-in-the-making whose detachment from Saturn was not completed." [ZS, *Genesis*:16 -18]. Scholars dismissed as myths Sumerian tales of moons on outer planets. But Sumerians said the Anunnaki saw moons circling Mars, Jupiter, Saturn, Uranus, and Neptune. In 1610 A.D., Galileo saw four of Jupiter's; before that "it was unthinkable for a celestial body to have more than one moon, since Earth had just one." Mars has 2; Jupiter, more than 16, Saturn, more than 21, Uranus, up to 15 and Neptune, 8. What Sumerians said about outer planets' moons supports the hypothesis that they saw these moons from beyond the inner solar system. [ZS, *Genesis*: 50]

Datum 5. SUMERIANS KNEW FIRST HOW THE MOON FORMED

4.6 billion years ago, when Tiamat–the proto-Earth--orbited Solaris beyond Mars, Tiamat's moon, Kingu, almost attained solar orbit. But 600 million years later, Nibiru entered the inner Solar System. Nibiru's moon, Evil Wind, hit Tiamat into orbit within Mars'and left Kingu circling Earth.

Our Pioneer and Voyager probes sent back evidence Kingu formed from Tiamat, the planet that became Earth. Tiamat, then beyond Mars, generated Kingu.

Glassy material with nickel in the Moon's rocks validate the likelihood that a moon of Nibiru impacted Kingu 500 million years after Kingu grew into a Tiamat's satellite, when Kingu had almost attained planetary orbit around the Sun. "Tiamat was split in two; one half shattered [and became the asteroids]; the other half, accompanied by Kingu, thrust into a new orbit to become the Earth and its moon." [Wood, J., 1984, *The Origin of The Moon*; ZS, 1990, *Genesis*: 107 - 131]

The collision depleted most of Kingu's iron, "resulting in decrease in its density. The mass of the Moon's core "bears the mark of the 'big whack' compressed the moon, just as the Sumerians related. Contrary to views the moon was always inert, it was found in the 1970s and 1980s to possess all attributes of a planet except independent orbit around the Sun: rugged mountains, plains and seas formed by water [or] molten lava. It retained a magnetic field caused by rotation of a molton iron core, heat and water, astrue of Earth and other planets" until the Evil Wind struck it.

"The Moon witnesses the accuracy of ancient knowledge." Nibirans, who ruled the Sumerians, knew the Moon's history long before our scientists did.

Datum 6. NIBIRANS GOT ASTEROID MAKEUP RIGHT FIRST

Nibirans described asteroids as pieces of Earth knocked into space when, four billion years ago, a moon of Nibiru struck Tiamat. "Debris from the lower half of Tiamat stretched into space. Sumerian texts and the biblical version thereof" said the asteroid belt, a bracelet of debris, orbited the sun between Jupiter and Mars, "but our astronomers were not aware of that" until in 1801 Piazzi found the first asteroid, Ceres. "It's taken modern astronomy centuries to find out what Sumerians knew 6,000 years ago.[ZS, *Genesis*: 51]

Datum 7. SUMERIAN STORY PREDICTED MODERN FINDINGS OF EARTH'S MAKE-UP AND HISTORY

"Earth's crust, plate tectonics, differences between the continental and oceanic crusts, emergence of Pangaea from under the waters, the primordial encircling ocean: the findings of modern science corroborated ancient knowledge. The only explanation of the way Earth's landmasses, oceans and atmosphere evolved is a cataclysm four billion years ago. What was that cataclysm? Mankind possessed the Sumerian answer six thousand years: The Celestial Battle" between the planets "Nibiru/Marduk and Tiamat." [ZS, *Genesis*: 88-106]

The Sumerian tale predicted Earth's geo-features. "In the aftermath of the Celestial Battle, Earth evolved into an independent planet and attained the shape of a globe dictated by the forces of gravity. Waters gathered into the cavity on the torn-off side. Dry land appeared on the other side of the planet. Earth's crust is 12 miles to 45 miles thick; but in parts taken up by oceans the crust is only 3.5 miles thick. While the average elevation of continents is 2,300 feet, the average depth of oceans is 12,500 feet. The thicker continental crust reached much further down into the mantle [rock layer], whereas the oceanic crust is a thin layer of solidified sediments. In the Pacific, the crust has been gouged out at some points 7 miles. If we could remove from the Pacific's floor the crust built up over the last 200 million years, we arrive at depths 12 miles below the water's surface and 60 miles below the surface." [ZS, *Genesis*: 93- 98]

Datum 8. NIBIRANS LONG AGO TOLD HOW LIFE EVOLVED ON EARTH

"Scientists now believe Earth's atmosphere reconstituted initially from gasses spewed out from wounded Earth. Clouds thrown up from these eruptions shielded Earth and it began to cool, the vaporized water condensed and came down in torrential rains. Oxidation of rocks and minerals provided the first reservoir of higher levels of oxygen on Earth; plant life added both oxygen and carbon dioxide to the atmosphere and started the nitrogen cycle with the aid of bacteria. The fifth tablet of the *Enuma elish* describes the gushing lava as Tiamat's "spittle" as it poured forth, "assembling the water clouds; after that the foundations of Earth were raised and the oceans gathered" just as the verses of *Genesis* reiterated. Thereafter life appeared: green herbage upon the continents and "swarms" in the waters."[ZS, *Genesis*: 134 (*Genesis* condenses *Enuma*.)]

3.4 billion years ago, "clays acted as chemical laboratories where inorganic materials were processed into more complex molecules. Inorganic proto-organisms in the clay acted as a template from which living organisms [one- celled microscopic algae like today's blue-green algae] evolved. Defects in the clays acted as sites where stored energy and chemical directions for the formation of proto-organisms developed." Green algae's "the precursor of chlorophyllic plants that use sunlight to convert their nutrients to organic compounds, emitting oxygen in the process after algae spread upon dry land. For plantlike forms to process oxygen, they needed rocks containing iron to bind the oxygen; free oxygen was still poison to life forms. Such banded-iron formations sank into ocean bottoms as sediments, the single-celled organisms evolved into multicelled ones in the water. The covering of the lands with algae preceded the emergence of maritime life" [ZS, *Genesis*: 136 - 139] .

Crick and Orgel, our Nobel laureate scientists, say, in "Directed Panspermia [*Icarus*, vol. 19], a technologically advanced society on another planet in a spaceship with due protection and a life-sustaining environment, seeded Earth" Crick and Orgel "rule out the possibility that the essential genetic material had time to evolve on Earth." They found the same twenty amino acids in all living organisms on Earth. All Earth's organisms, when they evolved, incorporated within themselves the same four nucleotides "that and no other.[ZS, *Genesis*:152]

The Nibirans "figured out evolution on Earth." Maritime vertebrates came 500 million years ago; land vertebrates, 100 million years later. 225 million years ago, fish filled the waters. Sea plants and amphibians moved from water to land. Plants lured amphibians to land; amphibians adapted into egg-laying reptiles. Some reptiles evolved into birds; reptiles on land grew to dinosaurs. 65 million years ago, dinosaurs died out. "Full agreement here" among the *Enuma, Genesis* and modern science." [ZS, *Genesis*: 141 - 145]

Datum 9. NIBIRANS AND EARTHLINGS SHARE DNA

"300,00 years ago, the Anunnaki jumped the gun on evolution and using genetic engineering, upgraded a hominid, *Homo Erectus*–to an intelligent, tool-handling *Homo Sapiens*) to be their serf. It happened in the Great Rift Valley zone of southeast Africa, just north of the goldmining land.

"The wild hominid of the Abzu had DNA similar enough to the Anunnaki's that just a little genetic mixing produced a Being that, according to Sumerians and the Bible, was akin to the 'gods' both inwardly and outwardly except for their longevity. All life on Earth, from birds to fishes, flora to algae, and down to bacteria and viruses–all have the very same DNA, the four nucleic acid letters from which all genes and genomes are made. The DNA of the Anunnaki was the same as the DNA of all life on Nibiru. The DNA on Earth and the DNA on Nibiru were the same." Our genome--less than 30,000 genes–holds 223 genes without evolutionary predecessors. These 223 genes, absent in vertebrae evolution, regulate the human body and mind.

The theory of panspermia, that Earth was "seeded from elsewhere," was inscised in clay tablets millennia ago. Nibiru gave Earth its DNA during the Celestial Battle. This "explains how life could begin on Earth in the relatively immediate aftermath of the cataclysm. Since Nibiru, at the time of the collision, already possessed formed DNA, evolution began there much earlier. Just 1% earlier would mean a head start of 45,000,000 Earth-years–more than enough evolutionary time for Nibiru's astronauts to meet *Homo Erectus* on Earth." The planet "Nibiru is the 'Creator of the Primeval Seed who 'furnished the Seed of Earth,' culminating with 'the Seed of All People, all life stemming from the same DNA." [ZS, *Giants*: 153 -160]

We *Homo Sapiens* "showed up suddenly, 200,000 years ago in the fossil record with differences from "any other anthrodoid or homanoid" which evolved on Earth. This sudden appearance supports the hypothesis that creationism–which Enki, Ninmah and Ningishzidda claimed on tablets their scribes wrote--was a component of our history (as are both devolution and evolution of earlier humans before the Anunnaki). "Darwin principles do not apply to our unique genesis and subsequent development except as a minor theme in our climactic and incidental regional adaptation."

Freer lists our differences from other humans on Earth before Enki, et. al. created us modern Earthlings: "we have foreheads, hardly any brow ridges, eye sockets far more rectangular than round; relatively tiny nasal passages; small flat mouths and a chin; far less muscular strength and bone density; our skin, sweat process and glands, body hair, throats, and salt management are completely different. Human females do not have an estrus cycle. We are bipedal. Our brains different. We are a product of a melding of two racial gene codes where quality control was conditioned by practical purposes [creating obediant slaves] have some four thousand genetic defects rather than none to other species." [Freer, *Sapiens Arising*]

Datum 10 **NIBIRANS JUGGLED GENOMES BEFORE WE DID**

Long before our scientists understood evolution, Nibirans knew the developmental sequence of organisms on Earth. More than 300,000 years ago, they decoded the pan-human genome. They isolated their own, various animals' and *Homo Erectus'* deoxyribonucleic acid (DNA) and mitochondrial DNA (mtDNA) chromosomal sequences. Enki's symbol, entwined serpents, "emulated the structure of the genetic code, the secret knowledge that enabled Enki to create the Adam and then grant Adam and Eve the ability to procreate."

Enki's built a sterile lab; its air-conditioned is "the source of the biblical assertion that after having fashioned the Adam, *Elohim* 'blew in his nostrils the breath of life.

Enki, Ninmah and Ningishzidda mapped chromosomes, genes and genomes. They fertilized ova in test tube flasks with sperm soaked in Nibiran blood serum and mineral nutrients. They experimented with cloning, cell fusion and recombinant technology--cutting DNA strands with enzymes, targeted viruses, absorbing sperm in genetic material to be used for fertilization and splicing in DNA patches of other species to create, at first, hybrids unable to reproduce.
Then Ningishzidda isolated the XX and XY chromosomes that allowed the creation of fertile Nibiran/Erectus mineslaves. [ZS, 1990, *Genesis*: 158 - 182, 202]

Datum 11 **NIBIRANS MAPPED ANTARCTIC LAND DELUGE DIVULGED**

"13,000 years ago, the Ice Age abruptly ended; Antarctica was freed of its ice cover. Its coasts, bays, rivers were seen." Nibiran Goldmining Expedition personnel, from spacecraft orbiting Earth, saw the Antarctic landmass after the icecap slid into the South Sea. Our ancestors didn't even know the Antarctic continent existed before "A.D. 1820, when British and Russian sailors discovered it. It was then, as it is now, covered by a massive layer of ice; we know the continent's true shape under the icecap by means of radar." Yet, in 1958, Antarctica appears on world maps– ice-free--from the fourteenth centuries A.D.–hundreds of years before the discovery of Antarctica."

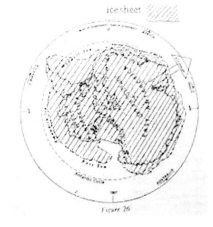

THE *OLDEST MAP OF AMERICA* DRAWN by *PÍRÎ REÍS*

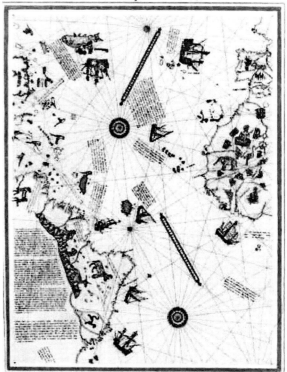

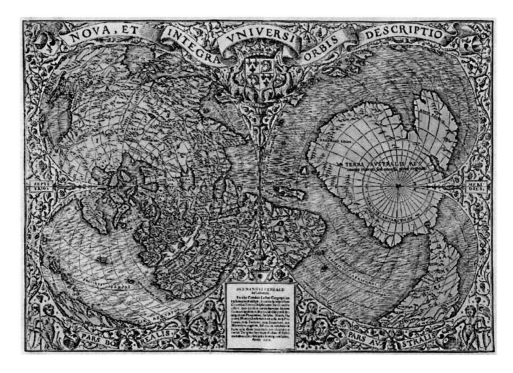

"Map makers in the Age of Discovery stated that their sources were ancient maps from Mesopotamia. No mortal seamen, even given advanced instruments, could have mapped Antarctica and its inner features in those early days, and certainly not an ice-free Antarctica. Only someone viewing it from the air could have done it. The only ones around at the time were the Anunnaki." [ZS, *Encounters*: 99-102]

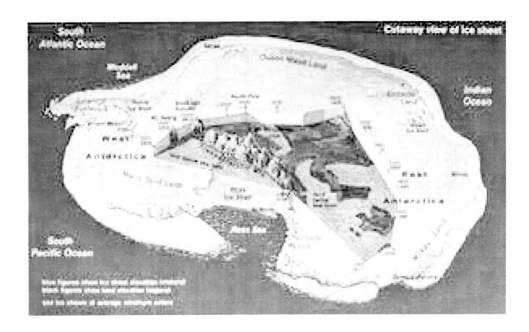

Datum 12 ETS LEFT HUGE DOODLES & ROCKETS TAKEOFF LINES

Evidence of the last Nibiran spaceport on Earth includes 740 take-off trails atop huge scraped drawings [geogylphs] of "known and imaginary animals and birds made by removing the topsoil several inches, executed with one continuous line that curves and twists without crossing over itself. Attempts to show that a horde of workers working at ground level and using scrapers could have created these images failed. Someone *airborne* used a soil-blasting device to doodle on the ground below.

"The feet-deep 'Candelabra' in nearby Bay of Paracas was obtained in the same way" by aircraft "equipped with some ray gun gizmo.

Candelabra, Bay of Paracas

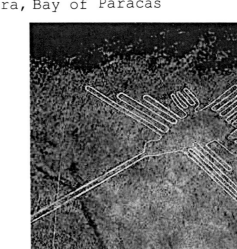

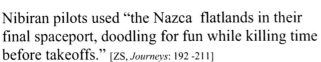

Nibiran pilots used "the Nazca flatlands in their final spaceport, doodling for fun while killing time before takeoffs." [ZS, *Journeys*: 192 -211]

In addition to the geoglyphs, there are actual lines, "the Nazca Lines, that run straight without fault. These stretch–sometimes narrow, sometimes wide, sometimes short, sometimes long–over hills and vales no matter the shape of the terrain." The straight lines "crisscross each other, sometimes running over and ignoring the animal drawings. These are not made with handheld ray guns. The lines are not horizontally level–they run straight over uneven terrain, ignoring hills, ravines, gullies. They are not runways. They are the result of takeoffs by craft taking off and leaving on the ground below 'lines' created by their engine's exhaust."

On a nearby mountain, lines of grooves outline a landing corridor; "circles and squares form a cross, as in a modern heliport." [ZS, *Journeys*: 212 -213]

Nazca Lines

Datum 13 ROCKET IMAGES, DESCRIPTIONS, ROUTE MAPS AND CALCULATIONS

Ancient engravings show spaceports, rockets, launch towers, helicopters, flying saucers, accounts of take-offs, landings and journeys. Rocket and airplane journeys of Anu, Enlil, Anu, Enki, Ea, Anzu, Marduk, Inanna abound.

3-Stage rocketship carving from Anu's temple in Uruk

Helicopter, two airplanes, Ziasudra's submersible on ancient relief frieze, twenty-five feet above the floor on an Abydos temple Egypt

Drawing from Anu's temple at Uruk shows "multistage rocket atop which rests the command cabin, engines at the bottom, Igigi Astronauts within.

Phoenician coin from Gebal, Lebanon shows a launch tower.

Hittite glyphs showed cruising missiles, rockets mounted on launch pads and a god inside a radiating chamber.

Nibirans on Earth had "craft that could appear over a place, hover for awhile, and disappear from sight again. Ezekial, on the banks of the Khabur in northern Mesopotamia, reported "a helicopter consisting of a cabin resting on four posts, each equipped with rotary wings–a whirlbird.

"Seal[9] found in Crete dated to the thirteenth century depicts a rocketship moving in the skies (above cart) and propelled by flames escaping from its rear."

Earthlings saw rockets and jets as fire- breathing dragons

The epic of Gilgamesh details an "ancient account of launching a rocket. First the tremendous thud as the rocket engines ignited ('the heavens shrieked'), accompanied by the shaking of the ground ('the earth boomed'). Clouds of smoke and dust enveloped [the Sinai Spaceport] the launching site ('daylight failed, darkness came'). Then the brilliance of the ignited engines showed through ('lightning flashed'); as the rocket began to climb skyward, 'a flame shot up.' The cloud of dust and debris 'swelled' in all directions; then as it began to fall down, 'it rained death!' Now the rocket was high in the sky, streaking heavenward ('the glow vanished; the fire went out'). The rocket was gone from sight; and the debris 'that had fallen had turned to ashes'" [ZS, *12th Planet*: 128 -172]

Datum 14 NIBIRANS MOVED HEAVIER STONES

Our science still can't cut, move and fit huge rocks as well as the Nibirans. They cut stones as large as 10 tons with huge cutting tools run on power pulled from the earth and capacitated and amplified by crystals that broadcast energy within pyramids such as the Great Pyramid at Giza and Enki's Pyramids in South Africa. They used white powder of monoatomic gold to lighten iron-laden, magnetically charged stones for transport to construction sites.

The chief Nibiran Architect, Ningishzidda, planned and Earthlings built the gigantic astro-navigation landmark pyramid and Sphinx at Giza. Nibirans made spaceports at Sippar, then on the Sinai Peninsula and the Nazca Plateau in Peru. Ningishzidda directed Lagash's King Gudea who built a temple for Ninurta. Nibirans used their know-how and Earthling labor to build rocket silos and airplane hangers in the cities and temple-complexes of Sumer.

Babylon

Lagash

Enlil designed a huge temple for Solomon in Jerusalem, following the same design for the landing platform there that he'd used for the landing planform at Baalbek, Lebanon.

In Mexico, Ningishzidda, Sumerian overseers, Olmec foremen and Indian laborers built Teotihuacan. In Yucatan, they built (at Dzibilchaltun, Palenque, Tikal, Uxmal, Izamal, Mayapan, Chichen Iza, Copan, Tolan and Izapa) huge stepped-stone temples like Sumer's.

ChichenIza

In South America, Ningishzidda and his Uncle Adad directed the construction of Mochica, Chan-Chan, Cuzco, Macho Picchu, Chavin, Ollantaytambu and "the Baalbek of the New World"–a metallurgical, temple, and observatory complex at Tiahuanaco, Peru. On Mars, Nibirans manned a spaceport and lasered a monument to one of their kings.

Tiahuanaco

Baalbek: Nibirans built a launch tower at Baalbek, Lebanon for the goldmining expedition, "on a vast horizontal platform, artificially created 4,000 feet above sea level, surrounded by a wall. The enclosed squarish area, 2,500 feet long, over five million square feet, built before the Flood" [13,000 years ago] was "held together without mortar, rising stage after stage, to incredible heights, placed on a vast stone platform. The massive stones formed an enclosure that surrounded a cavity, a hollow within which stood the rocket about to be launched. The encompassing walls were multileveled, rising in stages to enable servicing the rocketship, its payload, [&] a command module. Arriving rocketships landed on the vast stone platform adjoining the launch tower, then would be put in place–as had been done to the colossal stone blocks–within the massive stone enclosure ready for launching."

Baalbek, Lebanon

"Baalbek was incorporated into the post-Deluvian Landing Corridor of the Anunnaki when they planned the planning of a spaceport in the Sinai to replace the one in Mesopotamia wiped out by the Deluge. They ran a line from the peaks of Ararat through Baalbek and extended it to Giza, where they built the pyramids. They placed the Great Pyramid and the anchor in Sinai that in the end delineated the Landing Corridor equidistant from Baalbek."

Baalbek included "stone blocks of incredible size, precisely cut and placed, including three colossal stone blocks that are the largest in the world, the Trilthon. The stone blocks that make up the Trilithon weigh more than 1,100 tons each and are placed upon older immense stone blocks, over sixty feet long with sides of fourteen to twelve feet, cut to have a slanting face that weigh 500 tons each. There is even now no man-made machine, no crane, vehicle or mechanism that can lift such a weight of 1,000 to 1,200 tons–to say nothing of carrying such an immense object over valley and mountainside and placing each slab in its precise position, many feet above the ground. There are no traces of any roadway, causeway, ramp or other earthworks that could suggest hauling these megaliths from their quarry, several miles away."

Stone quarried for Anunnaki Landing Platform, Baalbak

"The stone blocks that comprise the platform are "so tightly put together that no has been able to penetrate it and study the chambers, tunnels, caverns and substructures hidden beneath," though Arabs did penetrate a "460-feet long tunnel at the southeast corner of the platform." They proceeded through "a long vaulted passage like a railway tunnel under the great in total darkness broken by green lights from puzzling 'laced windows."

Nibirans "not only lifted and placed such colossal stone blocks but also carried them from a quarry several miles away. The quarry has been located and in it one of those colossal stone blocks had not been completed, still lies partly attached to the native rock; its size exceeds the Trilithon blocks. [ZS, *Stairway*: 168 - 176; *Expeditions*: 166 -179]

Datum 15 SINAI RESIDUES SHOW NUKES HIT

Nuking, which soil analysis documents, changed the soil of Sinai in 2024 B.C., the year Enki said Nergal and Ninurta bombed there. Sitchin [http://www.sitchin.com/evilwind.htm] wrote that in 1999, scientists determined that abrupt climate change depopulated Sumer [*Geology*, April 2000; *Science*, April 27, 2001]. DeMenocal, cited a correlated abrupt change in the area's vegetation with appearance of rocks called *tephera*--"burnt-through pieces of blackened gravel-like rock" usually associated with volcanos. Tephera still cover Sinai--which lacks volcanos. Sinai's tephera resulted when Ninurta's bombed of the Spaceport. The bombs left a huge black scar on the Sinai plain (where the shuttlecraft runway and launch platform had been) so large you can see it only from satellite. You can find millions of black-blasted rocks, north northeast of the scar in an area where all other color rocks. [See photos, *ZS, Wars*: 332-334]

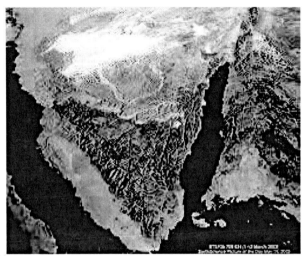

Datum 16 ETS TAUGHT SUMERIANS 2150 YEAR PRECESSION OF EQUINOXES

The detailed, multigenerational observation Sumerians needed to predict the sun's apparent shift backward along the line of Earth's orbit requires 2150 years for each degree of shift. [Lloyd: 2-36]

"The sun's apparent movement from north to south and back, due to the tilt of 23.5 degrees--causing the seasons--results from the fact that Earth's axis tilts relative to the plane of its orbit around the sun and is associated with the equinoxes, when the sun passed over the Earth's equator (once coming and once coming back) times when daytime and nighttime are equal.

"Because of the wobble, the Earth's orbit around the Sun is retarded each year; the retardation amounts to 1 degree in seventy-two years. Observance of sunrise on the spring equinox in 2160 years is in the preceding [not the following] zodiacal house. In zodiacal time, matching the clockwise direction of Nibiru [all the other planets orbit counterclockwise; this means that] on Earth, in zodiacal time, the Past is the Future."

Enki devised the division of the ecliptic (the plane of planetary orbits around the sun) into twelve to conform to the twelve member composition he invented. "That gave 30° per house. So "retardation of all twelve houses "added up to 2,160 years. The complete Processional Cycle or "Great Year" added up to 25,920 years. Relating 2160 to the then 3,600 cycle of Nibiru's return to the inner Solar System, Enki gave us the sexagesimal system of mathematics which multiplied 6 by 10 by 6 by10." [Sitchin, *Time*:20 - 26]

The Precessional movement is so slow ordinary people could not possibly notice this movement in single lifetimes. Sumerians said Nibirans gave them the 2150 year formula so they could determine which of the twelve zodiacal houses–indications of which Nibiran ruled was ascendant.

Contention as to where on the ecliptic the Spring Equinox occurred was critical in the conflict between Ninurta and Marduk in 2156 B.C..

The advanced astronomical observation and its precise recording over hundreds of Earthling lifetimes needed to predict the precession of the equinoxes is totally beyond the capacity of Earthlings without the help of Nibirans' advanced instruction. [Lloyd: 2-36]

Datum 17 ANCIENT POWER-CUT CRYSTAL SKULLS, COMPUTER, BATTERY

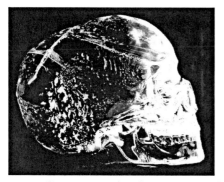

CRYSTAL SKULLS from South America remain in the British Museum; staff there said the skulls were "made with a powered cutter." Powered cutters are shown in carvings from Olmec sites in Mexico the Sumerian metallurgy complex in Peru.

"A COMPUTER dated one hundred years before Jesus discovered in 1900 of the island of Antikythera near Crete contained a system of differential gears not known to have been used until the sixteenth century."

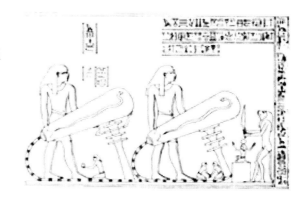

BATTERY: "A small vessel containing a copper cylinder with an iron rod inside, discovered in an Iraqi village and dated 220 B.C." is a battery. "Alkaline juice added to it produced a half volt of electricity. [Marrs: *Rule by Secrecy*: 361 - 362; ZS, *Lost Realms:* 105 -107]

In the *Enuma Elish*, Marduk, pursued by Inanna and Ninurta, ran past luminous crystals in the Giza Pyramid. The signal from these crystals were spun upward toward the pyramid's top, creating a toroid signal able to speed faster than light to Nibiru. [Sereda, D., 2012]

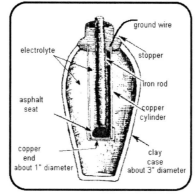

ANUNNAKI DATA BEST EXPLAINS OUR HISTORY

Compare and contrast the variants of Gardiner, de Lafeyette, Tellinger, Sitchin, Icke, Cremo, Thompson, Pravupad and others for the elements they have in common. Use the principle of parsimony--which explanations best account for all the data--and leave the least ooparts (data and artifacts that the explanations out their comprehension.

All our theories are hypothetical formulations, words and mathematical models we employ to account for our observations. Our observations are in turn directed by our theories. In science we test the null hypothesis--what data would disprove our theories.

Re: replilians: Sperry long ago showed that we *Homo Sapiens* are part reptile (Anunnaki?) in our brainstems. Brainstem impulses impel us to automatically, without conscious consideration, seek homeostasis and survival, this overlaid with our mammalian brains (limbic systems), in turn overlaid by our intellects (cortex) and, lately, overlaid in some, by a growth in our pineal areas--meditative brains [Ma, 2011].

Is Jimmy Carter a reptile or did he act like one to rise in the elite illuminati hierachy, then become a real human being (conscious enlightened person) in later years? I like the idea of reptilian as metaphor. David Icke, a personal friend, actually sees people's reptilian forms, I don't. Yet I, as a professional psychotherapist encounter many who see the world very differently than I. I accept each client's symbol system as valid for him or her.

Consensus determines social reality but does it predict the chemical composition of asteroids or the shape of the landmass beneath the Antarctic icepack the way ancient Sumerian tablets do? We're left with alternate explanations of much. Enjoy them, wonder, and keep asking what to cut away with Occam's razor. We grasp the elephant of reality from varying perspectives. See them all and get a clearer picture of the beast and the blind who generalize from their particular vantages to the nature of the whole and its context.

An explanation or theory that most parsimoniously (simplest, with least words, numbers, adumbrations) accounts for the all the data and makes more accurate predictions of future behavior as well as past accumulated data is more useful for our understanding than one that uses more words and symbols and must exclude exceptions to work. Thus, Copenicus's heliocentric explanation of the apparent movement of planets takes less math than Ptolomy's epicycle system, though the latter also can predict apparent planetary movement.

Freer writes: "I am convinced of the correctness of Sitchin's thesis and of Sir Laurence Gardiner's by utter coherence; they are the only explanations which contain no inexplicable elements, no contradictions and in which all the facts dance together in total consort. Our species' internecine violence, a product of Babel-factoring for crowd control that has carried through to great wars and the religious mayhem of crusades, jihads, inquisitions and persecutions and not intrinsically of human nature.

The Roman Church, a continuation of the fear of the god Enlil [Yahweh] type of subservient religion came into ascendance by an alliance with the gradual assimulation of the Roman empire and adopting its practices. Suppression of our true history through promulagation of the Hebrew Old Testament forgeries done to make Enlil their single monotheistic diety affected a racial amnesia and the ancient Sumerian culture was forgotten and only rediscovered in the late 1800s. Military and political controllers have suppressed the knowledge and data about alien presence on this planet by denial and ridicule." [Colaw, 2004]

All explanations and theories are but symbolic hypothetical variable sets that our limited mental capacities apply to phenomena. They are not the phenomena, any more than a map is the territory or a menu is the meal (menus taste lousy compared to food.

Theories are always influenced by the mental set of those who promulgate them. Theorists first, have guesses of what they expect to find--hypotheses--which they subject, hopefully, to the test of what data would disprove their guesses (null hypotheses). If their prejudices lead them to not even think of what to guess, they may never find it. Thus 18th century Christians thought Earth only 8000 years old and even Sitichinites did not look for the fossil humans Cremo cites in Earth's strata millions of years before Anunnaki settlement 450,000 years ago.

Writers of the Bible painted Jezebel as a whore, when a modern scholar points out that her "whoring" was no more than religious tolerance, which her intolerant and woman-hating enemies like the Anunnaki Yahweh wished to discredit [Hazelton,, 2007]

The establishment, fundamentalist Jews, Muslims and Christian fear the more efficient explanations Sitchin and the Vedas cited by Cremo and Thompson, for they would undermine research monies, social control and sinecures they treasure.

Part III: PERUSE THE APPENDIXES
TRACK THE TIMELINE

4.5 billion years ago
Our Sun created the planet Tiamat, the proto-Earth. Tiamat orbited the Sun counterclockwise.

200 million years ago
Nibiru's moon, Evil Wind, and Nibiru hit Tiamat and left no crust at all in the Pacific Gap, only a gaping hole.

654,000 years ago
Nibiru unified; North/South truce and treaty installed An as Nibiru's King.

500,000 years ago
Nibiru's protective shield weakened. The atmosphere thinned. Nibirans considered mining gold on Earth to powder Nibiru's air, save their atmosphere and keep heat they needed.

450,000 years ago
Nibiru's deposed King Alalu nuked to Earth, said *"Gold's here"* and threatene Nibiru. Nibiran Chief Scientist Enki rocketed to Earth to deal with Alalu.

400,000 years ago
Enlil, Commander of the Earth Expedition, built seven centers in Sumer: Sippar the Spaceport; Nippur, Mission Control; Badtibira, Metallurgical Center; Shurrupak, Med Center.

380,000 years ago
Anzu, Alalu's grandson, and the Igigi Astronaut Corps rebelled, seized Lebanon Landing Platform, immobilized Sumer. Ninurta, Enlil's and Ninmah's son, defeated and executed Anzu.

300,000 years ago
Enki, son Ningishzidda and lover/sister Ninmah created us, the slave species.
Nibiru's perigee killed Marsbase.

70,000 years ago
South African slaves, the Bantu (devotees of Antu, wife of Nibiru's King Anu) fled to India, after the super volcano at Lake Toba in Sumatra erupted. "Prevailing winds carried dust and poisonous gasses westwards towards eastern and southern Africa, caused a mini ice-age. Southern Africa, where the first civilization lived" got ost dust and gas. [Tellinger, *Temples*: 122 - 124]

49, 000 years ago
Enlil, enraged that Enki and Ninmah let Earthlings rule Shuruppak, vowed Earthlings' genocide.

31,000 - 11,000 years ago
10,800 years ago, Nibiru reached its furthest point (apogee] from Earth and debris at perigee, the opposite LaGrange point in its orbit, created a sudden warming of Earth's northern oceans and began the catastrophic melting of Earth's ice sheets. [Lloyd, *Dark Star*: 248] Earthlings' living standard worsened and we regressed to living in caves and in the bush. Each generation's life became poorer.

15,000 B.C.
Aztec legend cited in the *Codex Boturini* relates a Nibiran god "whose symbol was a seeing eye on an elliptical rod" guided four clans in boats from the land of stepped pyramids (Sumer?) to Guatemala. "The four clans trekked inland, split into several tribes. One, the *Mexica,* reached Tenochtilan." Tenochtitlan means "'The City of Enoch'-- the son of Cain." [ZS: *Time*: 261]

11,000 B.C.
Nibiru perigee tore Nibiru's gold shield, slid Antarctica's Icecap into the sea and caused the Deluge.

Galzu (sent by the Creator-of-All) gave Enki a program for a submarine. Enki's downloaded the program in his hybid son Ziasudra's computer bank. Enki sent his genetically pure Nibiran son Ninagal to Ziasudra. Ninigal piloted the ship to Mt. Ararat (Turkey).

Nibiran Goldmining Expedition leaders got Enlil to rule through Ziasudra and Shem, Japhet and Ham–Ziasudra's sons–and their descendants.

Enki and Ninmah recovered genetic starts from diorite vault in Ed-In.

11,000 - 10,900 B.C.
Anunnaki renewed Earth's crops and beasts and created the Age of Domestication (Neolithic). Ninurta built dams and drained floodwaters into rivers for Sumer. Enki reclaimed the Nile Basin. Ningishzidda built new Sinai Spaceport with controls on Mt. Moriah, the Jerusalem to-be.

10,900 B.C.
Uranus drifted away from the Sun and sped Nibiru toward Earth sooner than 3,600 years. As Nibiru flew by, Uranus caught Miranda, a moon of Nibiru. Miranda, now a moon of Uranus, circled it instead of Nibiru.

9380 B.C.
Marduk, Enki's first son, divided Egypt between his sons, Seth and Osiris. Seth killed Osiris, ruled the Nile.

8970 B.C.
Pyramid War I, Osiris' son Horus beat Seth, who fled, seized Sinai and Canaan

8670 B.C.
Pyramid War II, Enlil's son's daughter Inanna and Enlilites defeated Enkiites. Ninurta broke and took Enkiite weapons, energy generation machines and communication devices in Giza Pyramid. Ninmah convened peace conference. Enlil and Enki replaced Marduk with Ningishzidda/Thoth as Nile Ruler.

8500 B.C.
Nibirans reserved Jerico for themselves and their hybrid offspring.

7500 B.C.
Anunnaki taught Earthlings pottery technology.

7400 B.C.
Ninurta built Kishi with fifty ME programs (for math, smithing, pottery, beer, wagons, wheels and law) Enki gave him.

3840 B.C.
Anu visited Earth, took Inanna as lover, saw Titicaca facilities and pardoned Marduk.

Ziasudra's sons ruled for the Nibirans--Shem' s descendants settled the ex-spaceport area of Iraq and the Landing Place at Lebanon. Japhet's issue ruled lands in Asia Minor, the Black and Caspian Sea areas, also nearby coasts and islands. Enki and his descendants ruled Egypt and Africa though successors of Ziusudra's son Ham the Dark. Ham's line ruled Canaan, Cush, Mizra'im, Cush, Nubia, Ethiopia, Egypt, and Libya from the highlands. Ham's descendants spread to the reclaimed lowlands.

Ninmah reigned for Nibirans and their descendants in Sinai.

4500 B.C.
Earthlings regressed, abandoned villages and stopped making pottery.

3760 B. C.
Inanna chose the first King, the Lugal, to direct, for the gods, Sumer's Earthlings, to create "a civilization in which our own is firmly rooted." The gods "picked Earthlings out of their decline and raised them to a higher level of culture, knowledge and civilization.' [ZS. *12th Planet*: 10 -11]

Enlil's Sons and grandsons gave Sumer assemblies, courts, schools, writing, printing, prospecting, mining, road- and ship building in a petrol-feuded money economy.

3460 B.C.
Marduk added Babylon on the Euphrates River to Enkiite fief at Eridu.

3350 B.C.
Nibiru, as it reached perigee at the edge of the Kuiper Comet Belt, caused solar flares and severe heating on Earth.

3500 B.C.
Anunnaki had Earthlings use surface deposits of oil in Sumer to fuel kilns, build roads, paint and fracture chemicals.

3450 B.C.
Enlil and Anu let Marduk marry Earthling Sarpanit to stop him from ever ruling Nibiru.

Inanna and Dumuzi flirted at Marduk's wedding. Marduk coordinated the rite so his astronaut (Igigi) allies who attended revolted. They abducted 200 Adapite Earthling women, conquered the on-planet Baalbek Landing Platform, forced Commander Enlil to recognize the women they kidnaped as legal wives. The Igigi forced Enlil to give them estates on Earth. They prepared to man the interplanetary launch platform Marduk said he'd build in Babylon. But Enlilites bombed Babylon, jumbled speech.

Marduk--aka Ra--deposed Ningishzidda--aka Thoth--as Egypt's ruler.
The present era identified in Hindu tradition and just ending, the *Kaliyuga,* began. Marduk got Dumuzi killed so Dumuzi wouldn't marry Dumuzi and rule Africa with Inanna. Innana went to Dumuzi's brother Nergal so he'd impregnate her for Dumuzi. Nergal's wife Ereshkigal killed Inanna. Enki's robots--the precursors of the Greys, revived Inanna.

3100 – 3113 B.C.
Ningishzidda/Toth/Quezelcoatl and his Olmec and Sumerian assistants built Stonehenge inEngland. They helped Adad/Viracocha design observatories and smelting facilities at Tiahuanaco, Peru. "The actual domain of Quezelcoatl/Thoth was Mesoamerica and Central America, the lands of the Nauhuatl-speaking and Mayan tribes, but his influence extended southward into the northern parts of the South American continent. Cajamarca in the north of Peru was where ancient roots in the gold land of the Andes, from the Pacific coast and from the Atlantic coast met and the latter followed the rivers." [ZS, Time:296]

2900 B.C.
Enlil's dynasty ruled Sumer from 2900 B.C. to 2024 B.C.. One of the kings through whom the Nibirans ruled, Gilgamesh of Uruk--a 3/4 Nibiran, 1/4 Royal Earthling (son of Ninurta's daughter Ninsun and Lugal Banda)--destroyed Enlil's robo-guard but unsuccessfully sought immortality and life-extending herbs the Lebanon Landing Place.

Inanna ruled The Indus Valley & Uruk, Igigi astronauts followed her to Indus Valley.

2600 B.C. Gilgamesh died; his successors buried him with his friends and attendants (killed for the occasion) in the Royal Cemetery at Lagash.

2500 B.C.
Nibirans shipped and flew Black Olmec managers across the Atlantic to Mexico [ZS, *Time:* 300]

2371 B.C.
Inanna and Sargon launched the Akkadian Empire from Agade.

2316 B.C.
Sargon invaded Marduk's empty stronghold, Babylon.

2291 B.C.
Inanna, Naram-Sin (Sargon's grandson) and the Akkadian armies captured the Lebanon Landing Platform and won Jerico, the private city of the Igigi astronauts' and their Earthling wives.

In Sumer, only Ninurta's city, Lagash, held out against Inanna and Naram-Sin. Inanna invaded Egypt.

2255 B.C.
Inanna recaptured Uruk, destroyed Anu's temple there and sent Naram-Sin to attack Enlil's minions at Nippur. She declared herself supreme to Anu, King of Nibiru and father of Enlil, her father's father.

2250 B.C.
Ninurta's Gutians beat Inanna and occupied Sumer. She fled to Nergal in Lower Africa.

2220 B.C.
Gutians left Sumer, returned to the Zagros Mountains where Ninurta gave them horse cavalry, which extended their reach thousands of miles.

Ninghzidda and Lagash's King Gudea built temple, hangar and Zodiac Time Observatory for Ninurta, who reasserted Enlilite power over Sumer.

2180 B.C.
Egypt split into Marduk's south, his rivals' north.

2113 B.C.
Nannar ruled Sumer from Ur, his commerce, manufacturing and cult center. He choose Ninsun's son Ur-Nammu King. Enlil sent High Priest Terah from Nippur to represent him at Nannar's court in Ur.

2096 B.C.
Ur-Nammu died in a chariot accident and the boat with his remains sunk; Earthlings rated Enlilites weak.

2095 B.C.
Shulgi succeeded Ur Nammu and wed Inanna. Shulgi and Elamites conquered Canaan but failed to drive Nabu from Sinai.

2080 B.C.
Marduk's Thebans under Mentuhotep I advanced on Northern Egypt.

2049 B.C.
Shulgi, unable to protect Mission Control at Sinai or the Landing Place in Lebanon from Marduk and Nabu, built a wall to defend Sumer's western border. Enlil, annoyed at Shulgi for orgying with Inanna in Anu's temple, ordered him killed for failure to protect the Enlilite realms.

2048 B.C.
Enlil replaced Shulgi with Amar-Sin and sent him to crush a revolt in the north and then fight an alliance of five kings along the Mediterranean in the west. Enlil also sent his general, Abraham (son of Ur's High Priest Terah), now trained in Hatti in Hittite military tactics, with cavalry to Canaan. After Abraham left Harran for Sinai, Maruk allied with Adad, ousted Nannar, moved in and cut Sumer's trade with the Hittites.

2047 B.C.
Marduk's son Nabu brought cities west of the Euphrates and Canaan against the Enlilites. Marduk's Egyptians in the south attacked his enemies in Northern Egypt. Elam's King Kudur- Laghamar threatened the Enlil's Sinai Spaceport.

2041 B.C.
Abraham with Enlil's men and camels and Northern Egyptians blocked both Nabu's forces and Ninurta's Elamites from the Spaceport.

2040 B.C.
Mentuhotep II, Marduk's Theban Pharaoh, took Egypt all the way to the western approaches to Sinai. Amar-Sin sailed to Sinai to block Marduk's Egyptians, defected to Enki and became his priest in Eridu, Enki's cult center in Sumer. Amar-Sin died suspiciously of a poisonous bite. Enlil madeShu-Sin Overseer of Sumer and built a shrine for Inanna's son Shara
at Nippur.

2039 B.C.
Ibbi-Sin succeeded Shu-Sin. Marduk returned to Babylon as Enlil left Sumer.

2025 B.C.
Marduk menaced the Spaceport. Abraham and Lot told Ninurta and Nergal the cities of south area of the Dead Sea defected to Nabu.

Enlil sent Abraham to the Negev Desert, then to Canaan. To brand Abraham's men as loyal Enlilites, Enlil made them circumcise each other.

Abraham's principal wife, Sarah, bore Isaac in Canaan. Enlil ordered Abraham to leave his secondary wife, Hagar, and Heir-Apparent Is-mael in the desert so Isaac, Abraham's son with Sarah, would rule Enlil's troops in Canaan.

2024 B.C.
Enlil said he knew where Enki hid Alalu's nukes. With Anu's okay, Ninurta bombed
Sinai; Nergal nuked Sodom, Gomorra, and killed the Dead Sea. But fallout engulfed Sumer, killing all
south of Babylon except people from Eridu whom Enki saved.

2023 B.C.
Sumerians fled throughout the Mediterranean and along the Volga to Geogia, Sumara and Finland.
They settled along the Danube to Dacia and Hungary. They migrated also to India and the Far East.
Marduk, now supreme, made Babylon Sumer's capital.

2016 B.C.
For forty days, with a crystal-tipped electrum stylus, Endubscar, Master Scribe of Eridu, Sumer,
wrote on a lapis lazuli tablet what Enki dictated.

2000 B.C.
Marduk said, "*I'm the gods' God.*" He renamed Nibiru "Marduk," and held New Year rituals that
enacted how he invaded the inner solar system and made Earth, then Earthlings.

Isaac sent his son Jacob/Israel to Harran to marry Isaac's Uncle Leban's girls. En-route, Jacob
watched Enlil and crew come and go from a skyship. Jacob worked twenty years for Leban. Then
Enlil ordered him *To Canaan return.* Jacob paused at the Jordan River, wrestled and pinned a
Nibiran ("angel" in Bible).

1800 B.C.
Sumerians took cuneiform writing, bronze weapons, chariots and walled cities to China's
Shang Dynasty.

1840 B.C.
Pharaoh Amenemhet III of Middle Kingdom's XII dynasty took Egypt's throne in 1842. He hired
Jacob's son Joseph to interpret dreams, then to oversee Egypt through drought to come. Joseph stored
water and invited descendants of Jacob/Israel to Egypt.

1833 B.C.
Jacob/Israel and his tribe joined Joseph in Egypt. For 300 years, they prospered and multiplied
till they numbered some 600,000.

1650 B.C.
Marduk's New Kingdom pharaohs took Egypt. Thothmose I invaded Enlilite Sumer to the
Euphrates River, where Abraham's kin lived. Thothmose knew Enlilites would strike back and
feared Jacob descendants in Egypt would join the Enlilites and strike from within, so he broke the
Middle Kingdom promise that Egypt honor "Children" of Israel.

1600 B.C.
The cluster trail of comets and rocks at the 180 degree position on Nibiru's orbit crossed the orbit of
Mars and Jupiter. This orbiting debris bombarded Earth.

1482 B.C.
Thothmose III attacked Enlilites abroad and brutilized Israelites within Egypt. Moses, now grown, killed an Egyptian overseer. Though Pharoh ordered Moses killed, he escaped to Sinai and there married a Midianite priest's daughter.

1450 B.C.
Amenhotep II, the new Pharaoh, let Moses' death sentence expire. Enlil told Moses, *"Go to Egypt, show the Pharoh magic. Tell him to let my people go."* But Amenhotep instead demanded the Israelites make three times more bricks. Enlil gave Egypt plagues, infestations, cattle diseases, darkness, weather disturbances. He killed all non-Israelite firstborn children and cows in Egypt. Finally, in 1433, Pharaoh told the Israelites, *"Go,"* then sent chariots to re-capture them. Enlil, with climate control devises, swept a path through the Red Sea, then let the sea drown the charioteers.

1433 - 1383 B.C.

For forty years,, Enlil led Moses and the Israelites through the desert to the edge of Sinai and Nights, he led with a "fiery beacon," days, he led with a dark cloud. He fed the Israelites and protected them from Amalekites. Enlil demanded they kill 3000 of their number who worshiped other Nibirans and kill 23,000 for sex before they married.[*Exodus* 32:26-28; *Corinthians* 10:8; ZS, *Divine:*295].

1383 B.C.
Enlil had Moses climb Mt. Sinai then relay demands to the Israelites. Moses told the Israelites what Enlil wanted. Enlil landed his aircraft on the mount and, with an amplifier, told the people himself what he wanted. They knew they had to say they'd obey or he'd kill them.

Enlil again flew to the mountaintop, ordered Moses up, and gave Moses stone tablets with commandments and showed him how to build a temple and a housing for the tablets (an "Ark of the Covenant") and a Talk-To-Enlil Comm unit. Moses' brother Aaron and his priest-lineage could message Enlil, pose questions, and get "Yes" or "No" answers. The ark and its stones weighed many tons. Enlil had Moses hide a monoatomic white powder of gold to lighten the ark. [Tellinger: *Africemples*: 86]. When Moses returned to the Israelites, he glowed with radiation from Enlil's shuttlecraft. His tablets told the Israelites to reject all other Nibiran gods, spend every seventh day worshiping him, subjugate women and kids, refrain from murder, adultery, theft and false witness. They must not crave others' homes, wives, slaves and property.

1394 B.C.
A comet hit Earth, disintegrated, made day last 20 hours as Joshua and the Israelites attacked the Canaanites near Beth-Horon and delayed sunrise 20 hours at Teotihuacan in the Andes.

1393 B.C.
Israelites, in *Genesis,* falsified how Enki, Ninmah and Thoth. The Bible writers used *Genesis* to justify a national religion that glorified Enlil as Yahweh, the one and only god.

1200 B.C.
Enlilite's King Tiglat-Pileser I of Assyria beat Lebanon and caught Marduk. Migrants and invaders flooded western Asia, Asia Minor, the Mediterranean coast and Arabia. Peoples of the Sea, repulsed in Egypt, invaded Canaan. Enlil choose Saul then David to rule in Israel.

Agamemnon, Menelaus and Odysseus led Greeks against Hittite allies of Adad and Inanna at Troy. Diamedes, a part-Nibiran Greek Earthling, hurt Inanna but she recovered. Her son, Aeneas, fought on the Trojan side, fled to Carthage, then, Virgil asserted, to Italy.

9th Century B.C.
Adad and Nergal again sent an Assyrian king--Shalmaneser III--with technologically-advanced artillery against Marduk's Babylonians. Shalmaneser won.

1000 B.C.
Ninghzidda and his followers ran high-civilization Yucatan temple centers.

1003 B.C.
Israelite leader David took Jerusalem and made it his Capitol.

931 B.C.
David's successor, Solomon, died; Abraham's descendants split their turf into the kingdoms of Judea in the south, Israel on the north. Until 910 B.C., Jeroboam, Rehoboam, Abijah, Nadab, Baasah, Elah, Zimri, then Omri ruled Israel.

872 B.C.
Ithbaal, King of Tyre gave his daughter Jezebel to Ahab, the successor to Omri as King of Israel to create Phoenician-Israeli alliance. Jehu (Enlil's agent) purged Ahab's dynasty and the alliance with Phoenicia and made Israel subject to Syria, which dispersed Israel's intelligencia throughout the Assyrian empire.

722 B.C.
Assyrian king Shalmaneser V captured Samaria in Israel. Sargon II, Shalmanser's successor, exiled Israelites from northern Israel.

689 B.C.
Sargon's son, Sennacherib, shelled then sacked Babylon on the pretext that Babylonians disappointed Marduk. Sennacherib sentenced the Babylonians to seventy years Assyrians would occupy their city. He took Phoenicia, Gaza and Judea. Then--without Adad's okay--attacked Jerusalem. Enlil, who controlled Mission Control Jerusalem, hit his erstwhile Assyrian allies with a techno-weapon that killed 185,000 of them. Sennacherib fled back to Nineva in Sumer and named his younger son Esarhaddon, his successor.

612 B.C.
Babylon's King Nabupolassar took Nineva, the Assyrian capitol; the Assyrians retreated to Harran. Sennacherib's older sons killed him, but the Nibirans hid Esarhaddon. Enlil sent Inanna to Assyria where she disarmed the Ninevan army, burned their weapons and made Esarhaddon King. She and her king attacked Marduk's Egyptian forces and she blinded them with a techno-weapon.

614-612 B.C.
Enlil let Babylonians conquer Assyria and sent Babylon's king Nebuchadnezzar II to take Lebanon.

610 B.C.- 650 B.C.
Most Anunnaki left Earth from Nazca.

600 B.C.
Ningishzidda left Central America. Native Mayas, for the next 100 years, revolted, drove Olmecs and their Sumerian bosses farther south and slew them.

587 B.C.
Marduk's Babylonian king Nebuchadnezzar overran Enlilite forces in Jerusalem. Nebuchadnezzer installed a puppet king, ordered worship of Marduk, and took leading citizens of the city as hostages back to Babylon.

586 B.C.
Nebuchadnezzar deposed the king he left in Jerusalem and burned the temple to Enlil that King Solomon had built there.

539 B.C.
Cyrus of Persia, whom Marduk welcomed, conquered Babylon and returned Nebuchadnezzar's hostages to Jerusalem. Cyrus' successor, Cambyses, brought Sumer, Mari, Mittani, Hatti, Elam, Assyria, Egypt and, of course Babylon, into the Persian Empire.

522 B.C.
Darius murdered Cambyses and ruled the extended Persian Empire.

490 B.C.
Darius unsuccessfully invaded Greece.

480 B.C.
Darius's successor, Xerxes, unsuccessfully attacked Greece again.

482 B.C.
Xerxes decided to destroy the tomb of Marduk, who'd recently died in Babylon. Marduk's son and prophet, Nabu disappeared.

400 B.C.
Mochica, coastal Peru, precursor to Chimu civilization, featured fifteen-foot wide roads, pottery, textiles, mud-brick pyramids and decoration showed Adad and other Sumerian gods–referred to as Giants--and art styles with gold from Andean highlands.

338 B.C.
Philip II of Macedonia united Greece. His son apparent, Alexander, thought Marduk had actually fathered him.

334 -323 B.C.
Alexander conquered the Persian Empire, the Indus and Egypt; Egyptian priests at Siwa confirmed Alexander as Marduk's son.

331 B.C.
Alexander reached Babylon and rushed to the ziggurat temple to grasp the hands of Marduk as conquerors before him had done. But Alexander saw Marduk's dead body preserved in oils in his ziggurat.

300 B.C.
Indian descendants of Ka-in killed remaining Olmecs and Sumerians in Central America.

2012 - 2112 A.D.

Nibiru, the sub-brown dwarf binary companion of our sun reaches its furthest point from the sun, and appears north of Sagittarius, in the constellation Delphinius, when the opposite (LaGrange) orbital point–Nibiru's perigee–loaded with a procession of rocks and comets, crosses the orbital planes of Mars and Jupiter and lines up with the center of the Milky Way Galaxy. Expect comets, rocks, magnetic pole reversal and increased earthquakes, volcanic eruptions, melting of all ice on Earth, intense global warming and rise in sea levels.

God's Gazette

ABGAL

Nibiran. Enki's planetary pilot, promoted to interplanetary pilot when Enki fired Anzu. Anzu captured Abgal but Ninurta rescued him. When Abgal took Enlil into exile in Africa for raping Sud, Abgal showed Enlil, unbeknownst to Enki, where Enki hid Alalu's missiles.

ADAD

Nibiran born on Earth. (aka Ishkur, Teshub, Baal, Rimac, Zabar Dibba, the Storm God and Viracocha), the youngest of Enlil's official sons with his wife, Ninti. Adad ruled and taught metallurgy to the Hittites and Cassites in the mountains of Anatolia. He ran the Lebanon Landing Place. In 3800 B.C., Enlil put him in charge of the gold and tin works at Tiahuanaco, where, as Viracocha, he "placed his symbol of the forked lightening for all to see from the air and the ocean, on a mountainside on the Bay of Paracas, Peru, the anchorage harbor for ships carrying tin and bronze of Tiahuanaco to the Old World."" [ZS, *Lost Realms:* 252]

ALALU

Nibiran, aka Chronos, Saturn. 450,000 years ago, Alalu killed Nibiru's King Lahma, took his crown, he said, to nuke the volcanos or mine for gold on Earth to shield Nibiru's atmosphere. Alalu displaced Anu, Lahma's heir as King. Anu served Alalu in exchange for legal succession of Kingship from Alalu to Anu's son Enki's son Marduk with Alalu's daughter, Damkina. Anu deposed Alalu; he out-wrestled him. So Anu, not Marduk, succeeded Alalu as King of Nibiru. Alalu stole a rocket with nuclear missiles (that later destroyed Sinai and Sumer). Anu rocketed to Earth and out-wrestled Alalu again but Alalu then bit off Anu's penis. Anu sentenced Alalu to die on Mars. Chief Medical Officer Ninmah, enroute to Earth, buried Alalu on Mars and memorialized him there in the statue at Cyndonia.

ANU

Nibiran, aka Cronos and Amen-Ra. Anu deposed Alalu as Nibiru's King and then ran Nibiru as a military dictatorship. Anu begat Enki, his eldest, Enlil, his legal heir and Ninmah and sent them and the goldmining expedition to Earth. Anu visited Earth 400,000 years ago to set up the Expedition, visited again 300,000 years ago to settle the Nibiran miners' strike Enki'd staged to justify hybrid Nibiran/*Erectus* mine slaves. When Anu visited again in 3,800 B.C., he took Inanna, his great granddaughter, as concubine. He divided Earth among his descendants and believed the Creator of All, through Galzu, got the Anunnaki to create and save the hybrid Earthlings.

ANZU

Nibiran. Alalu's grandson. Enki fired Anzu as interplanetary pilot, though he nuked Enki through the asteroids enroute to Earth. Anzu stayed with Alalu on Mars while Alalu died. Ninmah gave Alalu men on Mars to start a station there. Anzu stole Enlil's computer programs, disrupted his communications system and led the astronaut revolt against him. Enlil's son Ninurta captured and executed Anzu.

BAU

Also known as Gula, Bau was Nibiran, the huge youngest Daughter of Nibiru's King Anu. On Earth, Bau married Ninurta, Enlil's Enforcer and they begat Ninsun. Bau ran the medical center for Earthlings at Lagash and died with them when nuclear fallout from bombs Nergal and Ninurta dropped on Sinai poisoned Sumer.

DAMKINA

Daughter of Nibiru's King Alalu. Damkina wed Enki and bore Marduk, Nannar, Nergal, Gibil, Dumuzi. She was the surrogate mother for Adamu and Ti-Amat.

DUMUZI

Dumuzi (aka Tammuz, Adonis), a Nibiran born on Earth, youngest son of Enki and Damkina, trained on Nibiru to foster animal husbandry for the hybrid Nibiran/*Erectus* Earthlings. An Enkiite, Dumuzi betrothed Enlilite Inanna and hoped to bring peace to the Enkiite-Enlilite conflict. But Marduk told their sister Geshtinanna to seduce Dumuzi, then say he raped her. Marduk's men ran Dumuzi to his death; Inanna mummified him and hoped he'd revive on Nibiru.

ENKI

Also known as Ea, Nidimmud, Adonai, Apollo, Poseidon, Yam, Neptune, Aquarius, Ptah, Khnemu, Buzur, Nahash, Hephaestus, Vulcan and sometimes, Melchzdek; Enki graphed as entwined serpents. Born Anu's Firstborn Son but not legal heir–that was Enlil–on Nibiru, Enki betrothed sister Ninmah but Anu forbade their marriage when Enlil impregnated her.

Enki instead married King Alalu's daughter, Damkina. They parented Marduk, Alalu's heir. When Alalu for failed to secure gold to sprinkle over and save Nibiru's atmosphere, Anu deposed him and Alalu fled to the Persian Gulf on Earth, aimed his nukes at Nibiru, and demanded his throne back. So, 450,000 years ago, Anu sent Enki to on Earth to pacify father-in-law Alalu. Enki and his pilot Abgal hid the nuclear missiles Alalu had brought to Earth.

Anu made Enki, under Enlil's overall command, master of Basara as well as Chief of Africa, Goldmining Operations and the Seas. Ninmah joined Enki and they had many daughters, whom Enki kept impregnating. Enki, his son Ningishzidda (whom Enki fathered with Erishkigal) and Ninmah, created our Nibiran/*Erectus* hybrid ancestors as the solution to a mutiny of Nibiran astronauts working in the South African mines. Enki fomented the mutiny just to get Enlil to support genetic creation of mine Earthlings to replace the Nibiran astronauts.

Each generation, Enki mated with the prettiest females born to the hybrids; he multiplied the ratio of Nibiran to *Erectus* genes in our stock. He gave his part-Earthling son Ziasudra a computer program that showed Ziasudra how to build the submersible to save his community.

ENLIL

A Nibiran, aka Set, Yahweh, Jehovah, Ba'al, Zeus, Jupiter. Assyrians called Enlil "Ashur; " Jews called him "Yahweh. Legal heir to Anu, Enlil commanded the Earth Goldmining Expedition. He fathered Ninurta with his (and Enki's) sister Ninmah. Expedition Leaders forced Enlil to marry Sud, whom he'd raped and impregnated. Enlil and Sud (elevated as his wife to "Ninlil) begat Nannar and Adad.

Enlil ordered Earthlings drowned in the Deluge (here he's *Yahweh*), but let Enki's line of Earthlings who survived rule Earth for the Expedition. Enlil murdered thousands of both his rivals' Earthlings and his own Earthling followers.

ERESHKIGAL (Allat)

A Nibiran born on Earth, Ereshkigal. Inanna's younger sister born on Earth of Nannar and Ningal. Enki mpregnated Ereshkigal with Ningishzidda as he took to Point Aguelus, South Africa, to run the climatological station. Ereshkigal married Enki's son Nergal and ran the station with him. She killed Inanna to stop her baring a son Nergal'd begat for Dumuzi but Enki revived Inanna.

GALZU

Galzu represented himself as Plenipoteniary of King Anu. Galzu lied to keepEnki, Enlil, Ninmah and the children of these three on Earth when they would have left. Galzu subsequently intervened to give Enki the computer programs Enki slipped into Ziasudra's wall computer, with plans for the submersible Enki's son Ninigal guided to Mt. Ararrat in Turkey and regenerate the hybrids, to be governed through descendants of Ziasudra.

Anu uncovered Galzu's ruses to keep the anunnaki fostering nibiran-earthling hybrids. Enki told Anu the dream he had of Galzu. In the dream, Galzu described an submarine for Ziasudra, Ziasudra's clan and the villagers who would help build it. Enki related how, on waking, he found plans for the boat engraved on a stone tablet beside his bed. "By that was Anu greatly puzzled. *'I never sent a secret plenipotentiary to Earth'*" said the Nibiran King.

Enki and Enlil exclaimed, "*On account of Galzu Ziasudra and the seed of life were saved. On account of GALZU on Earth we remained. 'The day you to Nibiru you return, you shall die', so did Galzu to us say.'*

"Incredulous of that was Anu; *'the change in cycles* [between Earth and Nibiru*] indeed havoc did cause, but with elixirs cured it was.'*

" *'Whose emissary, if not yours was Galzu?'* Enki and Enlil in unison said. *'Who the Earthlings to save wanted, who on Earth made us stay?'*

"*'For the Creator of All did Galzu appear.'*" Ninharsag asserted that the creation of the Earthlings was also destined by the Creator of All.

"*While fates we decreed, the hand of destiny at every step directed,*" Anu said. "*The will of the Creator of All is: on Earth and for Earthlings, only emissaries are we. The Earth to the Earthlings belong, to preserve and advance them we were intended.*" [zs,Enki:271].

Galzu sent Enlil a dream Marduk would prevail in Mesopotamia and conveyed to the Nibirans that the hybrid Earthlings they created should be allowed to develop. In the dream Galzu told Enlil that the Creator wanted him to choose Abraham as general of his cavalry to stop advances and preaching in Canaan and the Mediterranean ports by Marduk's son Nabu that could lead to Enkiites from overrunning the Spaceport. Enlil kept his vision secret, but chose Abraham to rule "all the lands from the border of Egypt to the border of Mesopotamia." [ZS, *Wars*:289 -297]

GESHTINANNA
A Nibiran born on Earth. To stop Inanna and Dumuzi union, Geshtinianna seduced their brother Dumuzi, then claimed rape so Marduk's men chased Dumuzi to death.

HORUS
Aka Horon, Hor, and the Falcon God, Horus was the son of Marduk's son Osiris/Asar and Isis, who impregnated herself with the dead Osiris' semen. In 8970 B.C. Horus won Egypt when he defeated his uncle Seth, Osiris' murderer, in an air battle above the Sinai,

INANNA
(aka Irnini, Ishtar, Ashtoreth, Astarte, Annutitum, Aphrodite, Athena, Anat, Venus, Eshdar, Innin, Lillith, Ninni, Kali and Shakti), genetically Nibiran but born on Earth, Inanna's parents, Ningal and Nannar, begat her and her elder twin Utu. Offsprings like Inanna, born to Nibirans on Earth matured faster than those born on Nibiru. Inanna's growth seemed stunted; she grew to 66 inches height, whereas Nibirans born on the homeplanet usually over 84 inches [ZS, *Giants*: 221]. Inanna visited Nibiru at least once. She, like many Nibirans, often wore flight goggles or sunglasses to deal with greater sunshine on Earth than on Nibiru.

Enkiite and Enlilite elders hoped that if Enkiite Dumuzi wed Enlilite Inanna, the deadly rivalry between their lineages would stop. But Marduk, ruler of Egypt and Babylon, induced Geshtinanna, his sister and also Dumuzi's to love Dumuzi then yell rape. Marduk's security team drove Dumuzi to his death. She then wanted Dumuzi's older brother Nergal to impregnate her for Dumuzi. Nergal's mate, Inanna's younger sister Ereshkigal, killed her but Enki sent medical androids who revived her.

In 8670 B.C. Inanna helped defeat Marduk and the Enkiites in the Second Pyramid War. Inanna blasted them with "an explosive beam that tore the enemy apart." She demanded Enlil make her Egypt's ruler in Marduk's stead, since Marduk caused Dumuzi's death, but Enlil gave Ningishzidda Egypt.

She saw Dumuzi in Earthling men she bedded, but usually killed them after sex. In 3800 B.C. Anu and Queen Antu, rocketed to Earth. Antu taught Inanna to channel sexual energy to elevate their whole clan, ten gave Inanna to Anu. As Anu and Inanna coupled, Antu and the Nibiran royals shared their ecstasy, epiphany and satori. Ani gave Inanna the temple where they loved and his survey plane. She'd run Uruk's temple through a priest/king, son of her brother Utu with an Earthling.

She seduced Enki for programs to expand her Uruk temple complex into a city. She got him drunk, seduced him and he gave her the ME programs. She slipped them to her pilot to hide in Uruk. Enki sobered, locked her up at Eridu but couldn't reclaim the MEs. *"By right the MEs I have obtained, Enki himself placed them in my hand placed them!* So did Inanna to Commander Enlil say; the truth Enki meekly admitted."[ZS, Enki : 281].

In 3760 B. C., Inanna chose the first King of Sumer, the Lugal. The Lugal represented the gods to the Earthlings. Lugals shifted their center to Inanna at Uruk, then to Akad. In 3450 B.C., Inanna and the Enlilites bombed Marduk's Launch Tower at Babylon. The Enlilite Council named the Constellation Twins, after Inanna and Utu and replaced Ninmah with Inanna both as member and as The Maiden [Virgo].

Inanna appointed an Adapite Hybrid Earthling Shepherd-Chief (descended from Dumuzi) King of Aratta. The Igigi Aryans moved east, following Inanna to the Indus Valley. She shuttled in her plane between Aratta and Uruk. In Uruk, "A House for Nighttime Pleasure she established." Her second ruler in Uruk, Enmerkar (Utu's grandson and a Earthling) sent an emissary to the Arattan King. Enmerkar sent his son, Banda The Short, to Aratta. On the way back Banda fell sick, to his death was Banda abandoned" but Inanna's brother Utu revived him. When Banda returned to Uruk, Inanna saw him as Dumuzi. "'*A miracle!' My beloved Dumuzi to me came back!'* she shouted. In her abode Banda was bathed. "*Dumuzi, my beloved*! she called him. "To her bed, with flowers bedecked, she lured him." In the morning Banda still lived. "Inanna shouted: '*The power of dying in my hands was placed, immortality by me granted.'* Then to call herself a goddess Inanna decided, the Power of Immortality it implied."[ZS,, Enki: 287-292]

At Baalbek, Inanna invited Gilgamesh to couple with her; when he said, "No,"she had a mechanical guard-bull attack him, but he killed it and escaped her.

With her techno-weapons, armies and power (she said) to bestow immortality, Inanna ran kingship of Sumer for 1000 years. In 2371 B.C., she chose her Earthling half-brother, Akkadian gardener, Sargon (who'd raped her) to lead her armies. Sargon and Inanna built their capital, Agade, in Akkad (near Babylon). They subdued all Sumer except Lagash, her Uncle Ninurta's fief. She led Sargon's army through Luristan in the Zagros Mountains. With the army and her mass-killing weapons, she and Sargon united Sumer. They spread spoken and written-on-clay Akkadian all over Sumer and spawned the Semitic languages (including Hebrew and Arabic).[ZS, Heaven & Earth: 95; Wars: 10 - 11].

In 2316 B.C. in Marduk's absence, Sargon invaded Babylon. To show disdain for Marduk, Sargon "took away the soil" for Inanna to build a launch site of her own and take interplanetary power. Marduk and Nabu returned from Egypt to Babylon, fortified the city and diverted rivers to it from the other Sumerian cities. Inanna and Marduk both loosed lasers on each other's Earthling armies. Marduk's minions besieged Sargon. [ZS, Giants: 270 - 274; Heaven and Earth: 97]

In 2291 B.C. Inanna, Naram-Sin (Sargon's grandson) and the Akkadian armies captured the Baalbek Landing Platform. Then they dashed along the Mediterranean coast for the Sinai Spaceport and inland for Mission Control in Jerusalem. The Akkadians crossed the forbidden Forth Region, the region forbidden to Earthlings. Inanna and the Akkadians conquered Jerico, which switched alliance from Nannar to her. Her armies, under Naram-Sin, joined Nergal's and conquered Egypt.

Nergal visited Inanna and asked her to help him contain Marduk and he tricked Marduk to leave Babylon, then took its power source, which controlled irrigation for all Sumer. In 2255 B.C., Inanna recaptured Uruk, destroyed Anu's temple there and sent Naram-Sin to attack Enlil's minions at Nippur. She declared herself supreme to even Nibiru's King Anu. Enlil sent Ninurta and Ninurta's cavalry and Gutiums to reconquer Sumer. They wasted most of Sumer. Enlil ordered death for Inanna's strongman, King Naram-Sin, for his attack on Nippur. Enlil's agents planted a scorpion to kill the King and ordered Inanna arrested but she fled to Nannar, then flew to Nergal's Lower Africa. For seven years, Inanna and Nergal plotted to overthrow the Council. [Ancient text, *Queen of all the MEs*; ZS, *Wars*: 254]

She returned to Sumer, where, in 2095 B.C., Shulgi succeeded Ur Nammu. Inanna invited Shulgi to Uruk and declared him "the man for the vulva of Inanna." They wed in the temple where Anu'd elevated her in tantric ritual.

In 689 B C., Enlil sent Inanna to Assyria to disarm the Ninevan army and destroy their weapons. *"Esarhaddon rules,"* she proclaimed. In battles in Arabia and in an attack on Marduk's Egyptian forces, she fired "an intense brilliance" on her helmet to blind enemies of Ashurbanipal (Esarhaddon's successor). She "rained flames upon Arabia." [ZS, *Wars* 12-19, 276 -279]

After Nuclear fallout from the Enlilite nuking of the Enkiite Dead Sea Cities destroyed all life in Sumer, Inanna fled to Anatolia, where, in 1190 B.C., as Aphrodite, she fought on the side of Troy and was wounded by Diamedes. Virgil said she helped her half-Earthling son Aeneas flee Troy, sojourn in Carthage, settle in Latinum, marry a local and begat descendants, among them, Numitor, King of Alba Longa. Numitor begat Rhea, the mother of Romulus and Remus whom Julius Caesar claimed as ancestor.

MARDUK

For a few decades on Nibiru Marduk (aka Ra, Ra-amon, Amon, Aten, Bilulu, Bel, Nimrod, Ares, Mars), son of Damkina (King Alalu's daughter) and Enki (Enki was son of Anu, Alalu's successor), could succeed Alalu. Until Anu overthrew Alalu, both Anu and Alalu proclaimed Marduk Heir Presumptive.

Marduk's father's brother Enlil (Commander on Earth) gave Marduk rule of the transhipment facility and the Astronaut Corps on Mars. But 350,000 years ago, Nibiru neared Earth and brimstones rained on Earth and Mars, loosed earthquakes and volcanoes on both planets, trashed Marsbase and forced the Corps to leave it. So Marduk lost his command. Enki took Marduk to the moon. They surveyed the moon as an alternative base.

On the moon Enki gave Marduk vast scientific information. Enki told Marduk he'd help him reclaim his right to rule. 9780 B.C.: Enki gave Marduk rule of Egypt and its Earthlings. Marduk divided Egypt between his sons Seth and Osiris.

Marduk said he'd marry Sarpanit, a hybrid daughter of Enkime (a direct descendent of one of Enki's Earthling sex partners). Marduk's marriage would bind the Earthlings to him; he'd wield them as weapons, and defeat Enlil on Earth. Then with armies of Earthlings, he'd reclaim his right as Alalu's heir to rule Nibiru. Enlil let Marduk and Sarpanit proclaim they'd wed at Eridu. But Enlil ordered the couple, after they wed, to Egypt. 200 Igigi astronauts occupied the Lebanon Airport, then flew to Eridu. After the wedding, each astronaut seized an Earthling woman. They took the 200 Earthlings back to Lebanon and radioed Enlil: *"Bless our Earthling marriages or by fire all on Earth shall we shall destroy."* Marduk, the astronauts' Commander, demanded Enlil ratify the unions. Marduk and Sarpanit stayed with other Igigi families in Lebanon and begat Nabu.

When Enlil ordered the Indus Valley developed as a dowry for Inanna and Dumuzi, Marduk had his sister Geshtinanna seduce their brother Dumuzi. After she got his ejaculate, Geshtinanna said, *"Marduk of raping me will accuse you."* Dumuzi drowned as he fled Marduk's agents. Inanna chased Marduk through the chambers of the Great Pyramid. When he came out, the Enlilites convicted him and sentenced him to die. Anu had Ningishzidda rescue Marduk. The Enlilites exiled him to North America. In Egypt, they now called Marduk *Ra- Amen* (Amen = hidden)

In 8670 B.C., Inanna & the Enlilites again defeated Marduk and his armies. Marduk and his forces fled to the mountains. Inanna blasted them with "an explosive beam and forced them south. Marduk, Gibil, Seth, Horon and Enki escaped into the Great Pyramid at Giza. In exchange for a peace treaty, Enki surrendered and replaced Marduk with Ningishzidda as ruler of Egypt.

In 3850 B.C. , Anu inspected the Earth Project, and at the Peruvian Spaceport pardoned Marduk. Sarpanit had died; Marduk and Nabu moved to Enki's place in Eridu. In 3460 B.C.E. Marduk "decided he would extend his father's privilege" of a base in Sumer at Babylon (within Eridu), as his headquarters." Marduk had his Earthlings built a "tower whose head shall reach the heavens–a launch tower.

Nabu gathered Earthlings and Marduk taught them to make bricks for Babylon, his spaceport. With a spaceport, he'd challenge the Enlilite spaceport on the Sinai. But Enlilites bombed the tower and Marduk's camp at Babylon and he fled to Egypt. Enlilites scattered Marduk's Earthlings and gave them different languages and scripts.

"Marduk, after a long absence, to the Land of the Two Narrows [Egypt] returned, Ningishzidda as its master he there found." For the next 350 years, armies Marduk and Nigishzidda clashed over Egypt. Finally, Enki ordered Ningishzidda to leave Egypt to Marduk. Enki hadn't passed rule of Nibiru to Marduk, but maybe he could settle Marduk in Egypt. Enki gave him computer programs to make Egypt prosper; he gave him all his knowledge except how to revive the dead.

Marduk replaced Ningishzidda s image on the Sphinx with Osiris'. Marduk told his pharaohs he'd mummify and rocket them to Nibiru for eternity with the gods. He rallied Egypt against the Enilites.

In 2316 B.C., Sargon and Inanna invaded Babylon, filled an urn with Babylon soil and planted it in Agade, symboling she'd build her own tower to launch rockets to Nibiru. Marduk returned from Egypt to Babylon. When Marduk fortified Babylon and diverted rivers to it before they flowed to other Sumerian cities and said he'd build his spaceport in Babylon. Marduk's waterworks stopped water to Sumer's Enlilite cities, Inanna loosed lasers on his Earthlings and he shot laser beams at her armies. The Anunnaki Council told Nergal to restore Sumer's water and disarm Marduk and Babylon. In Uruk, Nergal allied with Inanna and asked Inanna to help thwart Marduk. Nergal and Inanna made love and planned to conquer the Earth.

Nergal and his Africans marched to Babylon, where Marduk greeted them. Nergal promised Marduk if he'd leave Babylon for South Africa, he'd get weapons–Alalu's hidden nukes--and computers hidden there. Marduk said that if he left Babylon, the waterworks would fail, and Sumer'd suffer floods, dried-up crops and cholera. Nergal said he'd respect the waterworks. Reassured, Marduk went to South Africa. Then Nergal destroyed the system and created floods, dried-out fields and canals throughout Sumer.

Marduk took Harran from Nannar and cut Sumer from trade with the Hittites. Nabu roused the cities west of the Euphrates and Canaan against Enlil. Marduk and Nabu threatened both the Spaceport. Nergal nuked Marduk's forces in Canaan. Nabu escaped westward to an island in the Mediterranean. The nuclear cloud blew to the Enlilites' Sumerian turf and killed all Sumer except Marduk's Babylon. Marduk made Babylon Capitol of Sumer and, around 2000 B.C., proclaimed himself God of the gods. He renamed Nibiru, after himself, "Marduk" and created New Years Celebrations there to enact "his" entry into the inner solar system and creation of Earth, then of Earthlings.

 He renamed Mercury, "Nabu." Marduk developed a priesthood which studied omens and a horoscope that predicted the effects the planets–and their namesakes--had on Earthlings. He degraded Sumer's astronomical observations, compassionate support of citizens, and the status of women, who were generally excluded from high office and the exercise of art.

In 587 B.C., forces of Marduk's Babylonian king Nebuchadnezzar overran Enlil's forces in Jerusalem. Nebuchadnezzer installed a king there, ordered worship of Marduk. In 539 B.C., welcomed by Marduk, Cyrus of Persia conquered Babylon. The Persian king Xerxes, in 482 B.C., decided to destroy the tomb of Marduk, who'd recently died. Alexander of Greece conquered the Persians. "Alexander reached Babylon in 331 B.C., Alexander went for blessings to Marduk's temple, but saw Marduk there, preserved in oils.

NANNAR (aka Sin, Allah)
Nannar, a genetically Nibiran--son of Commander Enlil and Ninlil–but born on Earth, in turn fathered Inanna, Utu and Erishkigal on this planet. 400,000 years ago, Enlil exiled Nannar, when he supported Anuzu's revolt, from Ur. Enlil appointed Nannar to Rule Ur again in 8670 B.C. .Nannar retreated to the moon when nuclear fallout killed Sumer in 2024 B.C. and again in

649 B.C., when Marduk's forces closed in on the Sinai Spaceport. Nannar's High Priestess Adapa Gupi got a messengering device of his, reached him on the moon and got him to return and rule Sumer again, this time (555 B.C.) through her's son, Nabuna'id.

NINGISHZIDDA

Humanity owes its existence and survival to Ningishzidda, the great architect, geneticist and musician. Genetically Nibiran, Ningishzidda birthed on Earth, son of Enki and Ereshkigal. Enki'd seduced Ereshkigal as he took her to run the Climate Station in South Africa. He left her there, pregnant with Ningshzidda

Ningishzidda (aka Thoth, Hermes, Dionysus, Kukulcan, Xiuhtecuhtli, Feathered or Winged Serpent and Quetzlcoatl) joined Enki and Ninmah to create Nibiran/Erectus hybrid Earthlings, Adamu and Adapa. Ningishzidda found the X and Y chromosomes that let us hybrids reproduce. Then he and brothers Adapa and Dumuzi rocketed to the planet Nibiru, where King Anu gave him grains for the Earthlings and told him to protect and foster the new species.

After the Deluge 13,000 years ago, Ningishzidda (as Thoth) built the Sinai Spaceport and the Giza Pyramids to guide rockets to the Spaceport. He built a model pyramid, then the Great Pyramid at the South end of a straight landing line--through the Landing Platform in Lebanon (Baalbek) to Mt. Ararat (Eastern Turkey) in the North. He installed the power generator, master computer programs and astronavigational equipment in the Great Pyramid and hid records (on indestructable tablets) in secret chambers (Halls of Amenti) under the Pyramid [Doreal, *Emerald Tablets*:1]. He also built and was the initial face on the Sphinx. He planned and supervised a castle, temple and fighter-jet hangar for his cousin Ninurta at Lagash.

Ningishzidda refused to fight for Marduk and Enki in the Second Pyramid War, though he did, when the Council of the Anunnaki, asked, tunnel into and rescue Marduk from the Great Pyramid. Enlilite considered Ningishzidda, though an Enkiite, an ally, since Enlil was, though his mother, Ereshkigal, Ningishzidda's grandfather. Both Enkiites and Enlilites accepted him, so Enlil, at the Peace Treaty of 8670 B.C., made him ruler of Egypt.

Ningishzidda held the Nile for 1,560 years when only pure-blooded Nibirans ruled for him there. But then Marduk returned from exile and for the next 350 years, sent armies in Egypt against Nigishzidda's, Enki, their father, ordered Ningishzidda to leave Egypt to Marduk.

Ningishzidda moved on: he guided the building of Stonehenge. In 3113 B.C., after he'd finished Stonehenge, he shipped Middle Eastern-looking Sumerian and Black African overseers and technicians with him to Mesoamerica, where descendants of Ka-in, whom he'd marked with facial hairlessness, called him called Quetzalcoatl, the Winged Serpent. He taught them math, astronomy, calendar calculation and temple-building. He showed them how to line up with the stars and the signs that Nibiru was nearing. Atop the Andes, he designed a spaceport and tin and gold-processing plants for his cousin, Enlilite General Adad/Viracocha. Ningishzidda built planetariums throughout Central America.

NINMAH

Ninmah (aka Ninharsag, Ninti, Mammi, Hathor, Isis, Athena, Minerva), Nibiran-born, youngest daughter of King Anu. The King cancelled her betrothal to her eldest brother, Enki, when she and Enlil, her next brother and Anu's heir, begat Ninurta. She took 50 female Nibiran Medical Practitioners and grape starts to Sharuppak (Iraq) on Earth. Enroute, she stopped on Mars where she found Alalu dead. She revived Anzu, who was marooned with Alalu. She set Anzu up with 20 men to start Marsbase and had him create the monument of Alalu's head at Cyndonia.

On Earth, she connected sexually with Enki, bore him many girls, and with him and his son Ningishzidda created the Erectus/Nibiran hybrid Earthlings. She tutored Enki's son Ziasudra, whom Enlil appointed the Earthlings' patriarch of Sumer. She voted on the ruling Anunnaki Council, where she repeatedly supported Earthlings. On Mount Ararat, Turkey, after the Deluge, 11,000 B.C., she got Enlil to spare the Earthlings and govern them through Ziasudra and his male descendants. He gave her rule of the entire Sinai--Tilmun (Land of Missiles)—as neutral turf between his Enlilite lineage and Enki's. In 8670 B.C. Ninmah mediated war between the Enlilite lineage which her son Ninurta championed and the Enkiites in the Giza Pyramid. Enlil, Enki and Ninurta installed her in a Sinai palace where Enlil titled her "Ninharsag, Mistress of the Mountainhead."

NINURTA

Ninurta (aka Ishum, then Mars; sometimes, Ashur; possibly Indra too) birthed on Nibiru, son out-of-wedlock of Enlil and Ninmah. Ninurta served as Enlil's second-in-command on Earth and ruled Mesopotamia from Lagash, defeated Anzu and Inanna and inadvertently killed Sumer when he nuked Sinai for the Enlilites.

OSIRIS

Osiris, aka Asar, ruler of Upper Egypt from 8970 B.C. to 9380 B.C, son of Marduk. Osiris married his half sister Isis. Astronaut Commander Shamgaz, Nephys and Osiris' brother Seth drugged, killed and dismembered him to win the fertile Upper Egypt fief. Isis impregnated herself with the dead Osiris's semen and bore Horus, who defeated and Seth. Marduk, replaced Ningishzidda/Thoth's visage on the Sphinx with that of Osiris.

SETH

In 11, 000 B.C. in Egypt, Marduk, Sarpanit, and their sons, Seth (aka Satu or Enshag) and Osiris (Asar) sheltered with Marsbase's Asstronaut Commander, Shamgaz. Osiris and Seth married Shamgaz's girls, Isis (aka Asra–Ningishzidda's child with Marduk's granddaughter). Shamgaz and Seth allied.

Osiris married Seth's half-sister Isis to block Seth fathering heirs to Egypt. Seth then married Nephys, his full sister. "The full siblingship of Seth and Neptys disqualified their offspring from rulership.

Osiris and Isis lived near Marduk in the northern lowlands of Lower Egypt. Seth and Nebat settled in southern Upper Egypt's mountains, near Shamgaz's villa and the Lebanon Landing Platform. Shamgaz and Nebat told Seth that while Osiris lived he and the Astronauts would lack good fiefs on Earth.

Osiris, Shamgaz argued, lived near Marduk. So *Osiris*, said Shamaz, *will succeed Marduk and rule of the fertile lower Nile. Only Upper Egypt for you and the Igigi.* In 9380 B.C., Seth, Nephys and Shamgaz killed Osiris. They invited Osiris to dinner, drugged him, and when he passed out, locked him in a coffin and threw him the sea. Seth said he, as Marduk's sole living son, ruled all Egypt. [ZS, *Enki*: 243 - 244.]

Isis, Sarpanit and Marduk retrieved Osiris's coffin from the sea. Enki had Isis extract semen from Osiris's corpse and inseminate herself with it. She said, "*I carry Osiris' son. Our son, not Seth should rule Lower Egypt.*" She hid and bore Horus to fight Seth and avenge Osiris

As the astronauts spread and their armies advanced toward Sinai, Gibil tutored Horus to fight Seth. Gibil taught Horus to pilot aircraft, made multi-headed missiles for him and showed him and his Earthlings to make iron weapons. Wh\en Horus' army marched on Seth, Seth dared Horus to an air battle. Seth hit Horus with a poison dart missile but Ningishzidda gave Horus an antidote and a "blinding weapon and a missilecalled "the harpoon," with which Horon hit Seth. Blind, Seth crashed, his testicles squashed; Horus bound him and dragged him before the Council.

The Council, though Canaan was reserved for Enlilites and their Earthlings, let Seth live there. The Council had ordered Enkiite Nibirans and Earthlings descended from Ziusudra's son Ham restricted to Africa, but the Ham-ites defied the Council and occupied Canaan. The Council let Seth live among these Enkiites. Seth soon ruled Canaan. Seth's rule in Canaan meant Enkiites controlled the Giza Spacecraft Marker-Pyramid, the control tower and runways on Sinai, and the new Mission Control Jerusalem.

In 8670 B.C., Ninurta, Inanna and the Enlilites attacked Seth's forces in Canaan. The Enlilites fought to regain the space-related marker peaks–Moriah, Harsag (Mount St. Katherine) in the Sinai and the artificial mount, the Ekur (The Great Pyramid) in Egypt." [ZS, *Wars*: 156 - 158]

In 8670 B.C., Ninurta, Inanna and the Enlilites attacked Seth's forces in Canaan. The Enlilites fought to regain the space-related marker peaks–Moriah, Harsag (Mount St. Katherine) in the Sinai and the artificial mount, the Ekur (The Great Pyramid) in Egypt." Enlil agreed to stop attacks if the Enkiites and the Earthlings descended from Shem left Canaan's Restricted Zone (Sinai Peninsula and Spaceport) and Jerusalem. Enki demanded his Enkiites keep Giza.
To this, Enlil agreed if Marduk, Seth and Horus were barred from ruling over Giza or Lower [Northern] Egypt.

SHAMGAZ
Commander of the Astronaut Corps, ally of Marduk and Seth. Participated in murder of Seth's half-brother Osiris.

UTU (Aka, Shamash)
Before the Deluge, Utu (aka Sin, Allah), Inanna's twin, born on Earth to Enlil's son Nannar and Ningal, . Utu commanded the Astronauts at Sippar. After the flood, he ran Mission Control at Jerusalem, then retired to Sippar. Later, he left South America on an aircraft, perhaps for Nibiru.

Royal Rules

ABRAHAM

Born 2123 B.C, son of Ur's High Priest. In 2041, Abraham led Enlil's forces and defended the Sinai Spaceport. He reported Sodom and Gomorra sympathetic Nabu and Marduk. In 2024 B.C. Enlil sent Abraham to the Negev Desert while Ninurta and Nergal nuked Sodom and Gomorra.

On Enlil's orders, Abraham left his wife Hagar and their son Ishmael to die in the desert and almost stabbed his son Isaac. Abraham circumcised himself and his men to brand themselves as Enlil's. Enlil rewarded him with Canaan.

BANDA (aka Lugalbanda, King Shorty)

Banda's father, Uruk's King Enmerkar (Utu's grandson and a Earthling) sent an emissary with message in written Sumerian to the King of Aratta in the Indus Valley. Enmerkar demanded Aratta swear feality to Uruk. But the Arattan couldn't read Sumerian . After ten years, Enmerkar told Utu to have Nisaba, the astronauts' scribe, teach him Arattan script. When he'd learned it, Enmerkar sent his son Banda to Aratta with a message in Arattan: "*Submit or War*! " The Arattan wrote back that he'd prefer trade--Aratta's precious stones for the MEs [computer programs] of Uruk, or if Enmerkar insisted on war, one champion of Aratta and one of Uruk could fight to settle the war. "On the way back to Uruk, Banda fell sick; his spirit left him. On Mount Hurmu was Banda abandoned.

"Inanna restless and ungratified, for Dumuzi she still mourned. In Uruk, "A House for Nighttime Pleasure she established. To this young heroes, on the night of their weddings, with sweet words she lured: long life, a blissful future to them she promised; that her lover Dumuzi was she imagined." But "each one in the morning in her bed was found dead." So when Utu revived Banda, Inanna saw Banda as Dumuzi. "'Dumuzi, my beloved!' she called him. To her bed, with flowers bedecked, she lured him."

Banda succeeded his father, Enmerkar, as King of Uruk. Banda married Ninurta's daughter, Ninsun, who bore Gilgamesh.

GILGAMESH

King of Uruk, Sumer, ca 2900 B.C., 3/4 Nibiran, 1/4 Royal Earthling line; son of Ninsun and Lugal Banda. Enki fashioned Enkidu, an android, to befriend Gilgamesh and had Inanna's temple priestess Shamhat tame Enkidu with tantric sex. Enkidu then tamed Gilgamesh and helped him reject Inanna and challenge Enlil's robot at Baalbek and Enlil's ban on Earthling longevity. Gilgamesh and Enkidu destroyed Enlil's robo-guard at the Lebanon Landing Place. Gilgamesh sought Ziasudra's help at the Sinai Spaceport, but a snake stole the life-extending herbs Gilgamesh obtained. Gilgamesh died 2600 B.C.; his successors buried him with his friends and attendants in the Royal Cemetery at Lagash.

JACOB

Born in 1963 B.C., Jacob, Abraham's son, ruled Canaan for the Enlilites. He went to Harran to find a bride, and on the way, saw a Nibiran flying saucer deplane and reboard Enlil and his aides 20 years later, after Jacob's bride service in Harran for two wives, Enlil sent him back to Canaan. En route, Jacob wrestled a Nibiran into submission and so was renamed **ISRA-EL** [he who fought a god]. Israel limped into his twin brother Esau's camp, took over as Patriarch of Enlil's loyalists, known now as "the Children of Isra-El." Jacob fathered Joseph, whom Egypt's Pharoh made Overseer of Egypt. [ZS, Encounters: 250 - 256]

JEZEBEL

In 872 B.C., Ithbaal, King of Tyre gave his daughter Jezebel to Ahab, the successor to Omri as King of Israel to create Phoenician-Israeli alliance. Jehu (Enlil's agent) purged Ahab's dynasty and the alliance with Phoenicia and made Israel subject to Syria, which dispersed Israel's intelligencia throughout the Assyrian empire.

JOSEPH

Born, 1870 B.C.), son of Israel, Joseph's half brothers, who hated how he analyzed dreams, sold Joseph into slavery in Egypt. Joseph, jailed as a sexual predator by the slaveowner's wife whom he'd refused to bed, won fame he when he interpreted dreams. When Pharaoh Amenemhet III of the Middle Kingdom's XII dynasty ascended the throne of Egypt in 1842 B.C. and dreamed seven skinny cows ate seven fat cows and seven scorched ears of grain ate seven healthy ones, he told Joseph. Joseph said Pharaoh's dream augered seven years good harvest, then seven famine years. Impressed, in 1840 B.C., Amenemhet made Joseph Overseer of Egypt and let him store water and grain from the seven good years for the seven lean ones.

Joseph ran Nile high flood waters into miles of canals and underground pipes to an artificial lake near Hawara. He made the Fayam area breadbasket of Egypt. When drought and famine hit the Near East, refugees pored into Egypt where vegetables, fruit and fish still, thanks to Joseph, abounded. In 1833 B.C., Papa Jacob (now 130 years old) and Joseph's half-brothers who'd sold him to slave joined the refugees from Canaan to Egypt.

JOSHUA

When Moses died, his general, Joshua, led the Israelites. Joshua, whom Enlil told of astronomical events and assisted with techno-weapons, conquered much of Canaan. Joshua killed 120,000 men and enslaved 200,000 women and children. Enlil had him kill a million Ethiopians too. With the weapons and engineered plagues, Enlil and Joshua slew 10,000 Canaanites and Perizzites and 10,000 Moabites. [Judges 1:4, 3:28-29; Tellinger, Slave Species:173 -191]

MOSES

(1391–1271 B.C.; aka Aminadab, Amenhotep III and Akhenaton). PharaohThothmose I broke the Middle Kingdom promise that Egypt honor "Children" of Israel. He'd work them to death and stop their breeding. He "ordered any newborn Israelite male killed at birth." In 1513 B.C., to save their newborn, a couple descended from Jacob/Israel laid the boy in a box and floated it down a stream where Thothmose's daughter bathed. She named the boy Moses and adopted him.

"In 1482 B.C. Thothmose III renewed hostilities against Enlilites abroad and the Israelites in Egypt. Moses, now grown, killed an Egyptian overseer who brutalized Israelites. Thothmose III ordered Moses killed, but Moses escaped to Sinai, where he married the daughter of a Midianite priest.

In 1450 B.C., Amenhotep II, the new Pharaoh, let Moses' death sentence expire. Enlil sent Moses back to Egypt to free the Israelites. Moses tried to scare Amenhotep with magic but Amenhotep resisted and instead ordered Israelites make three times more bricks than before. Enlil hit Egypt with plagues, infestations, cattle diseases, three days of darkness and weather disturbances. He killed all non-Israelite firstborn children and cows in Egypt. In 1433 B.C., Amenhotep told the Israelites, *Go*. When he thought them caught between the desert's edge, lakes, then the Red Sea, he sent chariots to re-capture them. Enlil either used his climate control devises to sweep a path through the Red Sea or showed the Israelites a way to cross. Egyptians chased them but Enlil let the sea sweep over and drown them.

For forty years, Enlil guided Moses and the Israelites through the desert to the edge of the Sinai Peninsula and protected them from Amalekites. Nights, he lit the way with a "fiery beacon." Days, he led with a dark cloud. He fed them and had them kill 3000 of their number who worshiped other Nibirans and 23,000 for sex before they married. [*Exodus* 32:26-28; *Corinthians* 10:8].

He ordered Moses to climb Mt. Sinai then relay demands to the Israelites. Moses told the Israelites what Enlil wanted. Enlil then landed his rocket on the mount and, with an amplifier, told, the people what he wanted. They had to say they'd obey. He had Moses make a temple and a box (an "Ark of the Covenant") that sported two gold cherubs) for tablets of his orders. Above a drawer in the Ark, Moses built a Talk-To-Enlil communicator. Moses returned to the Israelites, glowed with radiation from Enlil 's aircraft.

NABU (Nebo, Ensag)

Son and Prophet of Marduk by Earthling Sarpanit, during his father's exile, Nabu made allies in Sodom, Gomorrah and the Dead Sea Cities. Nabu escaped the nuclear holocaust to an island in the Mediterranean. After Marduk prevailed, Nabu returned to his home in Borsippa, Iraq, and visited Marduk in Babylon each year for New Years ceremonies.

SARGON

Inanna's gardiner, then lover, founded Sumer's Akkadian Dynasty. In 2371 B.C., she chose her gardiner, Sargon (her Earthling half-brother), who'd raped her to lead her armies. They built their capital, Agade and won all Sumer except Lagash. Sargon's army followed Inanna through Luristan in the Zagros Mountains. Sargon spread spoken and written-on-clay Akkadian all over Sumer and spawned the Semitic languages. [ZS, *Heaven & Earth:* 95; *Wars:* 10 - 11].

In 2316 B.C. in Marduk's absence, Sargon invaded Babylon. To show disdain for Marduk, Sargon "took away the soil" for Inanna to build a launch site of her own and take interplanetary power. Marduk and Nabu returned from Egypt to Babylon, fortified the city and diverted rivers to it from the other Sumerian cities. Inanna and Marduk both loosed lasers on each other's Earthling armies. Marduk's minions besieged Sargon. [ZS, *Giants*: 270 - 274; *Heaven and Earth*: 97]

In 2316 B.C., Sargon and Inanna invaded Babylon, filled an urn with Babylon soil and planted it in Agade, symboling she'd build her own tower to launch rockets to Nibiru.

Inanna stayed beautiful and sexy but Sargon aged and "crumbled into a pathetic drunk who died cursing Inanna." [Ferguson, "Inanna Returns," in *Heaven and Earth*, ZS, Ed.: 97]

SARPANIT

Sarpanit, daughter of Enkime (a descendent of one of Enki's hybrid lovers) wed Marduk at Eridu in 3450 B.C.. Their marriage to Marduk and birth of their son, Nabu, proclaimed Marduk's bond with the Earthlings with whom he planned to defeat Enlil. At the wedding, the astronaut corps seized 200 Earthling brides and took Baalbek's Landing Platform. When Marduk had Dumuzi killed and Inanna and the Enlilite Council sealed Marduk to die in a sealed chamber in the Great Pyramid, Sarpanit got Anu to let Thoth save Marduk from dehydration and starvation.

Earthlings

ABAEL
Second son of hybrids Adapa and Titi (Enki's Nibiran/Earthling son and daughter). Titi bore twins (first, Ka-in; second, Abael) sometime 300,000 - 200,000 years ago at Enki's lab in Zimbabwe. Enlilite Enforcer Ninurta taught Kai-in farming; leading Enkiite, Marduk, taught Abael animal husbandry. Ka-in killed Abael.

ADAMU
The first successfully test-tube-conceived and surrogate-carried Nibiran/Erectus Earthling. He gestated in Chief Medical Officer Ninmah's womb. "Adamu learned to speak. His skin was "smooth, dark red," his hair, black. Adamu, unlike Nibirans, sported a foreskin." [ZS, *Enki,*: 148,168-170].

ADAPA (aka Utu-Abzu, Enoch)
Enki's son with an Earthling woman descended, some 300,000 years ago, from Adamu. "To Adapa, Enki himself teachings gave, how to keep records he was him instructing." Enki boasted, *"A Civilized man I have brought forth. A new kind of Earthling from my seed has been created, in my image and after my likeness. From seed they from food will grow, from ewes sheep they will shepherd. Anunnaki and Earthlings henceforth shall be satiated."*

Adapa rocketed to Nibiru with Ningishzidda and Dumuzi. There, Enki's father, Nibiru's King Anu, denied Adapa the Nibirans' extreme longeivity and sent him back to Earth to breed and teach his descendants–Earthlings enhanced by more of Enki's genes each generation--to run farms, herds and estates. Nibirans considered Adapa and his line better servants than the hybrid Earthling miners descended from Adapa's ancestor, Adamu. [ZS, *Enki:* 168-170]

BATANASH
Wife of Lu-March (Enki's foreman before the Deluge) made love with Enki and bore Ziasudra as result.

HAGAR
Slave, then secondary wife to Abraham; their son, Ishmael, had been Abraham's heir but Enlil had Abraham and his son with first wife Sarah begat a child to displace Ishmael. Enlil ordered Abraham to leave Hagar and Ishmael to die in the desert. Abraham obeyed but Hagar and Ishmael survived and Ishmael bred the ancestors of the Arabs.

KA-IN
Ka-in was the first son of Adapa and Titi, Enki's Nibiran/Earthling son and daughter. Titi bore twins, first, Ka-in; second, Abael sometime 300,000 - 200,000 years ago at Enki's lab in Zimbabwe. The Expedition Council banished Ka-In East of Sumer for killing his brother Abael and had Ninghzidda mark Ka-In genetically to lack facial hair.

LU-MARCH
Enki's pre-Deluge Workforce Foreman, husband of Batanash with whom Enki begat Ziasudra.

TI-AMAT

The first hybrid girl carried by .Ti-Amat's ova provided part of the genetic material for all subsequently bred humans. Ti-Amat was blonde, white & blue-eyed like Nibiran girls. To create a female, Ningishzidda planted Ti-Amat, as a zygote, prepared with Adamu's blood, in Damkina, and, when it grew to a viable female fetus, excised her. He then put ova from Ti-Amat into seven test-tubes and planted them in the same female Nibiran doctors who'd borne hybrid but non-reproducing males. He anesthetized Enki, Ninmah and Ti-Amat. "From the rib of Enki the life essence he extracted; into the rib of Adamu the life essence he inserted. From the rib of Ninmah the life essence he extracted; into the rib of Ti-Amat the life essence he inserted." [ZS, *Enki*: 148]

Enki, Ninmah and Ningishzidda hid how they'd altered Ti-Amat. She and Adamu stayed in Enki's Persian Gulf orchard, while her fetus gestated. Ti-Amat made leaf-aprons for herself and Adamu. Enlil banished T-Amat and Adamu when he saw she and Adamu wore aprons and made Enki confess that Ti-Amat's fetus would breed. Enki put Adamu and Ti-Amat in an enclosure in Zimbabwe where Ti-Amat bore the twins Kai-in and Abael, then others who, in turn, bred with each other and with Nibirans.

TITI

Enki's daughter Titi and his son Adapa started the line of superslaves, hybrids with enhanced genetic input from Nibiran genes–Enki's: 200,000 years ago, Titi and Adapa begat Ka-in and Abael in Zimbabwe.

ZIASUDRA

Enki surreptitiously impregnated Batanash wife of Lu-March (Enki's foreman) before the Deluge; she bore Ziasudra as result. Ninmah loved and cared for Ziasudra; Enki taught him to read Adapa's writings. Enki conveyed his son Ninagal and plans and instructions for submersible and its provisions for life-form starts to Ziasudra's wall-computer. Commander Enlil choose Ziasudra's sons Ham, Japhet and Shem to rule us hybrids for the Nibirans and granted Ziasudra and his wife extreme longeivity.

BIBLE FUSES NIBIRAN ROYALS INTO *ONLY* GOD

Q: WHAT DIFFERENCE DOES THIS HISTORY MAKE FOR OUR LIFE NOWADAYS?
A: Frees us from godspell and Illuminati control.

In parts of the Bible, the ET called "Yahweh" is *Enlil*–where Yahweh hates Earthlings, wants them dead, and teaches them to hate women, obey blindly. Yahweh is Enlil when he orders his branded followers to murder any among them who honored other Nibirans. He sends them to kill followers of his rivals. Bible authors also allude to *Enki* as Yahweh. Other places, the Bible, calls members of Enlil's lineage–Ninurta, Adad and Nannar Yahweh."

When, in 1393 B.C., Israelites captive in Bablylon, wrote *Genesis*, they fused well- known writings of how Enki, Ninmah and Thoth made us and thwarted Enlil. Bible writers spun the tale to justify a national religion that glorified Enlil–the Nibiran Expedition Commander, who forbade us reproductive ability and wanted us all drown in Noah's flood--as Yahweh, the one and only god. The clay tablets and stone engravings, before Genesis' authors distorted them for their propaganda, show "two Nibiran brothers, Enlil and Enki, always at odds with each other. Enki, with his half-sister Ninmah, created humans and was always favorable to them. Enlil had reservations about Earthlings and dominated them with severity."

Freer wrote: "Our species' internecine violence, a product of Babel-factoring for crowd control that has carried through to great wars and the religious mayhem of crusades, jihads, inquisitions and persecutions and not intrinsically of human nature." The Bible's compilers "make Enlil their single monotheistic deity. Religious, military and political controllers "suppressed the knowledge about the alien presence."

The Old Testament called god *Adonai* (Enki) when he did good things to or for the Hebrews. When god murdered, Bible writers called him *Yahweh* (=Jehovah, alias Enlil), whom they worshipped in fear. They "sublimated Enlil--a disagreeable, harsh, peevish individual, cruel toward humans--into a cosmic being. The establishment, fundamentalist Jews, Muslims and Christian fear the more efficient explanations Sitchin and the Vedas cited by Cremo [2003, *Human Devolution*] and Thompson [*Alien Identities*,1993], for they would undermine research monies, social control and sinecures they treasure." [Freer, 2004, *Sapiens Rising*]

Contrary to Genesis, literature written 4000 years before the Bible's propagandists made their spin on the tale, Enki, his son Ningishzidda, and half-sister Ninmah, created our Nibiran/Erectus hybrid ancestors to resolve Nibiran astronauts' strike in the goldmines. The hybrids replaced the astronauts in the mines. Each generation, Enki mated with the prettiest females born to the hybrids; he multiplied the ratio of Nibiran to Erectus genes in our stock. He gave his part-Earthling son Noah a computer program that showed him how to build the submersible to save the bloodline and to save and rule humanity.

NOTICE THE NOTES

1. Nibiru is also called Planet X, Phaeton, Lord of Hosts, Wormwood, Destroyer, Purifier, Frightener, Doomdragon, Red Sun and Planet of Crossing. [Freer, 2008 *Sapiens Rising*: 106]

2. I edited quotes, substituted nouns and pronouns for clarity, modernized some of Sitchin's renderings of Nibirans' utterances.

3. "It has been discovered that gold in its mono-atomic state defies the laws of gravity and is, it's a super conductor," said Tellinger. See www. michaeltellinger. com or visit http://ufoscience consciousnessconference.blog spot.com/

4. Anu, "in addition to his official spouse, Antu, had six concubines; his offspring were eighty in number." [ZS, *Giants*: 127.]

5. On Nibiru, Anu's cabinet of eleven top officials "included a Chief Chamberlain, three Commanders in charge of the rocketships, two Commanders of the Weapons, a Treasurer, two Chief Justices. two Masters of Written Language." Five Assistant Scribes took notes. The rank and file of Anu's staff ('Anu's Heavenly Ones.') carried out the orders. Five military men made up almost half the cabinet of eleven–a military government. There is a stress on weaponry. The palace proper was protected by two awesome weapons systems." [ZS, *Giants*: 127, 153.]

6. The Bible referred to E.DIN, the Garden of Eden, "the abode ("E") of the DIN ("The Divine Ones of the Rocketships") at the head of a body that served as the confluence of four rivers on the Arabian Peninsula--the Tigris (Hiddekel, Idilbat), the Euphrates (Prath, Purannu), the Karun (Gibon) which we still see and the Pishon, the buried river of Sumer which flowed until 4,000 years ago, when the climate changed.'" No surface trace of the Pishon, buried beneath the mud of the Deluge, 13,000 years ago, was recognized until modern ground-penetrating radar showed, under layers of sand, its bed and "ground -level inspections confirmed the existence of the ancient river."

The PISHON (Kuwait River): "under the sands of the Peninsula flowed for 530 miles from the mountains of western Arabia eastward to the Persian Gulf," merging at Basara, Iraq, with the Tigris and Euphrates "was fifty feet deep throughout its length and more than three miles wide at some points" and left deposits of "rocks from the Hijaz Mountains in Western Arabia." The Pishon "was an ancient source of gold and precious stones. Between 11,000 and 6,000 years ago, the Arabian climate was wet and rainy enough to support such a river. 5,000 yeras ago the river dried up. Wind-driven sand dunes covered the river''s channel, obliterating evidence of the once-mighty river" until "high-resolution imaging by Landsat sattelites" showed it joined the Tigris and Euphrates at their confluence at the Persian Gulf. [ZS, *Encounters*: 19 -26]

7. Enki knew the 223 genes in his genome differed from *Homo Erectus'*. "Our genome contains less than 30,000 genes. It contains 223 genes that do not have any predecessors on the genomic evolutionary tree. These 223 genes involve physiological and cerebral functions peculiar to humans." Enki withheld genes affecting longevity. "Anunnaki did not give us the relatively extreme longevity they possessed because it did not suit their purposes. We were invented as slave workers. Records show, that, over time, a handful of humans were granted immortality as a reward for being good subordinates as kings/foremen or for carrying out some critical mission." [Freer, *Sapiens Arising*; ZS, *Giants*: 162]

Sitchin said to test Enki's version of our creation with DNA of a body in the British Museum, the body of famous party-giver, demigod Nin-Puabi of Ur, buried in the royal cemetery next to the robbed grave of her brother, Gilgamesh. Puabi's burial goods included gold pieces Anu gave Inanna in 3800 B.C.. Puabi's grave also contained Sud's ceremonial gold tweezers. The last reigning demigod of Ur, Puabi's body rested with the royal family's golden artifacts.

Puabi inherited short-stature genes from Banda (King Shorty) and little Inanna. Puabi's skull, long-headed as Nibirans', measured capacity of 1600+, "250 c.cm., above the mean for European women." [ZS, *Giants*: 332]

Environmental factors, especially the speedier, 1-year revolution of Earth around Solaris compared with the lengthier revolution of Nibiru around Solaris, may also have shortened Inanna. Inanna, like Puabi, herself was short, as a result both of her birth and maturation on Earth.

Inanna gave Puabi's genome its mitochondrial DNA, "leading though Ninsun and [Anu's youngest Daughter] Bau to the Olden Mothers on Nibiru. If tested, her bones could reveal the DNA and the mtDNA differences that represent our genetic Missing Link--'alien genes' (223 of them) that upgraded us from wild hominids to Modern Man some 300,000 years ago."[ZS, *Giants*: 221, 337 -346]

8. "Recent experiments at the Universities of Minnesota and St. Louis showed copper compounds can carry pharmaceuticals to living cells, including brain cells [ZS, 1990, *Genesis*: 203].

9. The Nibirans on Earth continued the sort of competition royals practiced on Nibiru. On Nibiru, lineages within the royal clan (descendants of An) vied "for Kingship, at times at war, at times seeking peace through intermarriage." So Enlil and Enki sought peace in an Inanna/Dumuzi marriage. [ZS, *Giants*: 133]

10. Native traditions tell of noah's flood of 13,000 years ago & warn of 2012 repeat. Freer writes: "Evidence from geology coupled with reports of the survivors passed down to us as warnings [of the return of Nibiru] from Hopi, Navajo, Choctah, Cshinaua of Brazil, Ovaherero, Kanga, Loanga, Wanoro of Africa, Maya, Aztecs, natives of Celon and India, China, and Australia: Purifier/Nibiru brings conflagration, celestial disorder, flood, darkness, hail and fire, hurricanes, bombardment, a collapsed sky, hell on earth."

Hawaiian say the flood sunk Mu, a continent that stretched from from Hawaii to Rarotonga and Fiji. Mixtecs of Mexico relate the sinking of Atlantis, East of America. The passing of Nibiru in 13,000 B.C., pushed up the Andes and left closed (live) clamshells atop Everest." Nibiru's return or the return of the comets and asteroids at Nibiru's 180 degree LaGrange points] "can also bring pole reversal, crustal slippage, geomanetic chaos, ice-bound conditions of whole regions, wholesale extinctions, raised mountain ranges, sunken continents." Freer, 2008:110]

11. Cylinder seals were inch-long cylinders cut from stone and engraved in reverse with a drawing and/or writing. Sumerians rolled the cylinder on wet clay as a positive image. The imprint lasted thousands of years. Cuneiform script, used thoughout the ancient world from 4,000 till 1,000 B.C. evolved from pictographs to "wedgelike signs" of "the syllabic sounds of the spoken words." [ZS, *Handook* : 52 - 53]

READ THE REFERENCES

Pages in citations are signaled by a colon [:] preceding the page number

Allan, D. & Delair, J.,
   1995, *When The Earth Nearly Died: Compelling Evidence of a World Cataclysm 11,5000 Years Ago*, Gateway

Alford, A.
   1996, *Gods of the New Millennium: Scientific Proof of Flesh and Blood Gods*, Eridu
   Books
   1998, *The Phoenix Solution*, Hodder & Stoughton

Arthur, C., 2002, "More Signs the Solar System Has Tenth Planet"
   http://www.news.independent.co.uk/world/story.jsp?story=360803

Bagby, J.
   1982, *Evidence for a New Planet or Massive Solar Companion Beyond Uranus*
   1984, "Further Speculations on Planet X", *Kronos' Journal*, Vol IX, No. 3.

Bauval, R., and Hancock
   1996, *The Keeper of Genesis,* Mandarin

Bauuval, R. and Gilbert, A.
   1994, *The Orion Mystery,* Mandarin

Bond, P.
   2004, "Brown Dwarfs Form in The Same Way as Stars," *Astronomy Now*, March: 13

Brooks, M.
   2005, "Thirteen Things That Do Not Make Sense," *New Scientist,* March 2005

Bramley, W..
   1989, *The Gods of Eden,* Avon

Chatelain, M.
   1979, *Our Ancestors Came From Outer Space*, Pan

Clark, D., W.,
   1959, History of the Primates, Phoenix

Childe, G.,
   1960, *What Happened in History,* Pelican

Colaw, J.,
   2000, A Neil Freer Interview, http://www.ufodisclosure.com/freer2.html

Cremo, M. and Thompson, R.,
   1993, *Forbidden Archeology: The Hidden History of the Human Race*, Torchlight

Cremo, M.,
   2003, *Human Devolution: A Vedic Alternative to Darwin's Theory,* Torchlight
   2001, *Forbidden Archeology's Impact,* Torchlight

Couper, H. & Henbest, N.,

    2002, The Hunt For Planet X, *New Scientist*, Dec. 14,

    2002 d'Arc, *J.,*

    2000, Space Travellers and the Genesis of the Human Form, Book Tree

Davies, J.,

    2001, *Beyond Pluto,* Cambridge

DoHerarty, J.,

    2011, *Did Enki Give Humans Knowledge Against Anunnaki Law?*
    youtube.com/watch?v=HkRAxC70-to

Diamond, J.,

    2011, *Collapse,* Penguin

Doreal, M.

    2002, *The Emerald Tablets of Thoth-The-Atlantian,* Source Books

Freer, N.

    1999, *God Games*, Book Tree

    2000, *Breaking the Godspell*, Book Tree

    2004, *Sapiens Rising,* neilfreer.com/SRPAGE2.html

    2004b, *The Alien Question,* neilfreer.com/SRPAGE8.html

    2008, Sapiens Rising: The View From 2100, Electronic Dragon

Gardiner, L.

    2000, *Bloodline of the Holy Grail*, Fair Winds

Goldschmidt, W.

    1959, *Man's Way*: 110 -117

Goodman, M.

    2008, *Rome and Jerusalem,* Vintage

Google Images, 2012 (source of all images in this book)

Hapgood, C.

    1997, *Maps of the Ancient Sea Kings*, Adventures Unlimited

Hauck, D.

    1999, *The Emerald Tablet*, Penguin

Hoagland, R. & Bara, M.

    2007, *Dark Mission: The Secret History of NASA*

Holland, T.

    2005, *Persian Fire,* Anchor

Kramer, S.

    1971, *The Sumerians*, University of Chicago

Lessin, S.

    2000, www.*enkispeaks*.com/wordpress

    2011, "ETs from Planet Nibiru", *UFOs and Supernatural Magazine*, Vol 1:2

    2011, "A Chat with Dr. Sasha Lessin", *UFOs and Supernatural Magazine*, Vol 1:2

    2011 "Extraterrestrials Engineered Our Species" *UFOs and Supernatural Magazine*, Issue 4

    2011, " The Anunnaki's Great Deluge: The True and Original Story " *UFOs and Supernatural Magazine*, Feb-March Issue

Lloyd, A.

    2001, *Winged Disc: The Dark Star Theory,* http/www.darkstar.co.uk

    2004, "Planet X: Past and Present," *UFO Magazine*, January 2004

    2005, *Dark Star*: *The Planet X Evidence*, Timeless Voyager

Ma, M.

    2011, *The Neuorbiology of Tantra,*
      http://community.onetantra.com/groups/group/search?q=One+Tantra+News

Matase, P., Whitman, P. And Whitmire, D.,

    1999, "Commentary Evidence of Massive Body in the Outer Ort Cloud," *Icarus* 141

McKee, M.

    2004, "Stray Star May Have Jolted Sedna,"
http://www.newscientist.com//news/news/jsp?id=99996204

Mills, C.W.

    1956, *The Power Elite*, Oxford

Mitchell, S.

    2004, *Gilgamesh*, Free Press

Muir, H.

    2005, "Brown Dwarf May Harbour Habitable Planets" *New Scientist*, Feb.8

Murray, J.B.

    1999, *Mon. Not. R.Astron. Soc*, 309, 31-34

Mruzek, J.

    1998, *The Abyddos Helicopter & The Golden Section,* vejprty.com/abyhelic.htm

New Scientist

    2004, "Rogue Star Smashed Up The Solar System" February, 2004

Pike, A.

    2004, "Exoplanets: What's New" *UFO Magazine*, February, 2004

Pye, L.

    *2000,Cyclostratigraphy*www.coastalvillage.com

Redfern, Martin, 1 Henbest and Nigel

    1983, "Has IRAS Found a Tenth Planet?" *New Scientist*, 10/11/1983

Santillalana,G. and Von Deschend, H.

    1969, Hamlet's Mill, Gambit

Schultz, D.

    The Earth Chronicles Time Chart, galactic2.net/KJOL/CCCA/timechart.html

Sereda, D.

    2012, *Breakthrough: Faster Than Light Communication with ET,* Open Minds

Sitchin, J.,

    2011, *Zecharia Sitchin Official Website* [*Website* in citations] Sitchin, Z. [ZS in text attributions]

    1976, *The 12th Planet*, Avon

    1983, *The Stairway to Heaven* [*Stairway*], Avon

    1985, *The Wars of Gods and Men* [*Wars*], Avon

    1990, *Genesis Revisited* Avon

    1990, *The Lost Realms* Avon

    1993, *When Time Began* [*Time*], Avon

    1995, *Divine Encounters* [*Encounters*], Avon

    1996, *Of Heaven and Earth*, Book Tree

    1998 *The Cosmic Code*, Avon

    2002, *The Lost Book of Enki* [*Enki*], Bear

    2004, *The Earth Chronicles Expeditions* [*Expeditions*], Bear

    2007, *The End of Days*, HarperCollins

    2007, *Journeys to the Mythical Past* [*Journeys*], Bear

    2009 *The Earth Chronicles Handbook* [*Handbook*], Bear

    2010 *There Were Giants Upon The Earth* [*Giants*], Bear

Strauss, B.,

    2006, *The Trojan War*, Simon & Schuster

Tellinger, M.,

    2006, *Slave Species of god* [*Slave Species*], Music Masters

    2009, *Temples of the African Gods*, [Temples], Zulu Planet

    2011,White Powder of Gold, *http://www.youtube.com/watch?v=7tp-WNrwQhk*

    2012a *Temples of the African Gods*,

    2012b *Michael Tellinger* Youtube: Bantu Fled African ET-ruled Civilization after Sumatra Eruption 70,000 Years Ago http://stargatetothecosmos.com/michael-tellinger-youtubebantu-fled-african-et-ruled-civilizat ion-after-sumatra-eruption-70000-years-ago/

TenBruggencate, J.,

    2002, "Asteroid Theory Explores Imact on Earth Life*" Honolulu Advertiser* 3/24/02

Thompson, R.,

    1993, *Alien Identities*, Govardham Hill

Trujillo, C. & Brown, M., 2002, "A Correlation Between Inclination and Color in th Classical

    Kuiper Belt" *The Astrophysics Journal*, December, 2002

UFOTV: Are We Alone? Geneis Revisited http://enkispeaks.com/2012/09/03/1603

Velikovsky, I.

    Undated, *In The Beginning*

Wilkins, H.,

    1945, Mysteries of South America, Rider

Wood, J., 1984, The Origin of The Moon, Lunar Planet Institute

 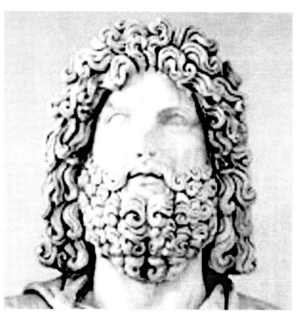

The Gods & Mount Olympus

ACCESS AUTHOR'S INFORMATION

Sasha Lessin Ph.D (U.C.L.A. anthropology Ph.D.), author of Anunnaki: Gods No More and

producer of the hugely popular web site, www.enkispeaks.com, studied with the late Zecharia Sitchin, for many years. Mr. Sitichin asked Lessin to create popular internet, book and college-level courses to revise ancient anthropology.

Sitchin asked Lessin to help disseminate written, graphic and traditional stories of ETs, hithertofore considered mythic "gods" on Earth from 450,000 years ago to 300 B.C. as well as the latest findings in astronomy that relate to the planet Nibiru from which the ETs came to Earth for gold to shield their planet, Nibiru. To this end, Dr. Lessin and his wife, Janet (a lifelong contactee) present public slide shows, radio and youtube programs and lectures.

EMAIL

sashalessinphd@aol.com

VIDEOS

Youtube: http://www.youtube.com/user/aquarianradio

WEB SITES

www.anunnakis.com
www.experiencersnetwork.com
www.extraterrestrialcontact.com
www.sashalessinphd.com
www.wetheanunnaki.com

Radio

www.aquarianradio.com

FOR MORE ON THE ANUNNAKI *see:*

www.enkispeaks.com and www.ninmah.com

hear: Enki Speaks at

www.aquarianradio.com - Thursdays, 2 -3 PM HST and archived anytime

#816.00

CPSIA information can be obtained at www.ICGtesting.com
Printed in the USA
LVOW09s1532260813

349577LV00007BA/186/P